MW00489330

Mexican Folk Art

From Oaxacan Artist Families

Arden Aibel Rothstein and
Anya Leah Rothstein

Schiffer Publishing Ltd

4880 Lower Valley Road, Atglen, PA 19310 USA

Dedication

To Sandy and Lenny Aibel who had the creativity to send their teenage daughter to Oaxaca,
and to all of our family members,
especially Chuck and Chloe Rothstein who have lovingly shared Oaxaca's treasures
and the excitement of preparing this volume.

Library of Congress Cataloging-in-Publication Data

Rothstein, Arden.
  Mexican folk art from Oaxacan artist families / by Arden and Anya
Rothstein.
    p. cm.
  ISBN 0-7643-1598-6
1. Folk art—Collectors and collecting—Mexico—Oaxaca. 2.
Artisans—Mexico—Oaxaca—Directories. I. Rothstein, Anya. II. Title.
  NK845.O2 R68 2002
  745'.0972'74—dc21
                        2002003859

Copyright © 2002 by Arden Aibel Rothstein and Anya Leah Rothstein

    All rights reserved. No part of this work may be reproduced or used in any form or by
any means—graphic, electronic, or mechanical, including photocopying or information
storage and retrieval systems—without written permission from the copyright holder.
    "Schiffer," "Schiffer Publishing Ltd. & Design," and the "Design of pen and inkwell"
are registered trademarks of Schiffer Publishing Ltd.

Designed by John P. Cheek
Cover design by Bruce M. Waters
Type set in Matrix Script Bold Oldstyle/Korinna BT

ISBN: 0-7643-1598-6
Printed in China
1 2 3 4

Published by Schiffer Publishing Ltd.
4880 Lower Valley Road
Atglen, PA 19310
Phone: (610) 593-1777; Fax: (610) 593-2002
E-mail: Schifferbk@aol.com
Please visit our web site catalog at
www.schifferbooks.com
We are always looking for people to write books on
new and related subjects. If you have an idea for a
book, please contact us at the above address.

This book may be purchased from the publisher.
Include $3.95 for shipping. Please try your bookstore
first.
You may write for a free catalog.

In Europe, Schiffer books are distributed by
Bushwood Books
6 Marksbury Ave. Kew Gardens
Surrey TW9 4JF England
Phone: 44 (0)20 8392-8585; Fax: 44 (0)20 8392-9876
E-mail: Bushwd@aol.com
Free postage in the UK. Europe: air mail at cost.
Please try your bookstore first.

Contents

Acknowledgments

It is impossible to adequately acknowledge the generosity and expertise of all the people who helped us bring this volume to fruition, but we must mention a few who gave a lot:

First of all, we thank Chuck (Arden's husband and Anya's father) and Chloe (Arden's older daughter and Anya's sister) for being supportive, both emotionally and strategically, in countless ways. They helped us brainstorm, tolerated our absences and our preoccupation with this work, translated, solved organizational quandaries, and assisted us by holding background fabric and unpacking vast crates of Oaxacan "goodies."

Constantino Jiménez López (Tino), truly our right arm, without whom this project could never have seen the light of day. His wide-ranging contributions included driving us to and from pueblos, arranging appointments, recording F-stops, dimensions, and prices for each transparency, verifying family trees and other tiny details, translating, drafting pueblo maps, shipping our treasures, and repeatedly reassuring us when we felt overwhelmed, "don waury" (don't worry). Telephone: (Oaxaca city code 95151) 34434.

Chloe and Chuck in the Benito Juárez market in Oaxaca City

Yorghos Kontaxis, our photographic consultant in New York, who outfitted and trained us, encouraged us enormously by ooh-ing and aah-ing at our photograpic yield following each trip to Oaxaca, and assisted us in selecting from the vast number of transparencies we shot the ones that best captured the beauty of Oaxacan artists and their work.

Panchita, Irma, and Alejandro at Casa Panchita, who nurtured us with their warmth, their fantastic meals, and the generally relaxing atmosphere of their guesthouse where we felt entirely at home. There we rejuvenated ourselves each evening after a fulfilling day's work and enjoyed sharing reminiscences of Oaxaca of the past. Telephone: (Oaxaca city code 95151) 51887.

Arden's sister and Anya's aunt, Wendy Aibel-Weiss, and our friends, Joan Erdheim, Linda Gunsberg, Jane Bland Honoroff, and Judy Smith (listed in alphabetical order) who closely and creatively read an early draft of the text and offered invaluable suggestions that immeasurably improved our final product.

Vera Kandt, an extremely knowledgeable Dutch anthropologist residing in Oaxaca, who suggested classes of folk we had initially overlooked, generously shared her contacts with several folk artists, critiqued our text, and became a good friend to boot.

Elizabeth Cuellar, an American anthropologist residing in Mexico City, who offered excellent suggestions about the scope of our volume.

Shira Weinert, Anya's photography teacher, who inspired her interest and contributed to her technique.

Sam Herschkowitz, a colleague, who unknowingly helped us make connections that are crucial to this book. By asking where we planned to spend our upcoming summer vacation, he put us in touch with two other colleagues and their wives, Harvey and Deborah Bezahler and Joseph and Peggy Coltrera, who he knew to be Oaxaca aficionados. This culminated in our introduction to Tino and our re-finding Casa Panchita.

Isabel Bertuna and Felix Cortés, Spanish teachers, who assisted us in correctly recording the book's many accents.

Carrie Wright, who inputted the extensive family trees.

And last, but by no means least, all the artists and their families who have so lovingly and informatively shared their work, their reflections, their histories, and their homes.

Yorghos Kontaxis

Introduction

In this book we introduce an indigenous folk art collector's paradise: Oaxaca (pronounced WAH-HAH-KAH) in southeastern Mexico. Within a small geographical radius, the visitor finds an extraordinary spectrum of folk art treasures at remarkably reasonable prices. Surrounding Oaxaca City (the capital of the state of Oaxaca), there are numerous indigenous "pueblos" (villages) in which artists produce art forms specific to that area. Belt weaving is practiced in one, rug weaving, woodcarving, black pottery, green glazed, multi-color glazed and terra cotta pottery in others, to name just a few[1]. Artists work entirely by hand, involved in every aspect of their creations, from start to finish. Their traditions have been handed down from generation to generation within that village, often over hundreds of years.

The art that results is a fascinating blend of diverse elements of their cultural, religious and physical environment: indigenous myths and legends, ancient patterns visible in preserved Zapotec ruins, the heritage of the Spanish conquest, and the region's natural earth products. While foreign in some respects, its expression of elemental fantasies and reverence for nature has universal appeal. As Nelson Rockefeller, an aficionado of the creative beauties of Oaxacan folk art and handicrafts as early as the 1930's, wrote, "In Oaxaca one sees the drama of this endless flow of creativity still pulsating with the vitality of a great people (Oettinger, p. 11)."

Collecting in Oaxaca is greatly enriched by familiarity with the family legacy of its creators. Our purpose is to highlight individual artists, their close-knit families and the persistent influence of their ancestors. In this spirit, we present a sampler of artist families who collaborate to create Oaxaca's many classes of captivating folk art and handicrafts.

Our Family Tradition: Inter-Generational Transmission

This volume is also a family collaboration based on transmission of traditions. A mother (Arden) spent three teenage summers in a program for American girls hosted by Franny Sciaky, an American woman who retired to this culturally and historically rich setting. A highlight of this experience was getting to know indigenous artisan families in their pueblos. Nearly 40 years later, I planned a return with my husband, Chuck, and teenage daughters, Anya and Chloe. By a fantastic coincidence we discovered that the Oaxacan driver hired in advance, Constantino Jiménez López (known as "Tino"), was a dear friend and neighbor of two of the people crucial to our summer experience. Panchita, our superb cook and friend, and her daughter Irma, still reside in this lovely home that has become a guesthouse. Casa Panchita offers outstanding hospitality by Irma and her husband, Alejandro,

and delicious meals prepared lovingly by its namesake. During this trip my love for and fascination with Oaxaca, and especially its folk art and handicrafts, was rekindled as I shared it with my family.

Since then a number of friends and colleagues, enjoying the many folk art treasures we brought home, were moved to travel to this previously unfamiliar area. We encouraged them to get to know our favorite artists in their own homes. High quality folk art pieces are available at affordable prices in the best shops in town (see our list in the Index). But viewing the artists' physical surroundings, and seeing their process of creation and their close-knit families in interaction, adds a very personal dimension to the collecting process. There are the added benefits of being able to commission pieces of specific size, design elements and coloration, and potentially to find lower prices.

A year later the pleasure of helping our friends led my daughter Anya and I to the idea of creating a book for beginning collectors. Intrigued by visiting pueblos and meeting artisans in their homes, Anya (now 14 years old, the exact age at which I first visited Oaxaca) joins me in preserving the artistic traditions of Oaxaca in photographs. In working on our project, we have traveled to the very same pueblos, relaxed in the very rooms, and eaten the very same food that I loved 40 years earlier.

Franny Sciaky in 1962

Our friend, assistant and driver, Constantino (Tino) Jiménez López

The "Casa Panchita" Family (left to right): Alejandro, Alejandro, Jr., Irma, Paco, Panchita

Panchita in 1962

Patio and gardens of Casa Panchita

Visiting the Artists: "Our Home is Your Home"

Artists who live in the pueblos are delighted when collectors visit their homes. Doing so requires no special contacts; it is standard fare in Oaxaca and leads to memorable collecting experiences. As their saying goes, "nuestra casa es su casa" (our home is your home). Tourists, accustomed to American standards of privacy, may feel reluctant to arrive unannounced. But here you are expected simply to walk in if the door is open, or to make your presence known by ringing a bell or knocking loudly on a closed metal door or wooden gate while yelling "buenos días" or "buenas tardes."[2] One can stop in briefly to get the flavor of the work produced, or linger while discussing the pueblo, the family, their artistic techniques, or asking prices, purchasing, placing orders.

These are several typical scenarios. After hiking up a rocky and jagged incline strewn with puddles from the previous day's late afternoon shower – an ascent too challenging for a car to negotiate – you see the entrance to a courtyard. It is populated by strutting chickens that weave in and out of lines of laundry hung to dry in the billowing wind. There is no address or name plaque to identify the spot, no signal that at any moment you will encounter an artist, often accompanied by several members of his family, engaged in various stages of inspiring artwork. A woman crafts a female figure out of clay, while her husband and daughter paint intricate designs on clothing or accessories created for other figures earlier that morning. In another pueblo you drive down a bumpy road behind a herd of goats meandering in the sparkling sun. A metal gate is slightly ajar. Looking through the crack, you see a large pile of wood fragments laid out to dry in the sun. Surrounded by wood shavings, a father carves a deer with delicate antlers out of one piece of wood, while his son decorates an already-carved reptile with brilliant colors. His wife and daughter paint the rabbit and armadillo hewn the day before.

In yet another pueblo, large patterned woven rugs wave like banners suspended from a massive but graceful arched home, encircled by its generous patio. Two vast whitewashed showrooms display a mixture of pre-Columbian patterns and woven reproductions of paintings by Diego Rivera and Escher. An expertly designed sign announces the success of this family. The click-clack of huge wooden looms, through which shuttles are woven, is created by a man whose devotion and industriousness is apparent. In these palatial quarters, a beautiful woman sits on the floor by his side, grinding natural substances with stone implements and overseeing the preparation of dyes. Many skeins waiting to be dyed are nearby, carded and spun by her daughter the previous day.

Our Selections

Because we survey most of Oaxaca's many classes of folk art and handicrafts, we do not intend our presentations to be comprehensive. How did we decide which artists to include? Our selections are guided by several considerations. We chose artists who are innovative or produce work of especially high caliber in other respects: coloration, quality of materials, degree of detail, and unusual juxtaposition of traditional elements[3]. More rarely, because the most precious work in a specific art form may be beyond the means of many collectors, we include an artist whose work is more affordable, although still of excellent quality.

Our wish to convey the spirit of creative collaboration and family tradition takes precedence over covering a greater number of artists. In some instances we feature all working members of a family, while in others we emphasize only a few members or one individual. Most often we feature individual members because they have distinct styles, or have developed reputations in their own rights. In other instances our coverage of a number of members is a tribute to the family's great importance in that genre of folk art. There are also occasions when the collaboration is so close that pieces are not attributed to a specific family member[4].

Finally, with one exception, we confine ourselves to the area no more than 45 minutes from the city of Oaxaca by car. This geographical radius - the one most often visited by tourists - roughly corresponds to only one of the seven regions of the state of Oaxaca: the Central Valleys. In addition to those in the city of Oaxaca or its immediate environs, we feature artists residing in twelve pueblos. Maps illustrating the relationship between these pueblos and Oaxaca City follow this Introduction.

What is Folk Art?

"Folk art" refers to objects created by common people for utilitarian, religious or purely decorative purposes. Their forms and designs are transmitted from one generation to another within a community. While the majority of artists originally produced their work anonymously, and many continue to do so to this day, there is a growing practice of signing pieces. This development may reflect the established economic success of some artists. In other cases, it derives from aspirations for personal recognition and efforts to prevent the false passing off of work. Even before artists signed their pieces, the work of an individual was often recognizable in distinctive features, such as a unique type of face, juxtaposition of elements or decorative motif.

Many folk artists engage in their chosen craft only a portion of the day, supplemented by work as farmers, homemakers, or herdsmen. More rarely folk art is the major means of support. They fill orders for domestic markets outside of their immediate pueblos or for foreign export. Most often skills are passed down from parent to child starting at a very early age, as soon as they are physically able. As several artists put it, "it was our play." In rare instances individuals teach themselves or learn from persons outside the family.

Background on Oaxaca[5]

Oaxaca is the name of one of Mexico's southeastern states *and* its capital city. The city (more formally known as Oaxaca de Juárez, in honor of Benito Juárez, the indigenous native son who became one of Mexico's great presidents), 330 miles from Mexico City, is typically reached by a 45 minute plane trip or a five hour highway drive. Located at the convergence of two Sierra Madre ranges, it offers spectacular views of puffy cotton clouds in brilliant blue skies over dazzling mountain ranges and verdant cactus-dotted valleys sprouting endless crops of corn. With its altitude of 5000 feet, Oaxaca enjoys a spring-like climate year round. Even during the so-called "rainy season" one typically awakens to sparkling sun interrupted only occasionally by a late afternoon or early evening shower. This provides the nutriment for its exotic vegetation, and dazzling bursts of color from flowering trees such as bougainvilleas.

Cloud formations
in the countryside

Mountain with corn
fields on the highway
to Ocotlán de Morelos

Distant view of corn
fields and valley

Bougainvilleas

Although Oaxaca remains unfamiliar to many, once a person has visited, he or she is deeply moved and intrigued by its magical cultural traditions, glorious vistas and the warmth of its people. This is epitomized by a sign prominently displayed en route to the airport: "Oaxaca es tu casa. Regresa pronto (Oaxaca is your home. Return soon)." In addition to its outstanding spectrum of folk art and handicrafts, Oaxaca offers startling indigenous markets, ancient Zapotec ruins of monumental proportions such as Monte Albán and Mitla, and world famous Spanish colonial buildings and churches housing exemplary 16th century gold leaf work. To convey the flavor and topography of the pueblos surrounding the city of Oaxaca, we provide "snapshot" descriptions immediately preceding the artists in that pueblo.

Woman selling scallions in Sunday indigenous market of Tlacolula

Bread vendor in Sunday indigenous market of Tlacolula

Woman selling carved gourds in Ocotlán de Morelos Friday indigenous market

Turkey vendor in Tlacolula Sunday indigenous market

Ruins of Monte Albán

Detail of gold leaf decoration from Spanish Colonial era, Tree of Life on ceiling of church of Santo Domingo in Oaxaca City

The Book's Organization

Our book is divided into ten chapters representing most major classes of Oaxacan folk art and handicrafts. These include Ceramics, Textiles (woven woolen rugs, cotton belts and handbags, cotton cloth, embroidery), Woodcarving, Metal Crafts (tin or "hojalata," and cutlery), Miniatures and Toys, Jewelry, Candles, Basketry and Dried Flower work.[6] In addition, there is a section devoted to folk art specifically produced for or influenced by the Day of the Dead, the major indigenous holiday of the year, and an important inspiration for many types of creative work.

In each section, spreads of two or more pages are devoted to individual artists and their families, including:

-Brief descriptions of each artist's current work, biography and technique;

-Photographs of individual artists' pieces, accompanied by their dimensions and estimated prices (the latter, based on research completed between August, 2000 and August, 2001, are subject to change);

-Personal photographs of artists with their family members and at work;

-The artist's address (and, where relevant, telephone number, as one would call from within Oaxaca.)

At the back of the book we provide:

-Family trees indicating all members[7] involved in this type of folk art, both currently and in the past;

-A list of shops, markets and streets in the city of Oaxaca in which folk art and handicrafts are sold;

-Individual maps of the twelve pueblos we have included, indicating the location of featured artists' homes;

We also provide a glossary of frequently-used terms and a bibliography of books on Oaxacan folk art and handicrafts, and the related subjects of travel in Oaxaca and the area's history, anthropology and sociology.

Detail of ruins of Mitla

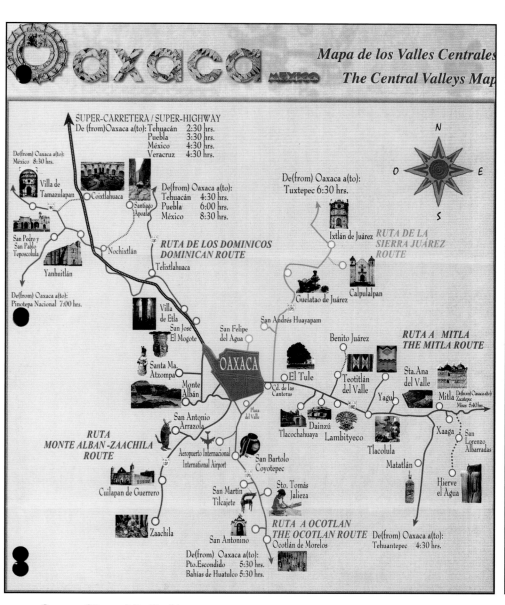

Oaxaca City and Its Pueblos

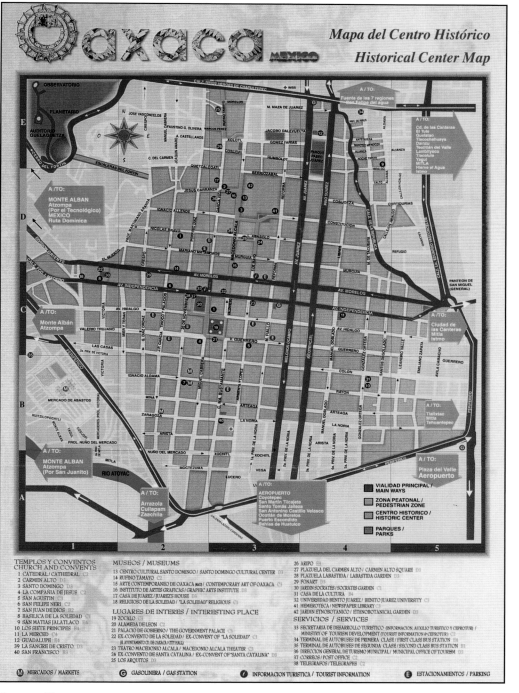

Oaxaca City

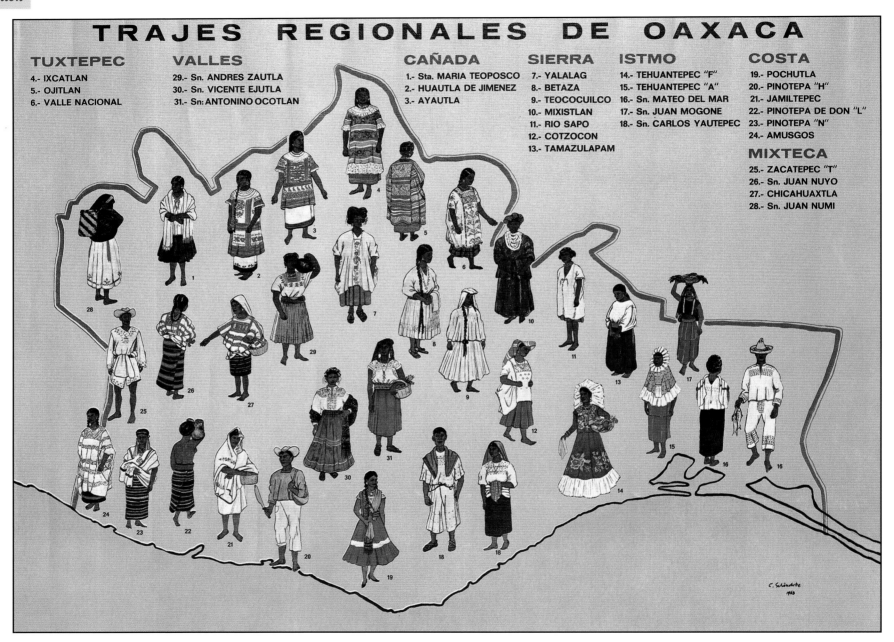

TRAJES REGIONALES DE OAXACA

TUXTEPEC
4.- IXCATLAN
5.- OJITLAN
6.- VALLE NACIONAL

VALLES
29.- Sn. ANDRES ZAUTLA
30.- Sn. VICENTE EJUTLA
31.- Sn. ANTONINO OCOTLAN

CAÑADA
1.- Sta. MARIA TEOPOSCO
2.- HUAUTLA DE JIMENEZ
3.- AYAUTLA

SIERRA
7.- YALALAG
8.- BETAZA
9.- TEOCOCUILCO
10.- MIXISTLAN
11.- RIO SAPO
12.- COTZOCON
13.- TAMAZULAPAM

ISTMO
14.- TEHUANTEPEC "F"
15.- TEHUANTEPEC "A"
16.- Sn. MATEO DEL MAR
17.- Sn. JUAN MOGONE
18.- Sn. CARLOS YAUTEPEC

COSTA
19.- POCHUTLA
20.- PINOTEPA "H"
21.- JAMILTEPEC
22.- PINOTEPA DE DON "L"
23.- PINOTEPA "N"
24.- AMUSGOS

MIXTECA
25.- ZACATEPEC "T"
26.- Sn. JUAN NUYO
27.- CHICAHUAXTLA
28.- Sn. JUAN NUMI

C. Schöndube
1963

Seven Regions of State of Oaxaca and their Regional Costumes

12

Chapter One
Ceramics

The wealth of ceramics in Oaxaca is truly extraordinary, and can easily fill many volumes. We sample five classes: terra cotta, green glazed, multi-color glazed, black and painted red. (Another attractive variety, unpainted red ceramics made in San Marcos Tlapazola near Tlacolula, is not included because of space considerations.) The first three – terra cotta, green glazed and multi-color glazed - are created in the same pueblo, Santa María Atzompa. By contrast, black pottery is specific to San Bartolo Coyotepec and painted red ceramics to Ocotlán de Morelos. We provide sketches of these pueblos immediately before the featured families.

Santa María Atzompa:
Pueblo of Terra Cotta, Green Glazed and Multi-Color Glazed Ceramics

Barely 15 minutes' drive from Oaxaca City is the pueblo of Santa María Atzompa whose elevated terrain affords expansive vistas of the valley below. A friendly sign greets the visitor: "Bienvenidos a Sta. María Atzompa" (welcome to Santa María Atzompa"). Here there is remarkable artistic sophistication side by side with age-old traditions. The experience of waiting in our red Suburban vehicle for the parade of oxen, burros and goats to clear the way captured in microcosm Atzompa's artistic contrasts.

This pueblo is home to various types of ceramic work, roughly classified as terra cotta, green glazed and multi-color glazed. (There is also a variety of utilitarian red ceramics that we have not included.) Many families of great talent carry on their longstanding traditions here, and others introduce remarkable innovations.

This pueblo has a very pleasant "plazuela" (centrally-located market) where approximately 20 artist families display their work. While worth a visit to appreciate the more traditional, utilitarian, commercial, and inexpensive types of work produced in this pueblo, visits to the artists' home are often more memorable. This is also a comfortable spot to drink a soda at well-shaded tables or to make a rest stop. With a few exceptions, the majority of ceramic pieces featured in this volume are not available in the market. However, because the homes of some families are difficult to reach or are not easily visible, they choose to display their work in this more accessible and frequented area.

Terra Cotta Ceramics
The Blanco Family

Teodora Blanco Núñez
Grand Dame of Allegorical Figures and "Pastillaje" (Surface Decoration)

See Family Tree #1, "The Blanco Family," in Appendix on page 163.

Teodora Blanco (deceased in 1980), was a renowned artist whose tradition is carried out today in the work of her son, Luis, two of her daughters, Irma and Leticia, and her brother, Faustino Avelino, and sister, Bertha. Teodora became famous in her own lifetime for the introduction of a new style of terra cotta pottery: highly imaginative "muñecas" (human doll-like figures). Many variations on these have developed. Teodora's signature pieces are of a fantastic allegorical type, human-like figures bearing animal heads or horns, nursing children or frogs. She also pioneered a type of decoration called "pastillaje" that became her trademark. Superimposing smaller pieces of clay on the surface of the figure, she created patterns or added elements to the original form.

Teodora's work expresses the great influence of traditional beliefs, especially the idea of "nahuales." In Santa María Atzompa a "nahual" is conceived as an animal spirit that serves as an individual's protector, originating at birth. However, it also has threatening implications. For example, if one's "nahual" dies, one may die as well. This is distinct from the concept of "nahual" in some other pueblos where there is a purely positive relationship.

Teodora's influence extends well beyond the boundaries of her family. Elements of her style were incorporated by many of her contemporaries, and continue to appear in the ceramics of the generations that follow. Nelson Rockefeller greatly admired her work, purchasing every last fragment she produced each time he visited her home (Oettinger, 1990).

Portrait of Teodora Blanco in 1958 by Paul Petroff

Family (left to right): Luis in front with his piece, "Muñeca" with "nahuales", and behind him (left to right) his children, Sandra, Adriana, Luis, Jr., Teodoro, and his wife, María

An early piece by Teodora Blanco.
Courtesy of Casa Panchita

A later piece by Teodora Blanco.
Courtesy of Casa Panchita

Luis García Blanco
(son of Teodora)
Maternal Tradition Combined with Personal Creativity
"My soul and my emotions go with each person who buys my work."

With a twinkle in his eye, Luis García Blanco lovingly perpetuates his mother's tradition of terra cotta figures combining human and animal features. At the entry to his courtyard stands one of his impressive pieces. A figure with a human body and animal head nurses an animal figure, while wearing a skirt covered with "pastillaje," from which small animals, such as frogs, are suspended. The family's special pieces are nativity scenes, mermaids and "nahual" figures, each "carrying a moment of our life."

Luis believes that he both conserves his mother's style and adds his own type of faces. His wife María Rojas de García, with whom he works closely, was also taught by his mother and has similarly introduced her own ideas. Luis comments, "A lot of people have copied my mother. I don't mind as long as they copy well." Luis's integration of tradition and personal innovation is further embodied in his living arrangements. He and his wife and children live in a newly constructed house on the site of his mother's original home, which is now occupied by his two brothers: Arturo, a pharmacist, and Roberto, a teacher.

Luis at work

**Tehuana woman,
20" x 9", $90**

Nativity, 10" x 7", $60

Luis is deeply involved in his work, each piece reflecting his philosophy, "If one does not have patience, one will not make anything valuable." When someone buys one of his pieces it pleases him intensely, as he feels his soul and his emotions are going with them. Luis also derives great satisfaction from seeing his work in museums and in the homes of others. He has exhibited his ceramic pieces in many museums in the United States, such as in San Antonio, Santa Fe and Tucson. Recently a German collector organized an exhibit of the best artisans of Oaxaca to tour Europe, in which he included Luis's work.

Luis's and Maria's children collaborate in ceramic work as well. Luis's greatest hope is that his mother's form of art will not die, and that the young will not forget their roots. He fears that in their eagerness to immigrate to the United States, they may fail to preserve artistic traditions and memories of the work of their ancestors. For this reason he implores the young to maintain more interest in their culture, including their art.

Biography

Luis, the eldest of Teodora's five children, began to work in ceramics at six years of age. Like all his siblings he started by playing with clay to form figures such as musicians and small pigs. By eight he became more formally involved in his work, seeing the necessity of learning as much as he could from his mother who became seriously ill. Luis made dancers that he sold in the main market in Oaxaca City. By the time his mother recuperated he had become a true artist, specializing in virgins.

Technique

Luis uses a carefully prepared mixture of white clay from Atzompa and black clay from San Lorenzo Cacaotepec. To make a large urn he initially forms the base and then its body, all by hand. Once the basic configuration is completed, he uses the "pastillaje" technique for decoration, following which the piece is dried for one or two weeks depending on the weather. Finally, after engraved decorative elements are added it is fired for approximately three hours. When the urn is removed from the oven, it either remains its natural beige tone or color is added with a substance called "esmalte," depending upon the client's preference. The entire process requires approximately fifteen or twenty days.

Address:
Avenida Libertad #502
Santa María Atzompa
Oaxaca
C.P. 71220
Telephone: 01 (95151) 27942

**Mermaid, 20" x 10",
$115**

Irma García Blanco
(daughter of Teodora)
Faithful Innovator
"Our work is done entirely by hand."

Irma García Blanco, an initially shy but actually warm expressive woman, continues to work in her mother's tradition. Especially known for her "muñecas," she also creates altars with crucifixes, angels, virgins bearing angels, nativity scenes, and mermaids. Two other specialties are fountains and Tule trees (based on the gigantic tree for which the pueblo of Santa María El Tule, close to and due east of the city of Oaxaca, is famous). These are decorated with elements from the seven regions of Oaxaca (see the map on page 12).

During our visit Irma sat on the ground working on a majestic female figure, while her older children proudly engaged in other phases of the work: creating smaller pieces, packing, and firing. Irma hopes that her children will carry on the family tradition. This aspiration has been actualized in the first and second prizes recently awarded both mother and daughter, respectively, in the same contest in Mexico City.

Irma hopes people will come and familiarize themselves with her work, which she sells in both her home and the "cooperativa" (ceramic marketplace) in Atzompa. She feels that it is only in watching the process of creation that people can appreciate the beauty of the work, and the fact that it is done entirely by hand.

Biography
Irma began to work at six years of age sitting by her mother's side, where she continued to carry out her creative work until she married at the age of eighteen. As a young girl she made only small objects, undertaking larger pieces by the age of ten.

Technique
Irma begins the creation of her large figures with the skirt that serves as a base. Following a drying period of three to four hours, she turns this portion over and builds up, subsequently adding the torso, arms, and head. Her son and six daughters aid her in this process. Finally, "pastillaje" decoration and carving is added. Large figures are formed in approximately eight days, requiring fifteen additional days to dry and three hours in the oven. Irma's work is almost exclusively in natural terra cotta colors, although she is receptive to special orders.

Address:
Avenida Juárez #302
Santa María Atzompa
Oaxaca
C.P. 71220

Family with completed piece, Muñeca, 55" x 18", $340
(left to right) Elena, Irma, Jaime holding Anita, Carolina

Irma at work with two completed pieces
Tehuana Woman, 9" x 8", $15
Mermaid,16" x 10", $55

Jug, 33" x 16", $225

Letty's lovely daughters were ever-present, helping to supply their mother with the moist clay she needed for her newly-emerging piece, showing us her completed pieces, and wrapping them up for sale. Letty deeply hopes that the children of Santa María Atzompa do not forget to learn and perpetuate the tradition of their pueblo: ceramics. She fears that increasingly many do not cherish their ancestors' life work as artisans.

Family (left to right): Cristina, Eloy, Alicia Leticia, Fernando, Reina

Nativity pieces range from 15" x 5" to 13" x 5", $275 for the collection

Alicia Leticia at work

Alicia Leticia García Blanco
(daughter of Teodora)
Creator of Small Evocative Figures
"I learned most from my mother."

Another of Teodora's daughters, Alicia Leticia García Blanco (nicknamed Letty) specializes in small, imaginative and well-crafted "pastillaje" and/or engraved figures, most especially mermaids. She also creates women at market, angels with candlesticks, figures riding burros, and nativity and procession scenes. At our visit the remains of what would have been a fabulously ornate nativity scene mounted on a round base stood next to Letty's completed work. Apparently a firing accident interfered with the completion of this treasure.

Small mermaid, 6" x 5", $2
Mermaid with frog, 8" x 7", $4
Mermaid "Vendedora", 10" x 4", $6

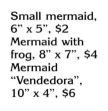

Biography

Letty grew up in the exciting innovative atmosphere of her mother's home. She began to make small figures with her mother at the age of nine or ten, becoming proficient by sixteen. At twenty she was able to form larger figures, most often mermaids. However, she has persisted with her love for the petite, creating imaginative combinations of human and animal figures.

Technique

Letty begins one of her signature small mermaids by forming the lower portion of the body. The next day she adds the base by which the mermaid is supported. After this has dried for one hour, she affixes the tail, followed by the hands, head and "animalitos" (small animals that project from the body) in the style invented by Teodora. Once completed, the figure requires one to three days to dry, depending upon the weather. Small pieces are fired for one and one-half hours.

Address:
Avenida Juárez #109
Santa María Atzompa
Oaxaca
C.P. 71220

Bertha Blanco Núñez
(sister of Teodora)
Inspired Sculptor of "Pastillaje" Virgins
"I would like people to come to know my work."

We encountered Bertha Blanco Nuñez in the artisans' market on the main street in Atzompa where she has a small stand, along with dozens of other ceramists. She accompanied us to her home and studio, a short drive away. Her best-known works are virgins, "muñecas," mermaids, angels, musicians, burros and nativity scenes. Her true artistic love is virgins, especially Soledad, the patron saint of Oaxaca.

Biography

Bertha began her work in ceramics at the age of six, helping her mother. Taught by both parents, she initially made miniatures. Her much older sister Teodora was a major influence as well. There was a time when Teodora signed and sold Bertha's work. By ten years of age Bertha began to do some work on her own, creating small muñecas. By sixteen she already produced the large virgins that remain her trademark. At seventeen Bertha had begun to be recognized herself. Since her marriage at the age of twenty-seven she has lived apart from her family of origin.

Technique

Bertha does her work entirely by herself. She described the 30-day process of creation of the huge Virgin that sat in the corner of her studio. During the first two days she makes the base: the portion of the body up to the figure's neck. On the third day she forms the head. The fourth day is devoted to one side of the cloak, and the fifth day to the other. The most difficult stage is creating the decoration, primarily "pastillaje." It dries quickly and can break easily. Last, the crown is formed and then decorated with "pastillaje." The huge figure must dry for a week, after which it is fired for four hours at a gradually increasing temperature.

Address:
García Vigil #301
Santa María Atzompa
Oaxaca
C.P. 71220

**Bertha Blanco
at work**

**Virgin of Soledad,
36" x 26", $400**

"Vendedoras" (vendors),14" x 6", $30 each

Mermaid "vendedora" (vendor), 19" x 9", $60

Faustino Avelino Blanco Núñez
(brother of Teodora)
A Blanco Pioneer in "Pastillaje"
"The day I don't work I'm not content. I love to talk to people, to relax, to sell, but work is a release, a cure."

In a pleasant, shady courtyard Faustino Avelino Blanco Nuñez (he prefers to be called Avelino) works with his two daughters and son to produce a large variety of ceramic pieces in terra cotta, green glaze, and multi-color glaze. In cheerful and prideful collaboration, they run the ceramic shop and small convenience store that stands at the entrance to their home. An enormous jug decorated with prominent "pastillaje" is being readied for a contest. On the floor nearby an ornate coffee and cup set is being painted before firing in preparation for another competition, this one in Guadalajara. Since the family enters many contests, they are always developing new designs that can later be produced for sale.

Their work ranges from the purely decorative (musician miniatures and "muñecas") to the utilitarian (jugs, planters, small plates, salsa holders, and cups) all with "pastillaje" flowers and leaves. Avelino's miniature musicians are especially lively, inspired by his thirty-two years as a guitarist in a band.

To Avelino it is most important that the young people of Atzompa not forgot its artistic tradition. He feels that even those who wish to become professionals can profit from remembering the original work of their pueblo. Although it is difficult to learn, it is worth it.

Family (left to right): Elizabeth, Noemi holding Emanuel, Avelino, Lucina

Avelino at work

Terra cotta jug, 17" x 13", $20
Terra cotta jug with blue glaze, 17" x 13", $30

Biography

Avelino began working in clay at eight years of age, making small figures. Although he learned how to fire from his mother and how to prepare clay from his father, he learned a great deal artistically from his older sister, Teodora, who was developing her "muñecas" during his childhood. Most of all Avelino regards himself as one member in the Blanco family's role as "pioneers in pastillaje."

He and his wife worked together closely for the thirty-five years of their marriage until her death in 1995. Their three children learned a great deal from her, developing the practice of producing some pieces together and others individually.

Technique

Some of Avelino's pieces are begun on a potter's wheel, while others are built entirely by hand. He creates his miniatures manually, shaping the desired figure from small lumps of clay. Avelino has designed various combinations of approximately twenty animals (such as dogs, cats, elephants, burros, goats) playing twenty instruments (for example, drums, trumpets, cymbals, violins, guitars). Working a very long day he can complete thirty such figures. Once formed they must dry for a day and then are fired for about two and one-half hours. When painted, they require a second firing of about one and one-quarter hours. Avelino makes both terra cotta miniatures (with and without paint) and green glazed miniatures, although terra cotta constitutes the vast majority of his work.

Address:
Avenida Libertad #408
Santa María Atzompa
Oaxaca
C.P. 71220
Telephone: 01 (95151) 27957

Animal musician miniatures, 3" x 1.5", $1.50 each

The Vásquez Cruz Family

See Family Tree #2, "The Vasquez Cruz Family," in Appendix on page 164.

This is an inspirational family, whose works we cherish in our personal collection. The best known member is Angélica Vásquez Cruz. Her evocative and elaborately detailed terra cotta pieces have won contests and are sources of enduring pleasure. Her success has brought attention to and catalyzed the creative work of her talented parents, Delfina Cruz Díaz and Ernesto Vásquez Reyes. In fact we first learned of them in a visit to Angélica's home outside of the pueblo's center, where some of their pieces are always on display. Delfina and Ernesto live closer to the center of Atzompa, their other daughter Enedina who produces her own distinctive terra cotta work on one side and their son Luis on the other.

Delfina Cruz Díaz and Ernesto Vásquez Reyes
Dignifiers of Everyday Life and Teamwork in Old Age
"We are pleased to be recognized for our work."

On a street accessible by car, and behind large metal doors, one finds this loving and closely-knit couple who have worked as a team throughout their 46 years of marriage. Early in their careers they made the exclusively utilitarian pieces (such as pots for rice and beans, planters and incense burners) for which Santa María Atzompa is well known. However, beginning at 40 years of age Delfina and Ernesto started to create soulful human figures and lively jugs sporting small animals and flowers - of moderate to large proportions - that are for purely decorative purposes. Some can be simultaneously used as planters. Their proud forms convey the vigor and vivaciousness of persons engaged in crucial everyday work.

Ernesto and Delfina at work

Jug with iguanas, 13" x 13", $90

Biography
Ernesto learned to work in clay from his father. Unlike many of the men of this pueblo, he did not like farming and has worked solely in ceramics during his adult years. His sister, Guadalupe Vásquez, also works in this pueblo, exclusively producing plates. Delfina's parents, who were not from Atzompa, did not work in clay. Nor did her mother endorse her choice to do this type of work. Instead Delfina learned from her half sister, Juana Martes.

Reminiscing about their lifelong involvement in ceramics, Ernesto and Delfina feel they have lost many opportunities for recognition. In keeping with their generation's custom, they devoted much of their creative lifetime to assisting artists who gained public acclaim. This often included creating entire pieces that were not attributed to them. Because Ernesto and Delfina had no direct commerce with the client and did not sign their works, their pieces were frequently mistaken for the creations of others. Now they proudly sign both of their names along with that of their beloved pueblo, Santa María Atzompa.

Ernesto and Delfina

Ernesto with three pieces:
Woman with jug, 26" x 12", $50
"Chocolatera", 21" x 17", $90
Woman with basket, 19" x 11", $50

Technique

Delfina and Ernesto's "non-commercial" pieces are made only upon order. Their "chocolatera," a seated female figure holding a baby while simultaneously stirring a pot of chocolate, is made in parts and requires approximately one week to complete. The couple begins with the base, which Ernesto decorates. Then the body and head are assembled, following which hair and earrings are added. Decoration consists of both "pastillaje" (pieces of clay superimposed on the figure to form elevated areas) and carving or stamping shapes or lines into the figure to delineate patterns. After a period for drying, the piece is fired for two or more hours depending upon the climate. The rainy season (May through October) poses a problem because moisture lengthens the process of drying the clay and firing.

Address:
Libertad #102
Santa María Atzompa
Oaxaca
C.P. 71220

Angélica Vásquez Cruz
Defender of Women's Self-Expression, Spiritualist and Raconteur
"Life is a Dream, a Dance, a Fair"

At the end of an ascending rocky road that must be negotiated on foot (cars can be parked at its base) one finds a deeply spiritual and reflective woman whose creative work and philosophy are inspiring. The challenging climb is well rewarded. Angélica Vásquez Cruz is an extraordinary raconteur who vividly relates her complex and moving history, and proudly explicates her ceramic pieces. Angélica's work is heavily influenced by indigenous legends and Mexican history.

Her house is her sanctuary. Surrounded by the trees and flowers that enchant her, Angélica pursues life as "a dream, a dance, a fair," always alert to its new possibilities. Her beloved maternal grandmother, an intensely spiritual person, confided in Angélica her "secrets" about life: "always be ready to find the beauty and intrigue in even the smallest experience or observation." "Enchanted by the night" she loves to work into the wee hours of the morning when, undistracted by the practical matters of life, the atmosphere is tranquil and she can enjoy the sounds of the wind. Angélica lives with her sons (her daughters have moved to the city of Oaxaca) and Don Juan, an animated American man originally from Texas. He has been her devoted life partner since the mid-1990's.

A staunch advocate of the rights and talents of women, Angélica's preferred theme is women, their significance and their multiple life roles. She has fought hard to defend her right to be a creative artist in a highly traditional culture which, from her perspective, discourages women's independent self-expression. One of

Family (left to right): Juan, Carlos, Angélica

her pieces, a woman with three personalities, is a vivid statement of this view. One side is a woman and the other a man; in the center stands a devil, signifying the image of women men cannot accept.

Angélica regards each piece she creates as special. No two are exactly alike. Nor does she produce a large volume of work. Her creations encompass a wide spectrum: small ethereal but spirited angels, to majestic female figures and large sculptural compositions. Due to their complexity and detail, the latter can take up to four weeks to create. Angélica refers to such pieces as "temas completas" (complete themes), in that they convey her interpretations of historical and contemporary subjects, such as the Mexican Revolution or the Abastos market, the largest market in the city of Oaxaca. Rather than a lot of people milling about, Angélica views the market as an embodiment of the universe. She explores its role in educating and transmitting cultural influences to those who engage in its commerce, and the interactional effects of "good" and "bad" people and produce.

Biography

Angélica dates her now very considerable success only to 1992. She began her work in clay as a child of seven, learning from her parents. Like everyone else in her pueblo she began by making cups, and graduated to vases at nine to ten years of age. When her father began to produce planters in the form of "muñecas" (dolls) Angélica was responsible for decorating them with details such as flowers and butterflies. By 11 she contributed the arms and faces. All the while she felt a yearning to do her own purely decorative (non-utilitarian) work. Her parents regarded it as "strange" and to no avail, convinced no one would buy such pieces.

Angélica married at the age of 18 and had four children in rapid succession. Ultimately abandoned by her husband and forced to live with her in-laws, she fought a hard uphill battle to be credited for her own artistic work. At present none of Angélica's four children carries on her tradition in clay. Although this makes her sad, she recognizes that, as a younger person, she did not wish to pursue this kind of work. One daughter, Nancy, wants to be a doctor. Another, Alicia, works as a secretary in the city of Oaxaca. Angélica's son, Ángel, creates painted carved wooden birds and the other, Carlos, is considering work in clay.

Technique

Angélica's use of two types of clay contributes the texture and varying coloration to her pieces, which she does not paint. She has, however, developed natural substances, "agobes," that are additional sources of color (further detail about this appears in the section on her sister that follows). Angélica begins by creating the base, to which other pieces are attached once it has dried for approximately an hour. Her pieces are fired at the home of her parents, in the oven shared by all members of the family.

Address:
Avenida Independencia #337
Santa María Atzompa
Oaxaca
C.P. 71220

Angélica with her piece, Revolutionary, 16" x 14", $1000

**"China Oaxaqueña",
12" x 8", $200**

23

Nativity Angel,
10" x 8", $275

Angels, 8" x 6", $40 each

Woman with Jug,
10" x 7", $135

Enedina Vásquez Cruz
Creative Historian of Regional Costumes and Religious and National Themes
"What really helps us live and keep working is not money, but when someone comes and says, 'I love that. It's different from anything I've ever seen.'"

Behind distinctive tin gates punctuated with bottle caps, Enedina Vásquez Cruz, a beautiful, slight woman, creates her original pieces with a loving spirit. She takes deep pride in having broken from tradition and being original. This includes her introduction of new designs and techniques, some of which she has developed along with her sister Angélica. Enedina distinguishes between artisans and artists. She believes the latter require more experience in life.

Enedina has a growing reputation for her female figures dressed in costumes of the seven regions of Oaxaca (see the map on page 12), and her two-sided pieces treating historical and religious subjects. One features the birth of Mexico on one side and the Virgin of Soledad on the other. In another the nativity of Jesus is visible on one side, and the Virgin of Guadalupe on the other. Some pieces double as utilitarian objects. An angel has a segment that serves as a pencil holder, and a bird bearing small figures has a recessed area that can be used as an ashtray. Enedina does not have a favorite style; all her pieces are inspired by her "sueños" (dreams).

Family portrait (left to right):
Verónica (daughter),
Enedina, Eduardo (husband)
holding Raymundo (son)

Woman in regional
costume of Ejutla,
20" x 10", $100

Enedina at work

Enedina does her own work from start to finish. Her husband creates green pottery, and her daughters are beginning to produce terra cotta figures. One table in their home bears Enedina's pieces, and two others display the work of her daughters and husband, with a few pieces of her own sprinkled among them.

Enedina hopes that her daughters will eventually perpetuate this art form, and will not forget its significance. It is also deeply important to her that they and others who appreciate ceramics will recognize her innovations.

Mermaids, 13" x 10", $90 each

Two-sided piece: (left to right) Birth of Mexico and Virgin of Soledad, 15" x 12", $200

Biography

Enedina began to work in clay at 12 years of age, making miniatures. Both of her parents influenced her. She recalls her father as the person who conceived the designs, while her mother made the forms such as the skirt, body, arms and faces of the figure. Her father then added the decoration. When she married at age 20 Enedina began to work independently, both out of necessity and creative inspiration. She experienced the calling of her own ideas and dreams. "One starts playing and ends creating." One of her first independent pieces was a collection of women wearing the costumes of the seven regions of Oaxaca.

Technique

Approximately six years ago, Enedina joined her sister Angélica's ongoing efforts to develop "agobes," natural substances distinct from paint that are applied to ceramic pieces to add color. They have created a wide range of colors to improve and distinguish their work. Enedina explains that this technique lends more life to a piece. This is in contrast to the limited number used by other artists in Atzompa. "Agobes" are laborious to make, based in clay and colored with natural substances such as volcanic ash and stone. Some change color when fired, while others do not. For example, green becomes beige and another type becomes gray if fired one way, and blue-white if fired another way.

Address:
Libertad S/N (without number)
Santa María Atzompa
Oaxaca
C.P. 71220

Luis Vásquez Cruz
Creator of Animal Figures
"My parents gave me this opportunity."

Luis has only undertaken work in ceramics since 1996, when he returned to Oaxaca from Mexico City where he was a mechanic. However, he originally learned from his father and mother as a young boy. His pieces, sold in the market, are very different from those of his sisters. Being less complex, he can complete up to 24 in a day. Luis proudly shared with us his list of the 22 small animals he produces, some of which are horses, pigs, rabbits, dogs and llamas. His favorites are ducks and dolphins.

Address:
Libertad #202
Santa María Atzompa
Oaxaca
C.P. 71220

Family (left to right): Esperanza (wife) holding Silvana (granddaughter), Luis

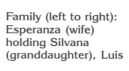

**Animal figures
Large pig, 7" x 5", $13
Lamb, 5" x 5", $12
Small pig 5" x 5", $12**

Green Glazed Ceramics

Guadalupe Aguilar Guerrero and Her Daughters
Embodiment of Dignity in the Creation of Green Glazed Ceramics
"This is my heritage. We hope you come to know us more directly."

See Family Tree #3, "The Aguilar Family," in Appendix on page 165.

In their courtyard, amidst strutting chickens and turkeys, many members of this huge extended family create lovely traditional pieces in the work for which Santa María Atzompa has long been known: green glazed pottery referred to as "loza verde." Guadalupe Aguilar Guerrero, a dignified and agile woman in her 70's and the proud mother of nine and grandmother of 15, sits on the floor of her patio lovingly shaping and then decorating a fruit bowl ("frutero"). She adds pieces of clay to the smooth surface to create grapes, leaves and flowers in relief.

Guadalupe's pieces are designed with utilitarian purposes in mind: cooking, serving, holding flowers and candles, and the like. She especially likes to make pitchers for mezcal (some in the shape of roosters through whose beaks the liquid pours), bowls for making chocolate and "atole" (a corn-based drink), salsa dishes and pitchers. Two daughters who live with her, Teresa and Juana Lorenzo, create their own styles in the same type of ceramic work. Teresa specializes in vases and pitchers of various sizes, and Juana Lorenzo in salsa dishes, many of which are decorated with birds.

In addition to selling out of their home, the family participates in the Mercado de Artesanías (artisans' market) in the city of Oaxaca on Tuesdays, Wednesdays and Saturdays.

Biography

The family's work in green glazed pottery extends back for two generations ante-dating Guadalupe's generation on her

Family (left to right): Front row: Guadalupe, Juan. Back row: Teresa, Lorenza

side of the family, and for one generation on her husband's side of the family. The first in Guadalupe's family to work in this folk art form were her grandparents, followed by her parents. Both of Juan's parents worked in this art form as well, the first in their respective families.

Guadalupe began her work in ceramics at eight. She learned how to make miniatures from her grandmother with whom she and her parents lived. By 10 to 12 she made her first pieces independently: miniature pots, cups and saucers that were used as toys. At 15 Guadalupe began to make jugs and other larger pieces, taught by her mother whose workmanship was considered superior. Because Guadalupe's mother came from a ranch in another pueblo, she learned this craft later in her life than most native residents of Atzompa. She was especially known for her large pieces: liquor pitchers, coffeepots, and jugs.

When Guadalupe married at 27 she stopped making miniatures, which she found too laborious, and worked exclusively in the pieces her mother taught her to make.

Technique

Guadalupe and her family purchase the clay they use from San Lorenzo Cacaotepec. Before drying it they take out its many stones and impurities with a filter. Two types of clay are mixed together to create the desired consistency for the utilitarian uses for which the pieces are intended.

To make a fruit bowl supported by a pedestal Guadalupe works entirely by hand, with the exception of assisting the formation of the bowl's bottom. She begins by placing a pancake-like piece of clay in a large saucer made of the same clay, something like a pie crust in a pie dish. She shapes it by hand, creating grooves and indentations with her hand and a toothpick. Other pieces of clay are formed independently and superimposed on the inner surface for further decoration: "pastillaje." This is the most common type of decoration used. The piece is dried for approximately 15 days, following which the initial firing of one and one-half hours takes place. The bowl comes out white at this stage. Then a yellow-colored glaze, "greta," is

Guadalupe at work

applied and the piece is fired a second time for two hours, resulting in a brilliant green. Guadalupe estimates that she can fire approximately 200 medium size pieces at once.

Guadalupe's daughter Teresa forms her pieces without any "mold," such as the saucer used by her mother, while Juana Lorenzo follows her mother's technique.

Address:
Corregidora #301
Santa María Atzompa
Oaxaca
C.P. 71220

Teresa's pieces:
Vase, 7" x 5", $3
Pitcher, 6" x 5", $3
Mug, 4" x 3", $2
Vase with handles, 5" x 3", $2

Guadalupe's pieces: Fruit bowl, 13" x 7", $7
Liquor vessel, 8" x 5", $3
Pitcher, 10" x 7", $4

Lorenza's pieces:
Incense burner,
8" x 6", $3
Small salsa bowl,
5" x 3", $3
Large salsa bowl,
8" x 6", $3
Ashtray, 7" x 7",
$3

Multi-Color Glazed Ceramics

The Regino Porras Family

See Family Tree #4, "The Regino Porras Family," in Appendix on page 166.

The extensive family of Dolores Porras and Alfredo Regino Ramírez, and their nine living children and countless grandchildren, produce a wide spectrum of ceramic work. However, they are best known for their multi-color glazed planters, vases, candleholders and platters.

Dolores Porras and her husband Alfredo Regino Ramírez
Pioneers in Multi-Colored Glazed Ceramics
"Tourism always comes. One day our children will carry on my tradition."

Dolores Porras Enríquez and her husband, Alfredo Regino Ramírez, are renowned innovators of the use of color. Their two-step firing process permits the production of multiple colors. Plates are boldly decorated with flowers, mermaids, human faces, iguanas, fish and birds, both painted and in relief. Vases sport multiple faces or swirling rows of color. While Dolores does create "muñecas" and mermaids with "pastillaje," in both terra cotta and multi-tones, the vast majority of her pieces are not figural. She and her husband Alfredo have an intimate working relationship. She creates the work, and he fires and sells it. Their many children and spouses create similar pieces, each one developing his or her trademark design elements.

Biography

Dolores Porras grew up with her father and stepmother. She began learning to work in clay at the age of 13, making utilitarian pieces such as casseroles and pots for cooking "frijoles" (beans) as she worked with her father, brother and aunts. Dolores continued to live with her parents until she married at the age of 18. Having established her own home and begun a large family, she continued to attempt to earn a living by producing cooking items, working in others' houses to produce the traditional green pottery ("loza verde") for which Atzompa was known. This continued for 10 years. Teodora Blanco was one of the people for whom Dolores worked and from whom she learned. Dolores adds that some of the pieces she produced were signed by Teodora, as was the custom at that time.

Still very poor Dolores began to create utilitarian objects decorated in distinctive ways about 25 years ago. Turtle heads and feet were affixed to flower pots, as were other animals. Faces were added to plates. This was the beginning of Dolores's recognition as an artist. She remembers her thrill when one specific promoter of folk art, Roberto Donis, placed the first large order of her work: twenty flower pots. She could not sleep, both because of her excitement and the need to produce such a large quantity of work in a short time. Teodora Blanco followed, buying Dolores's turtle planters for re-sale.

Dolores at work

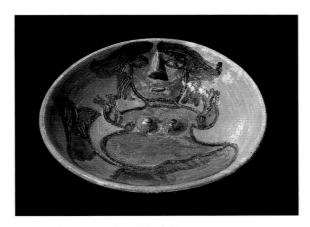

Mermaid plate, 17" x 17", $17

Family (left to right):Front row: Maricela, Vilma, Leticia, Dolores, Alfredo, Itzel (child in front). Back row: Clara, Luis, Rolando

Another important turning point in the careers of Dolores and Alfredo was the visit they paid to a painter friend. Observing her work they thought, why not paint on ceramic pieces? They researched how to do so with the help of another friend. Recognition soon followed. Dolores's work has been shown in museums in Mexico and brought to the United States since 1980. She has had multiple invitations to the United States, the most recent one in July, 2001.

Technique

Dolores uses a mixture of black and white clay to create a stronger substance, less vulnerable to breakage. The mixture is prepared by Alfredo. Black clay is mined in San Lorenzo Cacaotepec, while white clay comes from the "terrenos" (hills) of Atzompa. Alfredo reminisced about how in former times he secured the black clay by traveling to San Lorenzo seated on a "petate" (a woven straw mat) placed on the back of a burro.

Dolores and Alfredo use a two-step firing process that is necessary to produce their multiple colors. Since her pieces are not only decorative, but sometimes used for cooking and sewing, Dolores is very careful to use non-toxic paints that she imports from Monterrey.

Dolores works on several pieces simultaneously. If she makes a mermaid, she simultaneously forms six plates. If she produces a "muñeca" (doll), she decorates the pieces she has created the previous day. The beginnings of 12 jugs can be completed in one day, following which another day is necessary for decoration. Some combination of engraving, painting colored stripes and/or attaching faces is used.

Address:
Hidalgo #502
Santa María Atzompa
Oaxaca
C.P. 71220
Telephone: 01 (95151) 27792

Face jug, 14" x 12", $15

**Striped pot,
12" x 10", $12**

**Dancing women,
20" x 10", $90 each**

Irma Regino Porras
(daughter of Dolores Porras and Alfredo Regino)
Master of Geometric and Cut-Out Decoration
"The legacy of my mother is strong. She has given me the heritage of knowledge of secrets of this art form"

Irma Regino Porras specializes in plates and vases, jugs and planters with open work (cut-outs) decorated in multi-colors. She also makes casseroles. Her particular designs are geometric figures and "alcatrazes" (callas lilies), the type of flowers Diego Rivera's paintings made famous. Many of Irma's pieces mix these two patterns together. Her 22 year-old son, José, specializes in geometric patterns. Unlike her mother and many other artists in Atzompa, Irma does not use "pastillaje."

Because her home is difficult to reach by car, and one must walk the last stretch on foot, Irma has a stand (number 73) in the ceramic market in her pueblo. She also sells out of the home of her brother Norberto and his wife "Rosy" (see page 33), and through middlemen.

Biography
Irma's work is strongly influenced by that of her mother, from whom she began to learn to work in clay at the age of 12. For Irma, "the legacy of my mother is strong." The first of nine

children, she recalls her mother's standards being strict, but eventually helpful. For example, when her pieces did not turn out well, her mother would break them. Irma's initial pieces were jugs and casseroles. Her original work was in green glazed ceramics, the traditional style in the pueblo at that time. But when she married she and her husband decided to change their decorative technique and to produce the multi-color pieces introduced by her mother.

Technique

Irma and her husband use a mixture of white clay from Atzompa and black clay from San Lorenzo Cacaotepec that results in a beige tone. To make a jug, they mold the clay until the desired form is achieved, after which it is dried for three hours. Cut-outs are created at this time, following which there is another period of drying for approximately eight days. The initial firing of the piece is for one or two hours. Colors are applied prior to the second firing for two hours.

Address:
Ignacio López Rayón #103
Santa María Atzompa
Oaxaca
C.P. 71220
Telephone: (95151) 515458415

Irma at work   **Cut-out glazed flower pot, 17" x 8", $14**

Family (left to right): Miguel Jr., Lady, Miguel, Rosa, Irma

Aurelia Regino Porras
(daughter of Dolores Porras and Alfredo Regino)
Versatility in Decoration of Multi-Colored Ceramics
"Please come to visit and get to know us."

Aurelia Regino Porras creates excellent quality multi-color and terra cotta ceramics with a variety of decorative elements, often in combination: "pastillaje," cut-outs and painted patterns. A thoughtful and quiet but articulate woman, she is exacting and methodical in her work, producing outstanding pieces of this type. Her workshop is in her own home on the main road leading into Santa María Atzompa, and across the street from her brother Norberto and sister-in-law Rosy (the next featured artists).

Biography

Aurelia began to work in ceramics at the age of 14, learning from her mother. She started later than her siblings because she was in school and wished to complete her education. However, given the family's economic necessities, she frequently attended for a few months, only to be withdrawn for a number of months. Therefore, she did not graduate until she was 21.

31

Aurelia's first pieces were the classic green glazed jugs used for meals. She continued to work primarily in green glazed ceramics between the ages of 14 and 22. However, when she married at 29 she and her husband, who had also made green glazed pottery, developed their own designs in multi-colored glazed ceramics. They also produced "natural" (terra cotta) pieces.

Aurelia has been distressed by the tendency of her fellow Atzompans to copy designs she introduces. For this reason she prefers to sell out of her own home, rather than the market.

Technique

Aurelia and her husband purchase their clay from San Lorenzo. She works entirely by hand, with the exception of the "wheel" created by placing two ceramic saucers back to back. After completing a piece, she partially dries it prior to adding decorative elements, such as flowers and animals, to the surface. Aurelia also decorates by "engraving" such designs into the surface with a nail. She fires pieces in terra cotta once, and glazed pieces a second time. In addition to chemical ceramic paints, Aurelia sometimes uses natural substances to add color to her work.

Address:
Libertad #619
Santa María Atzompa
Oaxaca
C.P. 71220

Aurelia at work

Family (left to right): Front row: Aurelia, Celestino. Back row: Patricia, Celestino Jr., Martha, Gabriela

**Glazed flower pots: 10" x 20", $20
10" x 20", $15**

32

Norberto Regino Porras and his wife Rosa Elena García López
(son and daughter-in-law of Dolores Porras and Alfredo Regino)
Contented Collaborators in Multi-Color Glazed Ceramics
"We are always imagining new things as we sit with the clay in front of us."

Norberto and his wife Rosa Elena García López (known as Rosy) live and work on the main road in Santa María Atzompa, a short distance from his mother and father, Dolores Porras and Alfredo Regino Ramírez. This handsome couple exudes an air of satisfaction and peace as they both carry on his mother's tradition, while also adding personal elements. Their attractive multi-colored casseroles, flower pots, vases and jugs are produced primarily for local consumption, given their practical nature and their heavy weight. Some have elaborate cut-outs and others are engraved and then painted with bold or subtler flowers.

Norberto and Rosy each produce their own pieces, with the exception of the especially large jugs on which they collaborate. Because these works are extremely time consuming, Rosy forms them and Norberto adds the decoration. All the small jugs are hers. Norberto takes most pleasure in creating vases, while Rosy's favorite pieces are "muñecas" with fine "pastillaje" decoration. However, this constitutes only a small portion of her work.

This couple has begun to earn recognition, exhibiting in other cities such as Guadalajara and Monterrey. When asked why they do not sign their pieces, Norberto and Rosy indicated they "forget." Upon further reflection, they believe this would take too much time, compromising their ability to produce a large volume. In addition to displaying and selling their plentiful ceramic work in their new and easily accessible home, Norberto and "Rosy" participate in the cooperative market of Atzompa.

Biography
Norberto began to work in clay at seven years of age, learning all aspects from his mother and father. By 16 he made his own piece, a plate decorated with flowers, mostly roses, on the border. Norberto began to work on his own when he married at the age of 19. Rosy's family did not work in ceramics. She too was trained by Norberto's mother, Dolores Porras, to whom she is very grateful.

Technique
The process of creation of a large jug takes approximately one month from start to finish. Rosy begins the basic form on a foot-driven wheel. Norberto contributes the decoration that requires three days. He cuts out delicate and plentiful openings with a narrow knife, or adds superimposed patterns of flowers or other figures. The piece must then be dried thoroughly, which may require eight days in the dry season or up to 20 days in the rainy season. This is followed by four to five hours in the oven. When the jug has cooled, paint is applied and a second firing is necessary: three hours at a higher temperature.

Address:
Avenida Libertad #622
Santa María Atzompa,
Oaxaca
C.P. 71220

Family (left to right): Rosa Elena, Carlos, Norberto

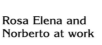

Rosa Elena and Norberto at work

Glazed flower pots:
13" X 23", $30
10" x 22", $40
13" x 17", $20

33

Fish pattern pot, 22" x 10", $60
Cut out pot, 28" X 14", $80

Black Ceramics
San Bartolo Coyotepec:
Pueblo of Black Ceramics

This village, approximately 12 kilometers (20 minutes) from Oaxaca, is known for its black pottery. Here clay is characteristically spun on two clay saucers placed back to back. The majority of the trip to Coyotepec is on a level, pleasantly re-paved highway. Prominent signs announce your arrival: "Coyotepec," "Welcome to the Artisans' Market. San Bartolo Coyotepec." A large white church also marks the spot. It is estimated that approximately thirty families work in the typical ceramics of this pueblo, about five of them creating work of outstanding quality. We feature two of these families.

Ceramics can be found both to the left and to the right of the highway. A left turn onto an unpaved, extremely bumpy road brings you to many small artisan shops. Along the way a local musical group, "Mariachi Coyotepec," advertises its work. On the left side of this road you come almost immediately to "Alfarería Doña Rosa," a famous landmark. It is the home and workshop of the descendants of the now deceased Doña Rosa, an artist who became famous for her outstanding abilities, including her application of the ceramic technique known as "negro brillante" (shiny black). Her son, daughter-in-law, four grandsons and three daughter-in-laws continue this work today.

On the right side of the highway is the home and workshop of many members of another extremely talented family, the Pedros. The other members live only a short distance away, also to the right of the highway. Just beyond the Pedros's home on the right side of the main highway, and in the center of town, there is a small market with a neatly arranged collection of stalls selling rather commercial but attractive pieces. The market is adjacent to a neatly manicured and pictur-esque park, complete with gazebo.

The De Nieto Castillo Family
See Family Tree #5, "The DeNieto Castillo Family," in Appendix on page 167.

Doña Rosa Real Mateo and her Descendants
Legends in Shiny Black Pottery ("Negro Brillante")

Doña Rosa, who died in 1980, is a giant in Oaxacan ceramics. Despite her diminutive size, she earned renown for her expertise in creating beautiful forms and applying quartz to the clay before firing. This resulted in a brilliant and intense black surface, in contrast to the previously dull gray appearance of the utilitarian ceram-ics of this pueblo.

The experience of watching Doña Rosa work, which Arden had the great for-tune to do in the 1960s, was unforgettable. A petite powerhouse of a woman, she sat on the ground on a "petate" (a woven straw mat) next to her "wheel," two gray ceramic saucers placed back to back, a method pre-dating the Spanish conquest. Without a wasted movement, she fashioned graceful shapes out of clay, as inspired ideas flowed through her fingers in a seemingly endless stream.

The son and daughter-in-law of Doña Rosa, as well as four of their sons and three daughters-in-law, respectfully carry on her legacy. Both their debt to her and their success are immediately apparent in the boldly displayed sign "Alfarería Doña Rosa" that cannot be missed as one approaches the pueblo of San Bartolo Coyotepec.

In their workshop and beautifully-designed display area on a grand patio sur-rounding a courtyard, the family creates and exhibits a vast range of primarily decorative, reasonably-priced pieces. Styles range from traditional to more con-temporary. A non-exhaustive list is large jugs, vases, small figures in a variety of poses (nursing babies, holding bowls of fruit, fishing, making tortillas, modeling regional costumes), small delicate boxes, candleabras, candlesticks, and masks. To maintain the shiny surface, pieces cannot be fired for the lengths of time requi-site for utilitarian purposes. For this reason they cannot actually be used for cook-ing or as vases for live flowers, since water disintegrates them.

Each member of the family, or couple, exhibits his or her work in one section of the grand showroom. However, this is not obvious since individual works are not identified as such. It was not until we had visited their workshop many times and inquired about personal styles that we came to identify these differences.

All pieces are hand-built and decorated in one or more of five ways: engraving (with the use of bamboo or a sharper tool), cut-outs (made with a knife), "pastillaje" (pieces of clay added to the surface to create a relief), superimposed pieces of metal, and colored paints.

On any given day, several family members are present to demonstrate their techniques and to man the eternally busy sale table frequented by tour groups and local residents alike. Don Valente (Doña Rosa's only child) and one or more of his sons create pots from scratch. His sons (all of whom are trained as professionals but also work as ceramists) and daughters-in-law have a rotating system for cover-age of the thriving family business.

Display of black pottery without quartz finish, courtyard of Alfarería Doña Rosa

Doña Rosa at work in 1963

In-ground oven at Alfarería Doña Rosa

Don Valente Nieto Real
(Doña Rosa's son)
Master of the "Wheel" in Black Ceramics
"I am grateful to my mother for having taught me this beautiful art, and in turn I can transmit it to my children so that the tradition will not disappear."

Don Valente's signature pieces are vases, jugs, candleholders and miniatures. Despite the introduction of many creative elements, Don Valente prides himself on perpetuating the fundamentals of his mother's work. To this day he goes to the Cerro del Coyote (hill of the coyote) on burro to collect the necessary clay. He utilizes the pre-Hispanic method of placing one convex plate upon another, back to back, and spinning them in a manner comparable to a potter's wheel to form pots. Finally, he uses a primitive oven run by burning wood.

Biography

Don Valente began to work in clay at 11 years of age, at the side of his mother and father. His first pieces were birds, pitchers and ashtrays. By 12 he made mezcal jugs bearing an array of figures. Clay molds were used at the beginning, but the rest was done by hand. Around this time his mother became expert in "negro brillante," which changed the tide of the family's work from utilitarian to decorative pieces. Don Valente has continued and perfected this tradition.

Family (left to right): Front row: Doña Rafaela, Don Valente, Fernando. Back row: María, Javier, Erasmo

35

Technique

Following the collection of clay, Don Valente carefully prepares it for many days. After mixing it with water, he filters impurities and stones, with the use of a cloth or plastic cover, until it is clear. It is a matter of pride to him that his clay is non-toxic, entirely free of lead. Finally, air bubbles must be removed by passing the clay from hand to hand. Work with clay is done in a closed room, so that variations in air or heat do not render the pieces more fragile. Quartz is applied before firing.

To make a jug, Don Valente begins with the base on one day, forming it on the convex dish "wheel." The next day he adds the mouth and decorates the piece in any of a number of ways. The piece is thoroughly dried in the sun before applying quartz and/or paint. Firing takes eight to ten hours. Don Valente estimates that he can complete 12 jugs in 30 days. (Because all family members employ the same basic technique, individual comments appear only when a feature is unique.)

Address:
Benito Juárez #24
San Bartolo Coyotepec
Oaxaca
C.P. 71296
Telephone: 01 (95155) 10011

Candelabras:
11" x 5", $5
8" x 6", $5

Jug, 9" x 8", $16
Small vase, 8" x 5", $6

Don Valente at work

Doña Rafaela Castillo Cardozo
(Don Valente's wife)
Elegant Creator of Graceful Female Figures
"We hope you will get to know our work in 'negro brillante.'"

Doña Rafaela, an elegant and gracious woman, creates graceful female figures. Some hold white flowers and others display regional costumes. She also prides herself upon producing an array of animals (especially cats and birds), masks and vases. The latter are among her favorites.

Doña Rafaela wishes visitors new to San Bartolo Coyotepec to appreciate that her family, beginning with her mother-in-law Doña Rosa, has been responsible for teaching many of the people in their pueblo in "negro brillante." The technique has been so widely disseminated that the tourist who makes a single trip may easily miss this historical fact.

While always remaining faithful to the basic methods of Doña Rosa, Doña Rafaela and her family are forever working to perfect their technique and to develop new style elements. She particularly enjoys studying nature and incorporating what she sees in her pieces.

Biography

Doña Rafaela began her ceramic work when she married her husband, Don Valente, at the age of 15. Learning from her mother-in-law and father-in-law, her first pieces were small jugs and female figures.

Cut-out jugs:
7" x 5", $8
6" x 3", $5

Doña Rafaela at work

**Woman with jug,
13" x 4", $12**

Erasmo Nieto Castillo and his wife Rita Rocío Andrés Calderón
(son and daughter-in-law of Don Valente and Doña Rafaela)
Blenders of Traditional and Abstract Design
"We hope visitors will appreciate the distinct quality of our work."

Erasmo Nieto Castillo and his wife Rita Rocío Andrés Calderón (she prefers to be called Rocío) specialize in decorative surfaces that are a blend of shiny quartz and matte finishes. These are used on vases, small animals and candleholders. Erasmo and Rocío have also created a collection of graceful modern configurations with purely shiny surfaces. Their pieces can be used for specific purposes (such as single and double vases for dried flowers) or simply to provide visual pleasure. In addition, they produce traditional pieces such as trees of life and vases with pre-Hispanic designs. In general, Rocío forms the pieces and Erasmo decorates them.

Erasmo and Rocío at work

Biography

Erasmo began to work in ceramics in his family's tradition. Rocío initially learned to work in ceramics at the age of 16 from her father who made utilitarian jugs and pitchers. He traveled the indigenous markets of Ocotlán and Tlacolula on his burro, laden with a huge number of pieces. Poorly remunerated, he gave up this work in favor of full-time farming. Rocío's serious ceramic work began when she married Erasmo at the age of 20. Her initial pieces were vases. The couple's first jointly created design was a pyramid of birds that many people in their pueblo have replicated.

Tree of Life, 12" x 10", $15

Vases: 10" x 5", $13
9" x 8", $9

Jorge Nieto Castillo and his wife Alejandrina Galán Morga
(son and daughter-in-law of Don Valente and Doña Rafaela)
Innovative Decorators of Black Ceramics
"Visit us and you will have a pleasant surprise. In our work we express the thoughts that occupy us."

This couple specializes in innovative methods of decorating pieces in shiny black pottery: cut-outs, engraved pieces of pewter that are superimposed on the ceramic work, and gold leaf decorative paint. Metal decorations, introduced in 1995, are applied to many types of pieces, such as pots, vases, boxes and small animals. Jorge and Alejandrina's signature pieces are candleabras, vases, trees with birds, turtles and birds.

The process of transmission of parental talents to the next generation was evident as we photographed this couple. As Jorge shaped a bird mounted on a base, and Alejandrina used a sharp knife to cut openings out of a wet pot, their lovely five year old daughter formed her own bird, no doubt influenced by her father's work.

Biography

Jorge began his work in ceramics at the age of ten, first making birds. Alejandrina has created black ceramics since childhood, taught to make simple pieces such as ashtrays by her mother. However, when she married Jorge she developed newer and more complex designs, such as cut-out jugs, pitchers, nativity scenes and vases.

Jorge, Diana and Alejandrina working

Technique
    Once pieces are fired and cooled, pewter applications are mounted with a special glue that is applied with cotton. After a day's drying, another liquid is used to shine the metal decoration. Cut-outs are created with knives specially designed for that purpose.

Jug with pewter, 10" x 8", $17
Box with pewter, 4" x 3", $9

Jug with cut-outs, 16" x 15", $70
Jug with cut-outs and gold leaf decoration, 17" x 15", $90

Javier Nieto Castillo and his wife María Mota
(son and daughter-in-law of Don Valente and Doña Rafaela)
Artists Specializing in Black Ceramic Boxes and Mask
"Working in clay is a noble profession that allows one to create in cly whatever one wishes to express."

Javier and Mariá's specialties are jewelry boxes decorated with engraving or cut-outs, vases, and jars with an unpatterned shiny surface. They are also known for their masks, small animals and busts.

Biography
    Although Javier has played with clay since he was eight, at 15 he began to help his parents with their work by making animals such as crocodiles, elephants, giraffes and deer. After their marriage he taught María this type of art. She learned rapidly and together they began to create their own designs with which they have had much success.

Technique
    Javier and María require approximately two hours to engrave their vases, and slightly more to create cut-out decoration. Following decoration the piece is dried for five or six hours

María and Javier at work

depending upon the weather. When semi-dry, decorative techniques are continued, for example rubbing the piece with quartz to achieve its sheen. Firing lasts about eight or ten hours, the entire process taking 20 to 25 days.

Masks, 8" x 7", $6

Vases :
10" x 5 1/2", $5
8" x 4", $6
8" x 3", $5

Vase with handle,
$17" x 6", $12

Fernando Nieto Castillo
(son of Don Valente and Doña Rafaela)
Outstanding Engraver and Vase Sculptor
"I, like many young men of the village, try to prepare myself to enhance this art to offer the tourist new designs in black ceramics."

The youngest of Don Valente's sons and still a student in accounting, Fernando works in ceramics part-time. In addition to his signature vases with huge handles and his elephants, he assists all family members, and most particularly his mother, in decorating their pieces. He is especially talented in "drawing," a technique similar to engraving designs, and in creating cut-outs.

Biography
Fernando began to work in clay at the age of five or six, initially learning from his grandmother and then continuing to learn by "practicing and living." At 16 he began to make jugs.

Fernando at work

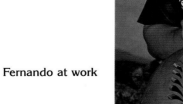

Vase, 7" x 7", $4
Lantern, 8" x 4", $4
Duck, 8" x 4", $4

The Pedro Martínez Family
Blending Tradition and Creative Genius in Black Clay

See Family Tree #6, "The Pedro Martínez Family," in Appendix on page 168.

This is an extraordinarily talented, productive and distinctive clan of artists who create purely decorative pieces in the black pottery for which their pueblo is renowned. What distinguishes this family is the remarkable diversity of their individual styles. Each of the parents, Antonio and Glafira, their five adult children (three sons and two daughters), and now a grandson, has developed his or her own type of work. One, Carlomagno, has achieved international fame for his outstanding interpretive pieces. Several other members have received significant acclaim, and their reputations are steadily growing.

Although they do not work collaboratively on individual pieces, family members are close-knit. This is evident in the mammoth, elegant showroom recently added to the home in which Antonio and Glafira live with two of their married children, Carlomagno and Magdalena, and their grandson, Antonio Eurípides. Pieces by all members of the family are displayed and sold there. The other three grown Pedro children live side by side in their own homes about one block away from this house. Departing from our custom of proceeding from eldest to youngest, we first present the family members who live together and then those with separate households.

Family (left to right): Front row: Glafira, Antonio. Back row: Federico (Magdalena's husband), Antonio Eurípides, Magdalena, a son of Abel, Carlomagno holding Carlomagno, Jr., Paula Maricela

Antonio Eleazar Pedro Carreño
An Artist Who Never Rests Self-Satisfied
"If you copy someone else's work, you also copy their errors. It is better to make your own errors."

A proud and dignified man, Antonio Eleazar Pedro Carreño never rests self-satisfied. Striving to improve his work and create new designs has been his lifelong credo. Many of his current pieces treat religious subjects such as the virgins most significant in Oaxacan culture.

Biography

Antonio began to work in clay when he was six years old. Although his father had been involved in ceramics, Antonio did not learn this craft from him. Because he was only one and one-half years when his mother died, Antonio was sent to live with his uncle. There he helped a neighbor when he was out of school, in exchange for instruction. Soon Antonio began to make human figures on his own, as well as hens and small dogs. When he left school at the early age of 12 because it ended at 4th grade, he spent more time farming than working in ceramics.

It was not until Antonio married at 26 that he completed his first major pieces: horses, bulls, and cows. He also continued to work as a farmer, an experience that inspired him to create figures of farmers as well. These he sold in the market in Oaxaca City, since few tourists visited the pueblos at that time. Over the years Antonio developed additional styles that he produces to this day: Virgins of Soledad and Guadalupe, mermaids and bells, the latter often in the form of "muñecas" (doll-like figures).

Antonio and Glafira with their pieces:
Virgin of Guadalupe, 26" x 12", $400
Angel, 8" x 2", $5
Mermaid, 9" x 9", $15

Technique

Antonio's distinctive virgins take approximately eight days to make. First he rolls out a clay "tortilla" (pancake) from which he creates the main portion of the figure with a clay mold designed for this purpose. After drying this for one day in optimal weather (and two to three days in the rainy season) he adds the head and crown and begins to decorate it with engraving. This work is done entirely by hand.

Antonio recalls the many years it took to perfect his expertise with the oven. When black pottery is fired too long it takes on a dull gray, rather than shiny black, appearance. Repeated experimentation has finally enabled him to correct for the tendency of ovens to hit sudden temperature peaks.

Antonio at work

Virgin of Soledad, 17" x 10", $45

Glafira Martínez Barranco
Motherly Creator of Small Figures and Animals
"I am proud to see my children continue with this tradition, each one in his own way."

Glafira Martínez Barranco is a gentle and warm, motherly woman who, in her own quiet way, bursts with pride at the combined perpetuation of tradition, creativity and success of her children. She produces small pieces based on ideas that occur to her. These include angels (both freestanding and for wall display), mermaids, and animals such as armadillos, pigs, and elephants.

Biography
Glafira began to work in clay at 12 years of age. Neither her father nor her mother was a ceramist. However, a woman who frequently visited their home taught her to make small male and female figures, and to decorate whistles, larger birds, and bells produced in the dull gray finish characteristic of work in Coyotepec at that time. Glafira sold these pieces very inexpensively to other artisans who had stands in the market.

When Glafira married at the age of 20, her husband encouraged her to charge more for her pieces and to diversify her styles. Together they began to make rabbits, fish, ducks and virgins. However, over time Glafira and Antonio developed their own designs and produced their own pieces from start to finish.

Technique
Glafira requires approximately one week to complete a mermaid. She begins by forming the body and then adds the face, hands and tail, leaving time for portions to partially dry before attaching them. For this reason she works on two figures at a time, alternating between them.

Address:
Guerrero #1
San Bartolo Coyotepec
Oaxaca
C.P. 71296
Telephone: 01 (95155) 10034

Glafira at work

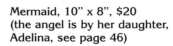

Angels, 9" x 3", $6 each

Mermaid, 10" x 8", $20
(the angel is by her daughter,
Adelina, see page 46)

Carlomagno Pedro Martínez
(son of Antonio and Glafira)
Unique Interpreter of Legends, Morality and History
"Popular art is a continuation of the contribution of the artists who worked before."

Address:
Guerrero #1
San Bartolo Coyotepec
Oaxaca
C.P. 71296
Telephone: 01 (95155) 10034

Carlomagno at work

A modest and somewhat reticent man, Carlomagno Pedro Martínez is a powerful and innovative artistic force. Since 14 years of age he has created unique sculptural forms and wall sculptures (or reliefs), based on his interpretation of legends, stories and cultural beliefs. In recent years he has gained extraordinary international recognition for his distinctive assemblages of figures and objects treating a range of subjects. These include beliefs associated with the Day of the Dead (such as skeletons and devils with carts, see one of these pieces on page 161 in Chapter Ten), Mexican history (soldiers and other historical figures) and morality (for example, the devil responding to the temptation of a couple making love). Carlomagno's figures range from "nahuales" (mythical figures pictured as humans with animal faces) to witches, devils and "muertos" (skeletons in human activity). Some are small, while others are collage-like (ceramic forms mounted on large canvases), and still others are major sculptural works of grand proportions.

While taking deep pleasure in the acclaim and the commercial success that he has achieved, Carlomagno wishes never to forget his place in a longer history of artistic work. He feels it is especially important that the cultural significance of Mexican folk art as a whole be remembered, along with its pre-Hispanic influences: "Popular art is a continuation of the contribution of the artists who worked before." He would like his children to realize this and to continue in this tradition, if they so choose.

With regard to his own work, he hopes collectors appreciate that in each piece lies a profound story.

Grandfather with devils, 9" x 9", $230

Biography
Carlomagno began working in clay at four years of age, taught by his parents. Initially he made small birds and then graduated to somewhat larger pieces by eight to ten years of age. By 15 he introduced sculptural forms, at which time his unique talent was already recognized in exhibitions of his work in Chicago and San Francisco.

Technique
Carlomagno begins by moistening the clay he will use for that day and then softening it with his hands. As a boy he participated in digging up the clay he and his family used, but now it is purchased. Carlomagno forms his pieces in parts, joining them together for his ultimate creation. Finally he uses pieces of quartz to rub the dry but unbaked clay to achieve contrasts between the shiny portions that result and those that will have a matte finish. Once completed his pieces are dried for eight days and then fired in the oven for seven hours. He leaves them in the oven, which has been turned off, for ten additional hours to cool gradually.

"Nahuales" with Bull, 15" x 5", $390

Butterfly mural,
40" x 22", $900

Detail of the history of the conquest (approximately 150 pieces), 88" x 30",
$2800

Magdalena Pedro Martínez
(daughter of Antonio and Glafira)
Physician and Ceramic Archivist of Regional Costumes
"I wish to preserve traditions in the form of regional clothing."

Magdalena Pedro Martínez is a sensitive young woman who is both an outstanding ceramist and a medical doctor. She currently devotes more time to ceramics than to medicine, but has a small office in her pueblo. Both she and her husband, also a physician, are available for house calls.

Magdalena specializes in female figures dressed in the traditional costumes of the seven regions of the state of Oaxaca (see map on page 12). She views this as her particular contribution to the broader cause of preserving the culture of her beloved ancestors. At present Magdalena has recorded 24 costumes in her ceramic masterpieces. She generally creates these figures in both sculptural and statuesque sizes. On occasion she fills a special order to produce a life-size figure whose face is a commissioned portrait. Magdalena is currently designing a collection of large costumed figures for a museum in Mexico City.

She works in a combination of shiny black and matte surfaces that capture, in the absence of color, the rich detail of costumes. Her favorite "traje" (costume) is that of the mountainous area of Tuxtepec, because of its brilliant colors and vibrant decoration, including flowers and ribbons. Magdalena especially admires the Tehuana women (from the distant Isthmus of Tehuantepec in the state of Oaxaca) who proudly preserve their traditional dress. She noted the irony of people who wear Tehuana "huipiles" (traditional tunic-like garments, square in shape with openings for the head and arms) with modern pants, as if they were peasant blouses.

Magdalena also produces a number of additional spectacular pieces: elegant and pompous "catrinas" (female figures for the Day of the Dead, see such a piece in Chapter Ten, page 161) sporting elaborate formal dresses and parasols, and a lamp that bears small female figures dressed in the costumes of the seven regions of Oaxaca.

Force of Passion, 12" x 8", $900

Biography

Magdalena was "practically born" working in clay, although she did not seriously dedicate herself to her art until the late 1980s at the age of 19. Prior to this she was deeply involved in her studies to become a doctor. Magdalena cited several inspirations for her specialty of women in costumes. When she was very young one of her father's pieces, a woman in costume, stuck in her mind. At one point she thought, "Why not make more pieces like those of my father?" She also loved to attend the annual "Guelaguetza," a regional dance festival, and especially enjoyed the richly detailed and colorful costumes worn by the female dancers.

Magdalena takes special pride in recording costumes that are no longer known. When her grandmother was still alive she created a vivid verbal picture for

Magdalena at work

Magdalena of the already-defunct traditional clothing of their pueblo, San Bartolo Coyotepec. Magdalena later captured it in clay. This was extremely difficult because the costume was all white, lacking the kind of detail more easily recorded in multi-tones of black.

Technique

Magdalena begins by making the faces of her figures. Then she creates the torsos separately. She rolls out a "tortilla" of clay and folds it over. The skirt and blouse are added to the torso. Finally the arms and face are attached. These segments are followed by accessories, such as a "rebozo" (shawl woven in cotton or wool) or pineapple. Each part must dry for two hours before being assembled. Magdalena estimates that it takes her a day to complete this portion of the process. Another day is necessary to engrave and otherwise finish the piece. The fully assembled and decorated piece requires eight hours to dry in the dry season, and up to four days in the rainy season. At this point quartz is ap-

plied to achieve the shiny finish. Pieces are cooked overnight and removed from the oven in the morning. From start to finish the process takes approximately one week.

Address:
Guerrero #1
San Bartolo Coyotepec
Oaxaca
C.P. 71296
Telephone: 01 (95155) 10034

Large figure in regional costume of Tuxtepec, 39" x 16", $1700

Figure in regional costume of Tuxtepec, 17" x 7", $225

Antonio Eurípides Pedro González
(grandson of Antonio and Glafira and son of Amando)
Creator of Assemblages Preserving Everyday Pueblo Life
"I transmit what I see of my people, their feelings and beliefs, to conserve the customs of my pueblo."

A lively young man whose career is off to a running start, Antonio Eurípides Pedro González is deeply devoted to the preservation of his cultural and religious tradition. His pieces reflect his cherished religious beliefs, daily and historical customs such as cooking, and the costumes of the seven regions of Oaxaca. Antonio loves to create assemblages of figures, such as processions in honor of the Virgin in which people carry religious objects. At the time of our visit Antonio had just completed a scene, an elaborate arrangement of many pieces, depicting how women traditionally cooked in the pueblos. He included utensils of olden times, and women making "tortillas" and cooking in casseroles. He also makes female figures in their regional costumes on a far smaller scale than those of his aunt Magdalena. Antonio Eurípides's work has recently been featured in a gallery in Oaxaca City.

Antonio's devotion to his culture was also evident in his preparations for dancing in the "Guelaguetza." This is an extraordinary annual celebration of traditional dances, performed in memorable garments. It takes place the two Mondays after the birthday of Benito Juárez (an indigenous native son of Oaxaca who rose to become one of Mexico's most revered presidents), July 18th. Antonio's vividly colored, plumed headdress for the "Danza de la Pluma" (dance of the feathers) sat in the corner of the new family showroom. This is the festival's highlight, in commemoration of the valiant struggle against the Spanish conquest.

Biography

Antonio began to work in clay at the age of six years, learning from the grandparents with whom he now lives. At seven he made his first personal pieces, animals such as birds and rabbits. By ten he introduced his beloved religious images, such as the Virgin of Soledad. At 17 he began to create "muñecas" (female figures) wearing regional costumes.

Technique

Antonio estimates that it took him a week to create his recent celebration of traditional indigenous cooking. First he makes the "muñecas." After forming their bodies, he adds the faces. Finally, he polishes the pieces with quartz to create a sheen. Then he carries out the decoration, creating the face, and eyes. Firing pieces in the oven takes only four hours, given their small size. However, when it is full more time may be required.

Address:
Guerrero #1
San Bartolo Coyotepec
Oaxaca
C.P. 71296
Telephone: 01 (95155) 10034

Antonio Euripides holding one of his figures

Antonio Eurípides at work

Kitchen Scene, including women making tortilla 10" x 4", table 8" x 3", large turkey 4" x 3", "metate" 4" x 3", small turkey 3" x 2", $230 for the scene

Adelina Pedro Martínez
(daughter of Antonio and Glafira)
Creator of Enchanting Angels and Mermaids and Inspired Raconteur
"Our work is to preserve our cultural heritage. It always carries a message about our everyday life."

Adelina Pedro Martínez, an extremely likeable and determined woman with distinct talent as a raconteur, specializes in enchanting black pottery angels and mermaids. Their distinctive faces are both cheerful and otherworldly. One of our favorite pieces is her large angel playing a mandolin whose flowing, matte and shiny skirt is punctuated by inserted baby angels and carved flowers. Adelina lives and works in the lovely home she shares with her husband and three daughters, for which she saved by selling her own work since the age of 15. Her house is located a few blocks from the home shared by her parents, her sister Magdalena and her brother Carlomagno. She is surrounded on either side by her two other brothers, Amando and Abel, and their families.

Adelina hopes that the pieces she currently produces become more valuable over time, and that her children continue in her family tradition: conserving the original style as well as introducing something of their own. She takes great pride in the fact that, even though very small, each of her daughters has started her career as a ceramist. With delight Adelina displayed a piece by her youngest daughter, only four years of age.

Biography

Several people have influenced Adelina's work. One is her two-year younger brother Carlomagno, whom she regards as extremely intelligent and enterprising. He impressed her in childhood by industriously building an oven while the other children played on their grandparents' grounds. Her father, a perfectionist, also taught her a great deal. In addition, Adelina incorporated into her angels and mermaids the extraordinary designs of a male artist in her pueblo who died tragically early. One was his style of placing candleholders on the heads and shoulders of his "muñecas."

Adelina's earliest memory of working in clay is of making necklaces at four years of age. To support the family, both her parents worked in the field in the mornings and then with clay in the afternoon. At six she made her first pieces intended for sale: small vases. However, when customers came to purchase her parents' work, they by-passed hers. She began to lose faith in

Family (left to right): Adelina, Federico and their children, Huitzilín, Quetzal and Citlalicue

her own abilities, and to longingly admire others' work as superior. Adelina's father encouraged her to persist with her own designs, cautioning, "If you copy someone else's work, you also copy their errors. It is better to make your own errors."

During Adelina's childhood, objects that did not whistle were difficult to sell. Though she considered this feature to be primitive and unimportant artistically, and despite her creativity (exemplified by her introduction of a distinctive bird design), Adelina continued to have trouble mastering this commercially necessary element. Her older sister, adept at this, tried to help her. However, Adelina frequently had to discard up to eleven pieces until she finally succeeded on the 12th. She also began to make other objects, such as turtles.

Adelina and her siblings spent many hours playing at their grandparents' house while their parents worked. They explored plants and animals, and unearthed small fragments of primitive ceramic work made long ago. The discovery of mermaids produced by past generations inspired Adelina to embark on this design beginning at age eight or ten. While the general idea of mermaids came from her ancestors, she created her own style: a non-whistling figure that consisted of a solid base and openings in the tail and body. The first person to see these figures commissioned 200 of them, affording Adelina instant success.

Technique

Adelina's pieces are created in parts. She begins her smallest angel candleabras with the skirt. Then she makes the musical instruments and finally the candleholder portion. This takes approximately four days, followed by firing for seven hours.

Address:
Zaragoza #3
San Bartolo Coyotepec
Oaxaca
C.P. 71296
Telephone: 01 (95155) 10175

Adelina at work

Angel with flowing skirt, 17" x 9", $100

Large mermaid, 16" x 14", $45
Small mermaids 9" x 8", $25

Amando Pedro Martínez
(son of Antonio and Glafira)
Designer of Multi-Purpose Pieces
"Traditional artwork is to conserve the culture. We have the serious problem that there aren't enough of us to meet the public demand."

Amando Pedro Martínez creates female figures, eclipses, and lamps that have segments encompassing multiple purposes (such as jugs and vases). He described the problem he encounters in his pueblo. Designs that are successful are readily copied by others. His solution is to ready himself with a steady flow of new designs, a talent that he feels he shares with his family. As an example he showed us his new style of a face composed of a half moon and half sun.

Biography
Amando first worked in clay at three years of age, "growing up with it." At five he made his first figures, miniature animals: lions, bulls, birds, horses, and frogs. By ten to 11 he created larger figures, partially made with molds.

Address:
Zaragoza #1
San Bartolo Coyotepec
Oaxaca
C.P. 71296
Telephone: 01 (95155) 10043

Family portrait (left to right): Front row: Xochipilli, Tonnantzín.
Back row: Misraím, Jovita, Amando

Amando at work

Abel Pedro Martínez
(son of Antonio and Glafira)
Celebrator of Life and Death
"I hope new generations will continue our tradition and not be distracted by other paths."

Abel Pedro Martínez creates ceramic figures, many of which relate to the Day of the Dead: skulls, skeletons, and female figures with skeletal faces. He also prides himself on his trees of life. When we visited, three of his children sat with Abel and his wife, each member of the family working on an individual piece. Cheerful mariachi music served as the background for their creative efforts.

It is Abel's cherished wish that his children, and the new generation in general, will not abandon the ceramic tradition of their family and pueblo.

Biography

Abel began his work in clay at the age of eight, making miniatures. At nine he created his own figure for the first time, a deer, for which he won a prize in school. When he married at 17 he began to make more complex figures such as mermaids, female figures with regional costumes, and masks.

Address:
Zaragoza #2
San Bartolo Coyotepec
Oaxaca
C.P. 71296

Piece combining jug, lamp, vase, mermaid, 20" x 7", $170

Eclipse, 8" x 5", $7

Family portrait (left to right): Front row: Jesús, Nextli, Alán, Abel Jr.
Back row: Gloria, Christián, Abel, Veronica, Paulina

49

God of Corn, 12" x 8", $60
Burro,   9" x 4", $25
Bird, 7" x 3", $6

Band of Monkeys, 6" x 4", $230 for the set of 11 pieces

Painted Red Ceramics
Ocotlán de Morelos:
Pueblo of Painted Red Ceramics

Ocotlán de Morelos, approximately 30 kilometers (45 minutes) due south of Oaxaca, is home to the extraordinary Aguilar ceramic family. Their ceramics and the fabulous cutlery and swords of another (unrelated) Aguilar family (see Chapter Five on metal work) are the major types of folk art produced here.

This is both a thrilling destination and a memorable trip. En route to Ocotlán a winding road ascends through the mountains, from which one looks down upon the verdant valley below on the right and up at hills on the left. The terrain is dotted with cacti and cultivated fields. Passing many other significant pueblos along the way, flat land gives way to lush vistas, with low lying puffy white clouds, so stunning that they hardly seem real.

Your arrival is signaled by a bold sign bearing the words, "Bienvenidos a Ocotlán" (Welcome to Ocotlán). Four Aguilar sisters live and work on the main street, which also leads to the indigenous market and town square. Their brother Jesus's studio is a short distance away. The homes of Irene, Guillermina and Josefina (in that order) come up very quickly on the right, while Concepción's home is on the left, just before this cluster. Their ceramic pieces, some very large, mounted on the exterior of their homes serve as a landmark.

A steady stream of "taxis" (bicycles attached to shaded two-seater vehicles) passes up and down this road. These transport local residents to and from the market that abuts the center square. On Fridays a wonderful indigenous market flows through this area, but a smaller version takes place daily. There is also a museum housing a fantastic ceramic collection, featuring most prominently the work of all members of the Aguilar family.

The Aguilar Alcántara Family
Joyful Celebration of Everyday Pueblo Life and Cultural Traditions

See Family Tree #7, "The Aguilar Alcántara Family," in Appendix on page 169.

Isaura Alcántara Díaz
Innovator of Colorful Decorative Indigenous Figures of Everyday Life
"Learn more than you already know and you'll be a great woman. Learn because this inheritance no one can take away."

Isaura Alcántara Díaz (who died in 1969 at the early age of 44) was the innovator of an important and delightful genre of ceramics. Departing from the utilitarian objects produced by her contemporaries in Ocotlán de Morelos, she introduced decorative human figures. These imaginatively captured the daily activities, passionate expressiveness and cultural richness of pueblo life. Her highly detailed, colorfully painted human figures embodied its vitality, depth of emotion and pulse. Women in indigenous garb were portrayed in every aspect of life: transporting their wares and possessions, displaying and selling their produce in the market, nursing their babies, arranging their flowers, attending funerals and weddings, praying, sitting on park benches with their "enamorados" (romantic loved ones), and celebrating fiestas. Isaura Alcántara was recognized as a major artistic figure by significant collectors of Mexican folk art such as Nelson Rockefeller and Alexander Girard.

Isaura had a profound influence on the creative lives of four of her daughters, Guillermina, Josefina, Irene and Concepción (from eldest to youngest) and her ex-son, Jesús. In addition to perpetuating her tradition in current day Ocotlán de Morelos, they honor her memory in their loving verbal tributes to her as a person. Most of Isaura's vast number of grandchildren, some of whom have developed their own personal (although clearly derivative) styles, are ceramists. The most famous and distinctive is Lorenzo Demetrio García Aguilar (a son of Josefina) who is increasingly recognized as a powerful artistic force.

In view of the great significance and size of this family, the work and family tree of each of Isaura's children that works in clay is individually presented.

Mermaid. *Courtesy of Casa Panchita*

Woman praying. *Courtesy of Guillermina Aguilar Alcántara*

Guillermina Aguilar Alcántara
Embodiment of Generativity, Wisdom and Spirituality
"A whole family working in clay is like a plant that eternally flowers."

See Family Tree #7-A, "Family of Guillermina Aguilar Alcántara," in Appendix on page 170.

Guillermina Aguilar Alcántara, the eldest of the four Aguilar sisters, is an extremely warm, spirited and pious woman. Inspired by her fertile imagination, her ceramic repertoire is rich. It includes female figures (large, medium and small) in highly detailed costumes, down to their dangling earrings. They engage in every facet of daily life, such as selling and carrying their wares and nursing babies. She also creates stunning trees of life standing nearly a yard high, and whimsical water jugs with animal heads (see one of her Day of the Dead pieces on page 160 in Chapter Ten). Guillermina clearly adores each figure she creates, caressing it as if alive. She regards the faces of her pieces, which are especially expressive, as her greatest contribution.

Guillermina's sense of connection to her mother permeates her life. It is evident in her work, in the prominently placed display case that preserves four of her mother's few remaining pieces – forming a kind of cherished shrine–and the altar dedicated to her mother's memory. The altar stands next to the outdoor wooden table at which Guillermina carries out her creative work for long hours each day. There is nothing somber about this celebration of her mother. Guillermina is a woman deeply involved in her current life with her many beloved children and grandchildren with whom she shares her home. She is extraordinarily proud of them and

Family (left to right): Front row: Estefam, Mauricio, Jaime, Guillermina, Leopoldo (husband), Julio. Back row: Juan, Guadalupe, Alejandro, Isabel, Rosario, Julián

has encouraged each one to introduce his or her own individual features or style. For example, her daughter Guadalupe specializes in making "Fridas" (female figures based on the very popular artist Frida Kahlo), while her son Julián is known for his "ladies of the night."

Biography

Guillermina learned to work in clay from her mother "since birth," first creating pots. In her earlier years she also produced bells, incense burners and water jugs. According to Guillermina her mother was an exacting teacher. When, at age 20, she made a candleabra that did not meet her mother's standards, Isaura indicated her displeasure by breaking it in her daughter's face. Although initially angry at her mother, in retrospect Guillermina feels that her pride in meeting her mother's high standards enabled her to successfully develop her talent. As the eldest child, Guillermina's assistance was crucial to the family's economic survival. For this reason she never attended school, something she claims she does not regret. Instead she learned at home, never hesitating to ask about whatever interested her.

Preservation of the family heritage is deeply important to Guillermina, who lovingly pointed out her "muñeca" that captures her grandmother's style of dress. When she married at 21, Guillermina taught her husband to paint her pieces. Later she offered the same instruction to her eight children.

Guillermina feels her success solidified only in the last decade of the twentieth century. Although she has always desired that all of her family members participate in this tradition, "like a plant that eternally flowers," before then her children were pessimistic about the viability of supporting themselves in ceramics. This was despite her efforts, guided by the spiritual presence of her mother whom she remembers with "mucho cariño" (deep love), to optimistically assure them that success would come.

Guillermina's sense of generativity extends beyond the boundaries of family. With sparkling eyes and infectious enthusiasm, she speaks of her trips to the United States (Chicago and several cities in Texas), Panama, Nicaragua and Costa Rica. She is especially thrilled by the exchange of ideas and techniques that come about when she participates in a clinic to instruct others in her way of working. In Chicago she taught students from six to 20 years of age. Transcending self-interest, Guillermina generously acclaims the work of innumerable artists and artisans unknown to her, both in the state of Oaxaca and in the world at large. She hopes that all governments will support their artists.

Guillermina at work

Technique

Guillermina begins her human figures by forming a "tortilla" (pancake) from which she shapes a skirt and a body in one full piece. Arms are created separately, as are heads. Guillermina emphasizes the need to work rapidly once she has begun a figure, in order to prevent it from drying before all parts are completed. It typically takes her four days to make a "muñeca" (a female human figure), which is fired for 16 hours. This is the optimal period to prevent the faces from turning black. Guillermina, who feels she does not paint very well herself, relies upon her son Polo to do the majority of the excellent painted decoration of her pieces. From start to finish a large "muñeca" requires 15 days to produce.

Address:
Prolongación Morelos #430
Ocotlán de Morelos
Oaxaca
C.P. 71510
Telephone: 01 (95157) 11109

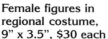

Tree of Life:
Large, 37" x 23", $335
Small, 27" x 18", $280
Mini, 23" x 15", $225

Female figures in regional costume, 9" x 3.5", $30 each

Market woman selling flowers, 13" x 6", $45

Josefina Aguilar Alcántara
Renowned and Faithful Carrier of the Maternal Torch
"Fame doesn't always carry money with it, but it does bring great satisfaction."

See Family Tree #7-B, "Family of Josefina Aguilar Alcántara," in Appendix on page 171.

Josefina Aguilar Alcántara, a serious and dedicated artist, is deeply involved in her outstanding work as a ceramist in her mother's tradition. The second daughter of Isaura, she resides in the left-most (if one faces them from the road) of three sequential residences of Aguilar daughters. Josefina creates "muñecas," human figures of both female and male gender, in a vast array of activities, venues and costumes (see also one of her Day of the Dead pieces on page 160 of Chapter Ten). She considers her specialities, either in their details or their entirety, to include headdresses, mermaids, crosses, "women of the night," the Last Supper and "zocalo" scenes (people seated on benches in the town square). Recently she has added male lovers.

These can be collected as individual figures or as remarkable assemblages depicting scenes such as a wedding, a funereal procession or a park. Josefina regards the faces, and especially the noses, of her figures as her trademark. In fulfilling the many requests that she has for "Fridas" (figures based on the very popular Frida Kahlo), Josefina emphasizes her practice of making different faces on each one. She produces the same figures in various dimensions: large, small, and even miniatures.

Women of the night by Guillermina's son Julian, 12" x 6", $23 per figure

Family (left to right): Front row: Josefina and José with their grandchildren, Gladys, Sara and Carina. Back row: Leticia, Rodrigo, Raquel, José Juan, Roberto, Elizabeth holding Frida, Arsenia, Demetrio

Josefina loves her work, and takes special pleasure in accompanying her pieces to the many exhibitions marking her success. Since 1985 she has traveled to San Diego, Austin, San Antonio, Dallas and Chicago. Equally rewarding to her are visits to her home by collectors to see her process of creation and her completed works.

Biography

Josefina began her beloved work in clay at eight years of age, learning at her mother's side. Initially she made small figures to which she refers as "novias" (sweethearts). At ten she began to contribute to her mother's larger pieces by making their faces and arms. By 15 she was creating her own figures. Josefina has similarly trained her own children in every aspect of the process of ceramics. She only signs pieces that are entirely her own, not engaging in the custom of some well-known artists of signing their lesser known relatives' work. She has encouraged her children, all of whom work in clay, to introduce their own designs. Her son, Demetrio (see pages 59 and 60) is a great talent who is recognized in his own right.

Josefina lives in the separate home she established upon marriage before her mother's death. She shares it with her husband, José, their eight living children and, in the case of those who are married, their spouses and children, Josefina's grandchildren. Nearly every member of this vast extended family is actively engaged in one or more aspects of the production of the ceramics for which they are famous: gathering the clay, preparing it for use, firing, painting, selling and preparing it for distribution.

Technique

The clay for Josefina's work is collected from five meters under the ground, following which it is put in the sun to dry for two to three days. It is then placed in a vat with water for two more days. Following removal to a "petate" (a straw mat) it is stamped by foot to make it smooth. For each piece, the clay is formed into a "tortilla" from which the skirt is cut. Next the arms, head and accessories are formed and added. Upon completion the figure is dried for about one week and then fired for nine hours. Painted decoration follows, typically with acrylic paints, although natural colors from the "sierra" (mountain ranges) were originally employed. The tones used range from brilliant to subtle, adding to the evocative qualities of her pieces. Josefina's husband, José, sits by her side hour after hour, responsible for a good portion of the painting.

Address:
Prolongación de Morelos #428
Ocotlán de Morelos
Oaxaca
C.P. 71510
Telephone: 01 (95157) 10214

Josefina at work

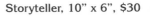

Storyteller, 10" x 6", $30

Frida, 20" x 5", $225

Market scene, 5-6" x 1-2", $7 each

Zocalo scene, 5" x 6", $225 for a 16-piece scene (some pieces not in photo)

Irene Aguilar Alcántara
Sculptor of Everyday and Mythical Scenes
"You don't need special clay to work. What is really special is the hands of the person working with the clay. I thank my mother for the great inheritance that her hands left me, her work. Now I carry it on in my hands and my heart."

See Family Tree #7-C, "Family of Irene Aguilar Alcántara," in Appendix on page 172.

As you step into Irene Aguilar Alcántara's home and studio, her vivacious and imaginative spirit is immediately palpable. Her cheerful, bright, and packed showroom conveys the broad range of her original work. She is known for her individual pieces such as musicians, devils, monks, "women of the night," "catrinas," (elegantly dressed female figures with skeleton faces for the Day of the Dead) and "fruteros" (fruit bowls). Sitting on the lips of these bowls is an array of figures, including lovers, the Three Kings, or "muertos" (skeletal figures engaged in human activi-

ties). In addition, Irene creates spectacular sculptural works, such as complex market scenes and an earth mother melded with foliage.

Irene is inspired by the rich customs of Oaxaca. She travels from pueblo to pueblo in search of thematic material, taking photos and mental pictures wherever she goes. She does not reproduce what she sees in its original form, but instead combines images from multiple settings to arrive at her own interpretation. Irene cites the example of her impressive sculpture of fruit vendors. One day, as she drank water in the square in the city of Oaxaca, she noted a woman in modern garb selling fruit. A few moments later she noticed a poor indigenous woman sharing "tortillas" with her little boy who was modestly clad only in underwear. She proceeded to mix these diverse aspects of Oaxacan life in her artwork. Another piece was influenced by her observation of the arrival of a large family - grandparents, parents and children - at a gathering. An indigenous funereal procession in a pueblo, in which all women bore flowers and men candles, was the stimulus for another piece. Noticing that people did not wear black, Irene drew the conclusion that, "Mourning is in the soul, not in the dress." This became the piece's central theme.

Irene's great talents have been widely recognized. Since 1986 she has regularly exhibited in the United States in cities such as Phoenix, Chicago and Santa Fe. She now spends time in Santa Fe each July where she exhibits at the Davis Mather Folk Art Gallery. Some of her pieces are on permanent exhibit in the Girard Collection of the Museum of International Folk Art in Santa Fe. She has also won first to fourth prizes in many competitions since 1990.

Biography
The fifth of Isaura's nine children, Irene began to work in clay at three years of age. As she put it, "My only toy was clay." Irene's deep involvement with her mother

Family (left to right): Nancy, Juan, Andrea, Irene, Socorro with Ana, Manuel is evident. She regards her mother, "standing at my side," as her "great teacher and friend." Irene only went to school for two years because of her responsibilities at home, especially that of caring for her brother.

As was the custom, she began her work in clay by making water jugs. Influenced by her mother's innovative figures, Irene began to create her own designs by the age of ten: weddings, baptisms, candleabras, angels, mermaids, nativity scenes. At 18 her mother died, "leaving me a lot of pain." While bearing a great deal of household responsibility, she also carried on her mother's work. This mitigated her sense of loss, as if her mother still lived on within her. When she married at age 20, she assumed the responsibility for her own household and family of three children. All three children now work in clay, perpetuating their mother's and grandmother's tradition.

Technique

Irene works entirely from her imagination. A large assemblage such as the fruit vendors takes her approximately one week, while the "madre tierra" (mother earth) takes about 15 days, as she builds one part that must dry before another can be added.

Address:
Prolongación Morelos #432
Ocotlán de Morelos
Oaxaca
C.P. 71510
Telephone:01 (95157) 10334

**Nativity fruit bowl,
12" x 10", $90**

Fruit Vendors. 16" x 8", $340

**Mother of the Earth,
15" x 24", $500**

**Irene with her piece, Deceased
Child, 16" x 8", $170**

Irene at work

Concepción Aguilar Alcántara
Inspired Interpreter of the Detail of Nature
"I want to make every piece I create better than the last one."

See Family Tree #7-D, "Family of Concepcion Aguilar Alcántara," in Appendix on page 172.

Inside a small, rather dark dwelling across the street from her sisters Guillermina, Josefina and Irene, Concepción Aguilar Alcántara and her husband Jorge Sánchez Ruiz sit side by side pensively creating their own individual pieces. She shapes a graceful female figure as he completes a nativity scene situated beneath a vast gnarled tree. One of their daughters lovingly tends to her two-year-old daughter and then joins her parents to paint the angel she molded the day before. Although Concepción has taught her own daughters and her husband to work in clay, she enjoys the fact that each one creates and paints his own pieces.

Concepción takes special pride in the great detail of her pieces, finding inspiration for her work in nature. She looks at pictures, but never copies them, instead filtering them through her imagination. In one of her pieces, brilliantly painted butterflies and delicately textured rocks are suspended from a vibrant cactus.

Concepción is also recognized for her Noah's arks and her elegant and expressive "Fridas," figures based on Frida Kahlo, the renowned artist and wife of Diego Rivera. She began to make these in the early 90s when a Japanese man visited her home to commission a great number of Fridas and Diegos for an exhibit he was arranging in Japan. (See also a Day of the Dead piece on page 160 of Chapter Ten). Concepción's dream is to be able to come to the United States one day for an exhibition of her work.

Biography
Únlike her older sisters, Concepción feels she learned more about her craft from her father than her mother. This is because she lost her mother at the very young age of eight. At first Concepción joined in the family tradition of producing market figures and assemblages. However, this style was not deeply satisfying to her. By the age of 12 she intro-

Family (left to right): Front row: Concepción, Jorge. Back row: Gabriela, Estela holding Jennifer, Ángel

duced her own designs: devils. Later she added whimsical and cheerful Noah's arks, butterflies, and small insects.

Technique
Concepción gets her clay from the river of Ocotlán. After re-moistening it for one night, she begins to mash it with her feet to remove all air bubbles. Concepción's figures are formed entirely by hand. A "Frida" is formed in parts. In the morning she makes the trunk and in the afternoon the neck and head. It is dried for three or four days, depending upon the weather, and fired for seven or eight hours. Painting is the final stage of the process that takes ten or fifteen days in all.

Address:
Prolongación Morelos s/n (without number)
Ocotlán de Morelos
Oaxaca
C.P. 71510

Concepción at work with her daughter Estela and husband Jorge

"Fridas", 14" x 5", $45 each

Noah's Ark, 20" x 10", $135

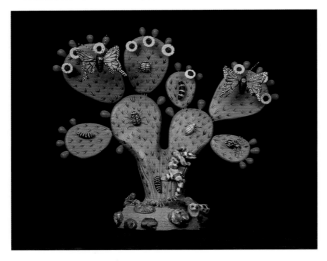

Cactus, 15" x 16", $70

Jesús Aguilar Alcántara
Sole Son to Perpetuate the Maternal Tradition
"I am proud to pass my mother's work onto my children."

See Family Tree #7-E, "Family of Jesús Aguilar Alcántara," in Appendix on page 173.

Jesús Aguilar Alcántara is the only one of Isaura's male children to carry on her work. He is especially known for his imaginative Fridas, some bearing monkeys, and his "chicas de la noche" (women of the night), frequently held in the arms of devils. Unique are his majestic, bare-breasted female figures to whose bodies an array of articles of clothing is attached. Also remarkable are his multi-figured displays, such as a dignified funereal procession. Several of these can be seen in the museum of Ocotlán (see his Day of the Dead piece on page 160 of Chapter Ten).

To Jesús his ceramic work is more than just a profession. It is a testament to the proud legacy of his mother. He is deeply respectful of the gift of her teaching, left to the many families whose pleasure and survival depends upon it. Jesús, too, takes great pride in his ability to teach his own children the beauty of his mother's art and the value of being industrious.

Biography

Jesús learned his art from his mother who died when he was 19 years old. He is the middle of the five Aguilar children who carry on her tradition; Guillermina and Josefina are older and Irene and Concepción are younger. Jesús began to work in clay at six years of age and continued until he was nine. However, not until the time of his marriage did he return to this art to earn a living. From 21 to 24 years of age he worked in clay but, because there was not much demand for folk art at this time, he entered the car business for many years. When he suffered a serious illness in 1995 Jesús resumed his work in ceramics, at the age of 45.

Four of Jesús's five children and their spouses work in clay. Each one has been taught to engage in all aspects of the creative process, including forming the figures and painting them. They all sat around a common table as we entered Jesús's studio. His eldest son built an enormous and detailed tree of life, on top of which a Noah's ark was perched. One of his daughters painted a "woman of the night," while another daughter painted a market woman carrying slices of watermelon on her head. She simultaneously cuddled her eight-month-old niece in her lap, while the baby's mother painted a devil. Although Jesús has signed all pieces made by his children until recently, some of them are starting to sign the works for which they are primarily responsible.

Family (around table from left to right): Pricila, Elizabeth, Juan, Yurít, Carlos, Concepción, Jesús Jr., Jesús, Laura, Margarita

Jesus at work with "Frida", 12" x 4", $25

Expulsion from the Garden of Eden, 14" x 13", $45

Woman selling fruit, 8" x 4", $7

Devil carrying woman of the night, 17" x 8", $40

Technique

Jesús emphasizes that all his work is done by hand. Portions of a figure are formed individually and then joined. The skirt is completed first, then the head and the arms. Decorations such as monkeys, snakes or veils, are added later. A "Frida" typically takes three days to make from the time it is initiated until the painting is completed.

Address:
Primera Calle de Libres #106
Ocotlán de Morelos
Oaxaca
C.P. 71510

Lorenzo Demetrio García Aguilar
(son of Josefina and grandson of Isaura)
Inspired Painterly Interpreter of Religious and Cultural Themes
"My pieces express the mystical inheritance of generations as well as my sentiments in dreams and fantasies. I work in dualities: life and death, day and night, man and woman, the cycle of life."

With extraordinary painterly and sculptural talent, Lorenzo Demetrio García Aguilar (he prefers to be called Demetrio), Josefina's eldest living child, creates a fantastic blend of his mother's tradition with his own unique style. His sensitive, rather quiet manner masks his artistic power. Demetrio's pieces, both "muñecas" (human figures) and plaques, are deeply personal interpretations of religious, cultural and family themes. They include the expulsion from the Garden of Eden, the good and bad (angelical and diabolical) sides of a person, scenes of the Day of the Dead (see one on page 161 of Chapter Ten), and a portrait of his mother in her creative, maternal and farming roles. Demetrio considers his Frida Kahlo and skeleton pieces bearing diverse emotions (such as happiness and sadness) to be his special designs. Although his wife sometimes paints small portions of his figural pieces, Demetrio generally carries out his work by himself. This is always true of his plaques.

Demetrio is delighted that his creativity has unfolded in ceramic work. He also loves to paint, an artform he regards as complementary to his ceramic creations. His rapidly building artistic reputation is evident in the invitation he received in 2000

Demetrio at work

to visit the United States, where he spent a month divided between Philadelphia and Boston.

Biography

Demetrio began to work in clay at 11 years of age, learning from his mother by making miniatures for Nativity and market scenes. As a very young man his abilities were recognized. As early as 1988 he won first prize in a competition for a piece he created in the church of Ocotlán. Since then he has also won numerous state and national awards.

Demetrio dates the discovery of his own style, a mixture of the old and the modern, to the age of 26. He regards his mother's influence on his process of working with clay as profound. However, his painting is quite different in that it is more realistic and more laborious.

Technique

To make a plaque Demetrio cuts the clay to the needed measurements. Depending upon the theme he forms figures in relief, which takes approximately two days. Once they have dried, he fires the piece for eight or nine hours. He then begins the painting, the most laborious and detailed phase of the process, to add depth and dimension. From start to finish a plaque generally requires six to ten days. A distinctive feature of Demetrio's work is his technique of replicating the texture of natural elements, such as rocks and trees, by mixing paint with clay. He is frequently asked if he has attended painting school, given the delicate and evocative brushstrokes for which he is known. For example, his rendering of "La Vida de Frida Kahlo" (the life of Frida Kahlo) takes four days merely for the decorative elaboration.

Demetrio holding a plaque

Address:
Prolongación de Morelos #428 (in the home of his mother)
Ocotlán de Morelos
Oaxaca
C.P. 71510
Telephone: 01 (95157) 10214

Good and Evil, 20" x 13", $280

Plaque: Mother of the Earth, 15" x 10 1/2", $120

Oaxaca is renowned for its wealth of textiles, of which we sample only a few. These can be divided into two broad categories: weaving and embroidery. Weaving includes woolen rugs and wall hangings created on shuttle looms; cotton belts, handbags and placemats produced on backstrap looms; and cotton cloth made on foot pedal-operated shuttle looms, sold as yard goods or used to make finished bedspreads, tablecloths, dresses and shawls. Embroidery in the immediate vicinity of Oaxaca City consists primarily of hand-made garments called "wedding dresses."

Some types of weaving are created in specific pueblos and others can be found in more than one pueblo. Rugs and wallhangings are woven on shuttle looms in Teotitlán del Valle, and backstrap loom belts, handbags and placemats in Santo Tomás Jalieza. Cotton cloth is produced in both the Xochimilco section of Oaxaca City and the pueblo of Mitla. In both venues it is used for tablecloths, bedspreads and yard goods. In addition, blouses, dresses and shawls ("rebozos") are specialties of Mitla. Embroidered wedding dresses are created in San Antonino Castillo Velasco, and its neighboring pueblo San Juan Chilateca.

Textile patterns derive from many sources, including Oaxaca's famous ruins of Mitla and Monte Albán. Others reflect the more specific heritage of an individual family's creative work.

In addition to these classes of textiles, many wonderful varieties come from distant regions of the state that far exceed our geographical radius. However, they can be seen in the markets of Oaxaca City, as well as in many of its better folk art shops.

Detail of the codices of the ruins of Monte Albán

Rugs and Wallhangings
of Teotitlán del Valle

Teotitlán del Valle, the pueblo known for centuries of rug weaving, is located approximately 26 kilometers (30 minutes) by car from the city of Oaxaca. It is the first pueblo founded by the Zapotecs more than 8000 years ago, and has been inhabited from its inception by painters, sculptors and weavers. Weaving on the traditional backstrap loom is dated to 500 B.C. Ancient traditions persist to a remarkable degree in this pueblo. For example, many families continue to speak the indigenous Zapotec language, either preferentially or bilingually.

The approach from Oaxaca City consists of varied terrain, ranging from flat portions from which impressive land forms suddenly emerge to lush green hills with a patchwork of rocks and cactus. A left turn into Teotitlán offers a breathtaking view of the mountains from every perspective. Off to the side are verdant flat plains nestled between gentle pastel blue mountains, peppered with cacti. Colorful houses, some bearing signs "Welcome to Teotitlán," announce the relative prosperity of many of the families who dwell here. One house is yellow with a purple dome. Another is a huge whitewashed structure with archways surrounding an expansive patio. The next is an imposing golden yellow, brick-arched home accented by striking blue trim. Along the way a disciplined herd of turkeys crosses the street and darts into a doorway.

At present there are approximately 150 weaving families in all, for a total of 600 weavers. However, they vary greatly in quality and style. The finest work is carried out by a few families (estimated variously from five to ten) that create dyes from natural substances and use pure hand-spun wool. Nearly all of them work on vertical shuttle looms operated with foot pedals and treadles, dating back to the 16th century when they were introduced by the Spaniards, This is in contrast to the vast majority of families using chemical dyes and acrylic fibers (introduced in the 1920s). These can be produced and processed far more rapidly and are less costly.

Detail of the "grecas" (stepped fret pattern) of the ruins of Mitla

The Vásquez Family
Renowned Weavers

See Family Tree #8, "The Vásquez Family," in Appendix on page 174.

This is one of the best-known weaving families in Teotitlán del Valle. Its members estimate that the family's tradition of weaving extends back for one thousand years. Isaac Vásquez García, the family's eldest living weaver, is a greatly respected member of the community because of his pioneering effort to bring about the renaissance of pre-Hispanic natural dyes and techniques. He and his eight children, three males and five females, and their families all carry on his artistic tradition. Each lives in his or her own house, with the exception of the two youngest siblings who continue to live with their father and mother.

In the Vásquez family, as in most of the best weaving families, there is great pride in preserving the ancient tradition pre-dating the arrival of the Spaniards. They wish to insure that weavers continue to work with natural colors and with pure wool that better absorbs these colors. This is despite the more time-consuming and expensive nature of these methods and materials, when compared with synthetics, such as acrylic blends. The Vásquez family guarantees their rugs for 40 years, in great contrast to the mere six month life expectancy of work created with chemical dyes and acrylic fiber.

Each member of the family creates personal patterns and weaves his own pieces, although there are many shared designs. While they conduct their own businesses, they have a cooperative spirit. For example, if a customer searches for a particular design or size that one member does not have available, he is directed to the home of another.

Isaac Vásquez García
Pioneer in Preserving the Ancient Tradition of Weaving with Natural Dyes
"I hope the next generation will continue to preserve the ancient manual techniques."

Isaac Vásquez García is one of the grand old men of this pueblo and the head of the renowned and successful Vásquez family. A warm and honest person, he narrates the story of his life in a captivating manner. He is famous for preserving and further developing the centuries' old dying techniques of the Zapotecs and Mixtecs. One example is the creation of red dye from the dried and ground "cochineal," an insect that is found in a type of cactus called "nopal." He has also devoted himself to conserving the carding and weaving methods introduced in colonial times.

Isaac's signature designs derive from ancient sources. He creates "estelas" (figures seen in stone carvings in the famous majestic Oaxacan ruins of Monte Albán) and "codices" (manuscripts), also from Monte Albán. These styles have been copied by many of his fellow villagers, but he was the artist who introduced them. Isaac weaves in a wide range of other styles, including patterns from prehistoric cave paintings, reproductions of Diego Rivera paintings, geometric stepped fret patterns from Mitla and the like.

Family (left to right): Front row: Isaac, Isaac and his wife María. Back row: Faustino, Isaac Jr., Juan Ramón, Jerónimo, Wilmer with Luis Enrique in front of him, Ludivina, Lila with Juan Isaac in front of her

Isaac at work

Biography
Isaac learned to weave at eight years of age, working daily at his father's side. By the age of 11 he began to weave by himself, and by 12 he produced pieces of good quality. As he worked with his father Isaac asked about colors used in generations past. By 1910-1915 his father, along with his contemporaries in Teotitlán, had relinquished the custom of creating colors with natural dyes in favor of less time-consuming synthetic substances. Nevertheless he was extremely knowledgeable about the practices of the past generation. Isaac's mother had used natural substances to dye the wool with which his father had earlier created "tapetes" (rugs and wallhangings).

Isaac's wife María and their daughter Ludivina at work

Jaguar, 4.5' x 4', $1100

Isaac has taught others in his pueblo to use natural dyes, although not as many families have availed themselves of this opportunity as he would have liked. For many the efficiency of chemical substances and acrylic fibers prevails over authenticity and fine quality.

Technique

There are four basic vegetable colors derived from varying ingredients that must be cooked over a fire for hours. Intense black colors are created from beans grown in local fields. Shades of yellow are created from "musgo de roca," a moss. Tones of blue are made from the indigo (or añil) plant that must be fermented for 27 days, washed together with firewood ash and then put in a filter to remove impurities. What results is a paste, in solid form, that is then ground with a "metate" (an elongated rounded stone, reminiscent of a rolling pin, that is rolled up and down a horizontal stone platform) to make powder that is subsequently boiled for two hours. Twenty-five tones of red are produced from the "cochineal," a dried insect. From these four basic colors, 126 different colors are created. The natural tone of the wool determines the intensity of the shade that results. Finally lime juice and salt are added to seal the colors and to render them more brilliant.

Traditional colonial methods of carding and weaving, carried out entirely by hand, are employed in contrast to some weavers who use machines for portions of their work. Isaac explains that pieces created in this way last three or four times longer than those produced in factories.

Weaving takes from a month or two up to eight months, depending upon the design to be executed. A simple geometric is the easiest, while designs that are not angular require the longest time.

Address:
Hidalgo #30
Teotitlán del Valle
Oaxaca
C.P. 70420
Telephone: 01 (95152) 44122

To Isaac conservation of the beauty and quality of the past was a calling. It was the tradition of his grandfather and great grandfather before him, and the heritage of Teotitlán extending back hundreds of years. Although not of interest to most of his fellow villagers or to the tourists who did not appreciate the superior qualities of natural dyes, Isaac found support for his research into the re-creation of pre-Hispanic colors in two famous Oaxacan artists. One was Francisco Toledo, the most famous living Mexican painter. He helped Isaac find a person who cultivated indigo and requested that he grow a larger crop for use in dying. Rufino Tamayo, the (now deceased) famous painter and native Oaxacan, offered to find "cochineal" in Peru.

Grecas of Mitla,
5' x 3.5', $340

Prehistoric pattern, 5' x 3.5', $450

63

Olmec butterfly, 4.5' x 4', $1100

Codice, 4' x 4', $1100
Zapotec diamond, 7' x 3.5, $550

Ernesto Vásquez Gutiérrez
Prince of a "Tapete" Kingdom
"I am grateful to God and to my father who have taught this craft that I plan to transmit to my children."

Ernesto Vásquez Gutiérrez, Isaac Vásquez García's eldest son, is an extremely successful weaver in his own right. He and his wife have their own home, a stunning piece of architecture consisting of high rounded white stucco walls with brick arches. Attractively suspended from the voluminous wall space are innumerable examples of his many creations. In one room there is a display of pre-Columbian and pre-Hispanic designs for which the extended family is famous. Another houses more traditional patterns that incorporate elements of the Zapotecs and the archaeological site of Mitla. At the same time Ernesto produces more modern representational designs such as birds, and reproductions inspired by artists such as Escher, Matisse and Diego Rivera.

To demonstrate the viability of his family's work, Ernesto showed us fabulous family heirlooms. One was 150 years old and the other 90 years old.

Biography

Ernesto recalls that, following tradition and "the predictable sequence," he learned to weave from his father at eight years of age just as his father had learned from his own father. Also in keeping with tradition, Ernesto's wife prepares the wool for weaving, just as his mother did in the past. As a very young boy Ernesto learned to spin the wool, and then to weave on chairs because the loom was too large for an eight-year-old. However, by 12 he assumed his place at a full-size loom.

Technique

Ernesto's family buys wool from the distant, mountainous La Mixteca area of Oaxaca, where the sheep's wool grows longer due to the colder climate. Since it is dirty when purchased, it has to be washed in the nearby river with natural soap made from the root of a local plant. This kills the insects it may contain. The wool is then sorted on the basis of its natural colors, dried, and ultimately combed to remove further impurities and to render it smooth. Following this it is spun and washed again. The wool is then ready to be dyed in large vats in the natural dyes that are a source of great pride for this family.

Once a pattern is designed, a model is produced, thread by thread. It is subsequently recorded on paper, including the colors that will be used to make a particular "tapete" (rug or wallhanging). Then the loom is strung and the process of shuttle weaving begins. Ernesto esti-

Family (left to right): Margarita (wife), Mayra (daughter), Omar (son), Ernesto

mated that a geometric rug of 9.5 feet by 6.5 feet takes four months to make working eight hours a day, while a Diego Rivera design of the same size requires six months.

Address:
Avenida Juárez S/N (without number)
Teotitlán del Valle
Oaxaca
C.P. 70420
Telephone: 01 (95152) 44144

Ernesto weaving

Escher pattern, 5' x 3', $375

Tree of life, 6' x 3', $390

Ernesto's wife, Margarita, preparing wool

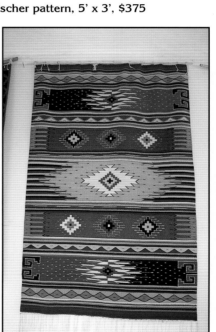

Prehistoric pattern, 5' x 3', $560

Zapotec star pattern, 10' x 6', $1300

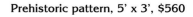

Prehistoric pattern, 5' x 3', $560

Aida Vásquez Gutiérrez
Versatile Female Weaver

"We dedicate ourselves to our work with all our hearts. We welcome you to our pueblo and to our house."

Aida Vásquez Gutiérrez and her husband Manuel Alavéz live and work in the prominent house across the street from that of her brother Ernesto. "Tapetes" (rugs and wallhangings) are displayed everywhere. They occupy all the walls of the patio where the family's looms are located and the enormous showroom on the second floor of their home. Aida and Manuel are best known for their original Zapotec designs. However, they are also dedicated to preserving more traditional patterns. In addition they produce lovely reproductions of paintings by Diego Rivera and Escher.

The couple work with two of their three daughters. The third works out of her own home. Although they are extremely helpful to each other, each member of this branch of the family works on his or her own rug from start to finish.

Biography
Coming from a very large family, Aida learned about weaving beginning at the age of six. She "played" with "tapetes," producing small ones in the course of which she learned "little by little" to card and wash wool and to select the high quality portions. Finally Aida learned to weave, a role that was unusual for females of this pueblo. The endeavor was entirely pleasurable since she did not have responsibility for earning a living: "Papa was in the front."

This changed entirely when Aida married at the age of 15. She had to work more seriously to sustain the family, along with her husband Manuel, with whom she closely collaborated. When their first child arrived soon after marriage, Manuel had to bear the major responsibility for the family's living. Prior to this, Aida looked for ways to earn more money. She spent years learning to make candles from Viviana Alavéz Hipólito, another native of Teotitlán del Valle (see pages 135 and 135 in Chapter Seven). Although Aida gave this up as a means of support, she still enjoys creating candles for her own pleasure.

Family: Manuel, Aida, Efren Jimenez Alavéz (Manuel's nephew), and Jessica Bautista Alavéz (Aida and Manuel's granddaughter)

Technique
In their earliest years Aida and Manuel owned sheep from which they got their wool. But as their work developed, they begin to buy wool from the Mixteca Alta (a distant region of the state of Oaxaca). They select the usable portions, and clean them, for example, removing thorns. Wool is then taken to the local river to be washed, following which it is dried on the patio. Carding, spinning and creating skeins is the next step, after which the wool must be washed again. Then colors are selected and produced from natural dye substances, and designs are drawn. Aida is adamant that all artists who make "tapetes" have to learn to draw.

Weaving can range from relatively uncomplicated geometric designs that require six or seven days, to the most difficult ones such as Diego Rivera reproductions that may take up to eight or nine months.

Address:
Avenida Juárez #119
Teotitlán del Valle
Oaxaca
C.P. 70420
Telephone: 01 (95152) 44132

Aida and Manuel weaving

**Tree of life, 81" x 52",
$1350**

Zapotec "caracol" (snail) pattern, 80" x 48", $500

Codice, 67" x 40", $800

Eagle, 62" x 41", $800

Bulmaro Pérez Mendoza
Traditionalist with a Forward-Looking Spirit
"I would like the tourist to visit Teotitlán del Valle to admire its art and traditions. Why not visit the house of the Pérez Mendoza family?"

See Family Tree #9, "The Pérez Family," in Appendix on page 175.

Bulmaro Pérez Mendoza is one of Teotitlán's best weavers. He is a gentle and warm young man who presents a wonderful blend of devotion to the preservation of tradition with a forward-looking, enterprising spirit, intent on developing new avenues of expression and commercial success. Like the Vásquez family, Bulmaro and his family take great pride in their tradition of natural dyes and pure wool. This is in contrast to the 75-80% of weavers in their pueblo who use more economical chemical dyes and acrylic blends.

While conserving the traditional approach, Bulmaro is simultaneously an innovator. He has discovered a range of colors well suited to both the old and new patterns that he produces. Many tourists have found great appeal in his signature combination of colors: greens, mustard, browns, turquoises and oranges. He has also created unique semi-abstract designs that he entitles "montañitas" (little mountains) and "símbolo de la lluvia" (symbol of the rain). Finally, in 1998 he introduced a different fiber, mohair, that he believes to be considerably more enduring. Bulmaro estimates that a rug created with mohair can be expected to last at least 80-90, and perhaps even 100, years depending upon the uses to which it is put.

Bulmaro's family practices the conventional division of labor. Although he is the primary weaver of the family at this point, he comes from a long line of men who practiced this art. His paternal grandfather was known for his designs based on the patterns of Mitla and Monte Albán, and his father produced "mil rayas" (a thousand stripes). Bulmaro's wife, mother and grandmother are intensely involved in processing, carding, spinning and dying the wool. It is a deeply moving experience to see female members of four generations of the family collaborating in the production of their cherished work. Bulmaro explained that a family is considered fortunate when there are enough men, so that the women do not have to weave.

Family (left to right): Front row: María del Pilar (Bulmaro's grandmother), Diego (son). Back row: María Luisa (sister), Aurea (wife), Margarita (mother), Bulmaro

It is his desire that the young people of Teotitlán will continue to learn the art of weaving, and thus preserve the tradition. Within his own family Bulmaro is dedicated to passing along his knowledge to insure that the next generation can produce their best work and protect the future of the pueblo of Teotitlán.

Biography

As is true of many weavers in Teotitlán Bulmaro began to learn from his father at seven years of age, weaving small pieces that served as place mats. He also helped his father in selling their work. Bulmaro was sent to a point in the highway, just as it passes his pueblo, for the purpose of directing tourists to his family's studio and home. His father also encouraged him to travel to the city of Oaxaca to study English because of its potential for enhancing business.

On market days, Bulmaro's father devoted himself to selling the work they had produced, traveling to the great markets on Saturdays in the

Bulmaro weaving

city of Oaxaca and on Sundays in Tlacolula. The other days of the week were reserved for weaving. Although there is a market in Teotitlán, Bulmaro's father and uncles declined to participate in it for fear that other artisan families might reproduce their original designs.

Technique

Bulmaro buys his raw wool in the markets of Oaxaca, especially in Tlacolula where people from the Mixtec region tend to sell their goods.

Aurea (Bulmaro's wife) grinding natural dye materials with a "metate"

The wool is washed in the nearby river and impurities are removed. Once it is thoroughly dry it is carded and spun into large skeins. Dying is done with natural substances exclusively (indigo for blue, "cochineal" for red, the "huisache" plant for black, alfalfa for green, nutshells for brown, marigolds for orange and pomegranate shell for gold), using secrets for combining various tones that were taught to Bulmaro by his father. Lemon juice is used as a sealer. When this process is complete, the loom is prepared for the particular design intended. A rug of two feet by three and one-half feet in the "montañita" pattern requires approximately 15 days from start to finish.

Address:
Centenario #27
Teotitlán del Valle
Oaxaca
C.P. 70420
Telephone: 01 (95152) 44011

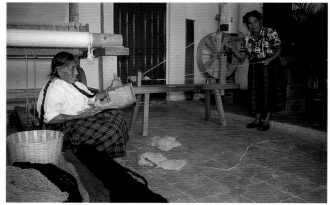

María del Pilar (Bulmaro's grandmother) and Margarita (mother) carding and spinning wool

Female members of the family finishing the tassels

"Tapetes" (Left to right):
Butterflies, 5.5' x 3', $300
Spring, 5.5' x 3', $300
Zapotec diamond, 5.5' x 3', $300

Montañitas, 5.5' x 3', $300

stances used for dying (for example, grinding them on a "metate"), while Fidel does the dying, prepares the loom and weaves.

Biography

Fidel began to learn to make "tapetes" at the age of nine. He helped to card the wool and to separate the dirty portions from those appropriate for weaving. Around the same time he wove easy patterns such as stripes, simultaneously improving his ability to modulate the tension of his weaving – a matter of great importance to him. He subsequently wove Zapotec diamonds and, by the age of ten to 11 years, undertook more complicated designs such as geometric "grecas" (stepped fret designs) from Mitla.

When Fidel married María at age 17 they "started a new life," creating "artesanías" on their own in all respects: entirely different designs, dyes and clientele. Feeling unsupported by their families of origin, and unable to afford the chemical dyes used by their families and most of the weavers in Teotitlán, they resourcefully experimented with natural substances. Struggling for many years, "fighting with colors," Fidel finally began to grasp the nature of these substances in the mid-90s. He perfected his techniques a few years later. This culminated in his winning first prize, in recognition of his extraordinary hues, in the national contest of "artesanías" held in Guadalajara in 1998. Even much earlier Fidel was invited to enter a contest for his colors, winning honorable mention at the ripe age of 17.

Fidel Cruz Lazo
Virtuoso of Color and Distinctive Patterns
"We are proud to have revived natural colors."

See Family Tree #10, "The Cruz Family," in Appendix on page 176.

Fidel Cruz Lazo and his wife María Luis Mendoza de Cruz are an outgoing and charming couple who have developed a glorious and exotic array of natural dye colors and distinctive designs. They also take pride in their practices of never exactly reproducing any one design, and of "signing" their pieces. Everything about their work is creative and first-rate, down to the unusually meticulous way in which they finish their fringes. Fidel's pride and excitement in discovering and producing new substances with which to create additional colors is infectious.

Being unique and distinct is of crucial importance to Fidel and María, a goal at which they succeed. To wit an American man residing in Oaxaca has written a book entitled *The Colors of Casa Cruz* that provides a wonderfully "intimate look" at their "art and skill." They have produced a video on their work as well. Fidel and María have a burgeoning international clientele as their extraordinary talents gain recognition, another source of pleasure. They guarantee their pieces since they are original designs and are washable.

Fidel prides himself on being intimately acquainted with every aspect of the work, although at this point there is a clear division of labor between Fidel and María. She is responsible for cleaning the wool and preparing the natural sub-

Family: María Luisa (Fidel's wife), Luis David and Emiliano (sons), Fidel

Technique

Fidel and María work with an unusual variety of substances for dying, resulting in a remarkable range of shades. To name a few, there is pomegranate, indigo, "cochineal" (dried mites collected from the nopal cactus), marigold and "palo de Brazil" (a tree). Their most exotic colors are tones of turquoise, red and blue. These dyes are not toxic and are extremely durable. Fidel ran us through his process of creating a vibrant red, dunking several skeins in a boiling mixture based in "cochineal." Over a two-hour period the wool went from pale pink to an increasingly deep rich red.

The time required for Fidel and María's pieces ranges widely from five days to two to four months. There are great variations in texture, fineness, complexity of design and size. The majority of their designs are in the Zapotec tradition. For example, a diamond is not simply a diamond, but one through which the symbol indicating that life continues runs. The "grecas" of Mitla have also been a strong influence. Like many of the best weavers in Teotitlán, Fidel and María work tirelessly, their day running from 4:00 a.m. to 6:00 or 8:00 p.m.

Address:
Casa Cruz
Avenida Juárez Kilometer 2
Teotitlán del Valle
Oaxaca
C.P. 70420
Telephone: 01 (95152) 44020

Fidel weaving

Maria Luisa grinding cochineal

Fidel dying wool with cochineal

Diamond interlaced with symbols of life, 68" x 26", $2700

Zapotec "caracol" (snail), 58" x 32", $400

Sun in diamond pattern,
53" x 32", $425

Zapotec jaguar, 56" x 32", $500

Diamond with Zapotec eyes,
108" x 24", $725

Additional weavers of rugs and wallhangings
Felipe Gutiérrez (Avenida Juárez #101)
Benito Hernández (Carretera a Teotitlán kilometro 1[highway to Teotitlán kilometer 1])
Jesús Hernández Jiménez (Avenida Juárez #100)
Arnulfo Mendoza Ruiz (although a resident of Teotitlán, see his work in his shop in Oaxaca City, La Mano Mágica, Macedonio Alcalá #407)
Jacobo Mendoza Ruíz (Avenida Juárez #39)
Zacaría Ruiz Hernández y Emilia González (Avenida Juárez #107)
Alberto Vásquez (Avenida Juárez #84)

Back Strap Loom Belts, Handbags and Placemats
of Santo Tomás Jalieza

In this pueblo, approximately 25 kilometers (35 minutes) from Oaxaca, spinning and weaving of cotton are carried out entirely by hand. The sign "Textiles de algodón hecho a mano" (cotton textiles made by hand) announces your arrival. Belts are created with the use of the back strap loom that dates back to 900-500 B.C. A left turn takes the visitor into the center of town. Neatly trimmed flowering trees, bougainvilleas, many in brilliant shades of magenta and rose, decorate the street.

Almost immediately to the left is a small market in front of which there are always several women and young girls demonstrating their techniques. This is where most tourists purchase the woven crafts of Santo Tomás. Friday is the day when the maximum number of artisans is present. About thirty women sell their products, as compared with ten on the other days of the week.

Cooperative market ("plazuela") in the pueblo's center

71

In 1940 a highway was built from the city of Oaxaca to Santo Tomás, bringing more business to the pueblo. Prior to that the only way to sell work was to take completed items to Saturday market in Oaxaca. In 1962 the weavers of Santo Tomás formed an organization with approximately 40 members. In 1963 they created a central location for selling their work, the "plazuela." These efforts to improve conditions and sales were catalyzed by Nancy Audiffred Bustamante, a Oaxacan woman who, with her brother Enrique, was dedicated to improving the lives and commercial prospects of Oaxaca's artisans. In 1994 the older plazuela was replaced by a newer one with a sturdier roof and better display space.

In addition to the two families we feature there are many wonderful weavers here and throughout the pueblo. Santo Tomás's union has resulted in the unusual practice of standardizing prices for items of comparable size, materials, and quality. All participants in the market produce excellent work, as do the families in our non-exhaustive list of weavers at the end of this section.

The Navarro Gómez Family
A Talented Ensemble of Weavers (and a Painter)
"It is very satisfying to us when people visit our house and see us working. It is not the same to see a completed piece in the market as to see an artist working."

See Family Tree #11, "The Navarro Gómez Family," in Appendix on page 177.

In their unusually spacious, tranquil and cheerful yard, replete with bursts of brilliant purple and pink bougainvilleas, Mariana Gómez Jiménez and her three grown daughters, Margarita, Crispina and Inés, sit side by side on the ground. Each works at her own back strap loom tethered to a tree. Having just returned from school for lunch during our visit, six-year-old Valbina, the youngest member of the family, joins them. She naturally assumes her place in the female cluster, proficiently continuing work that is in process. Adjacent to this touching scene is a multiple-room house with an expansive patio where the family's wide array of woven goods is displayed. Mariana's only son, Gerardo, paints in his light-strewn studio off the patio. His many paintings are proudly exhibited along with the family's weaving.

The women of the Navarro Gómez family produce an unusually large number of woven cotton items. In addition to the traditional belts, bags, place mats, coasters, "centro de mesas" (table liners) and napkins, they have added to their repertoire wallets, change purses, belts with leather trim, eye glass cases, and pillows created with woven segments mounted in leather. Gerardo used to participate in the family's craft by contributing the leather portions of belts. However, this was not to his liking, and in 1994 he began instead to develop his talents as a painter, at which he has had considerable success. A cousin now produces the leather belt trim.

Biography
Mariana learned to weave on a back strap loom from her aunt. Her mother was herself unfamiliar with this work, having grown up in another pueblo: Santa Cruz Papalutla (see Chapter Eight). When her mother and father married they chose to

settle in Santo Tomás, although neither one was a native. It was important to Mariana's mother that her only daughter, who was born and raised in Santo Tomás, learn this craft.

Technique
Cotton thread that has already been spun and dyed is purchased from a local man. The large family spinning wheel is constructed of wood and split pieces of bamboo mounted in a cement base. It is used to arrange the unwieldy skeins of thread in preparation for cut-

Family at work (front to back): Inés, Mariana, Margarita, and Crispina weaving, Gerardo painting

Valbina weaving with her aunts after school

Table centerpiece, 59" x 12", $8
Large belt, 63" x 4.5", $9
Narrow belt, 63" x 1.3", $4
Medium size bag, 12" x 9", $8

Bags: Small, 8" x 6", $4
Medium, 12" x 9", $8
Large, 16" x 13", $9

Juice of the Moon by Gerardo,
39" X 31.5", $550

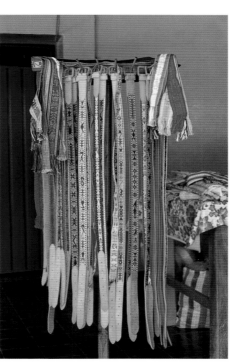

Belts with leather trim, $7

ting them to the proper lengths necessary for setting up each loom. Cotton thread is placed on a wooden mount and then cut.

It takes approximately two days to make a "centro de mesa" (a runner used for table decoration), three days for bags and one day for belts. Crispina specializes in extraordinarily fine patterns that are distinct from the traditionally bolder work in this pueblo. Pieces created from this type of weaving can be purchased in the form of belts and fine evening bags composed of multiple very thin belt strips sewn together. These can take up to three months to complete and are considerably more costly.

Address:
Calle Benito Juárez #42
Santo Tomás Jalieza
Oaxaca
C.P. 71507
Telephone: 01 (95151) 46994

The Chávez Family

The Chávez family has been involved in the craft of belt weaving since 1915. They occupy three households in the pueblo of Santo Tomás, all children of Cirila but the product of several marriages.

See Family Tree #12, "The Chávez Family," in Appendix on page 178.

Cirila Chávez Luis and Patricia Hernández Chávez
A Mother and Daughter Collaboration
"We carry out our artisans' work with a lot of love. We think this is the key to our success, to people throughout the world coming to know our craft."

Cirila Chávez Luis lives and works with her daughter Patricia Hernández Chávez. Using the back strap looms that are prominently suspended in their home, they create cotton belts (narrow and wide), place mats, table runners, napkins, and bags. Mother and daughter incorporate approximately 20 designs in their weaving. These are not recorded on paper, but

Family (left to right):
Natalio, Cirila, Patricia, Miguel

rather passed down in the oral tradition from one generation to the next. They consist of both traditional pueblo designs (such as dancers, animals, geometric patterns of the ruins of Mitla) and several that are unique to this family, such as an earthen jar accompanied by a pomegranate, and a carnation with stars.

Biography

Cirila's mother and father taught her how to weave beginning at five years of age. Carrying on the tradition generally sustained by the females of the family in this pueblo, she began with smaller pieces such as narrow belts and then progressed to wider belts. Gradually she undertook the larger and more complex types of weaving: bags, place mats and center pieces for tables. Her brothers, who died long ago, worked as well.

Patricia also began to weave at five, first working on small belts. By 12 years of age she graduated to the full size loom that she works on to this day.

Technique

Prior to weaving, Cirila and Patricia purchase cotton thread that has been spun and dyed by a man in their pueblo known to use materials that are of excellent quality. Cirila and Patricia thread their looms vertically according to the colors and configuration that form the selected pattern. Seated on the ground, balancing on their knees, Cirila and Patricia weave the hand shuttle horizontally, in and out of the appropriate vertical threads.

Multiple pieces are often created from the same piece of weaving. It is marked with divisions, and later cut into individual segments. For example, eight place mats woven in one long piece are subsequently turned into eight individual segments. The same process is used for bags and belts.

Address:
Matamoros #2
Santo Tomás Jalieza
Oaxaca
C.P. 71507

Large bag, 16" x 12", $9
Small bag, 8" x 6", $4
Four table centerpieces, 59" x 12", $8
Medium size bags, 12" x 9", $8

Agustín Chávez and his wife Asela Valentín Mendoza
Inventive and Enterprising Weavers
"We feel very moved that tourists, day after day, are interested in our work. This motivates us to continue to improve."

Agustín Chávez, his wife Asela Valentín Mendoza and their children create an unusually diverse range of items woven in cotton on a back strap loom. In addition to the traditional belts, bags, place mats and napkins of their pueblo, they make pillow covers and bath mats. They have also begun to produce dresses and pants many of which are decorated with narrow pieces of traditional weaving, the width of the narrowest belts.

Patricia (left) and her mother Cirila (right) weaving on backstrap looms

**Asela and Agustín showing their work
Bathmat,
22" x 20", $13
Table centerpiece,
59" x 12", $8**

Backpacks, 10" x 9", $10
Placemat sets of 8, 17" x 12.5", $15

Dress for 2-year old, $17

two bags from the four segments of which it is composed. The couple estimates that it takes two days to make four bags.

Address:
Zaragoza #4 (entrance on Guadalupe Victoria)
Santo Tomás Jalieza
Ocotlán
Oaxaca
C.P. 71507
Telephone: 01 (95151) 46994

Additional Weavers of Cotton Belts, Handbags and Placemats
Faustina Aragón Mendoza and her daughter Leonor Mendoza Aragón (Benito Juárez #22)
Josefina Aragón (market)
Blandina Chávez Méndez (inquire in the market since her street is unnamed)
Felipe Gómez Mendoza (Galaeana #6)
González family (Melchor Ocampo #4)
Abdón Mendoza (Guerrero #7)
Cándido Mendoza (Nicolas Bravo #10)
Elena Mendoza and her sister Paula Mendoza Ignacio (Zaragoza #7)
Celia Reyes and her daughters (Benito Juarez #22)

Agustín and Asela weave approximately 20 designs, some universal in the pueblo and others unique to them. Two of their exclusive patterns are snails with shells, and flowers. Agustín travels to Puerto Escondido (a distant beach town on the coast of the state of Oaxaca) to sell their products, since there is less competition than in his native pueblo.

This family lives and works in a well-appointed house, replete with white tile floor and multiple red brick arches. Matching brick ceiling beams are punctuated by electric lights surrounded by stars of the same color.

Biography

Agustín is the exception to the rule in Santo Tomás Jalieza in which women are generally the weavers of belts on backstrap looms. He worked as a farmer until the age of 23. As a newlywed his wife taught him the craft she had learned from her mother. Asela began to weave at the age of seven. By 13 she was working on a full-size loom, creating the types of pieces she continues to make. Now the two teach all their children, male and female.

Technique

Agustín and Asela begin by spinning the thread they will weave. Then they pass the "comb," a wooden object to which the spindle threads are attached. A wooden machete is employed to pack the horizontal threads. On the day we visited Agustín had worked from 8:00 a.m. to 2:00 p.m. to weave a piece that would be turned into

Woven Cotton Cloth
of Oaxaca City and Mitla

Woven cotton cloth is used for home decoration (finished tablecloths and bedspreads, and unfinished yard goods suitable for curtains and pillows) and clothing, including shawls ("rebozos"). Cloth for home decoration is produced primarily in the Xochimilco section of Oaxaca City and in the pueblo of Mitla. We feature two families involved in this type of work, one in each location. Woven cotton cloth for clothing is produced for the most part in Mitla. One of our Mitla families creates cloth for home decoration as well as for clothing, and another specializes in "rebozos," a long tradition in this pueblo.

Mitla, located approximately 45 kilometers (50 minutes or more) from Oaxaca, is home to the famous Zapotec ruins that inspire many woven patterns. The artisans of this pueblo create a vast array of weaving, primarily in cotton, for blouses, dresses, shawls ("rebozos"), shirts, pants, bedspreads and tablecloths. They encompass many decorative elements, including patterns (especially those based on the geometric shapes of the local pre-Hispanic ruins), lattice-work within the weaving itself, and embroidery and crocheting added to the weaving.

Surrounding the archaeological site is a fence of cactus. A daily market with all types of goods, but most especially clothing and other woven items, stands adjacent to the ruins. The winding road leading into the pueblo's center (5 de Febrero), where the ruins are located, is similarly flooded with countless shops sporting rich displays of woven products.

The route from Oaxaca City to Mitla is also the highway leading to the state of Chiapas to the east. It is a primarily flat road surrounded on both sides by expansive vistas. Cacti are prominent in the landscape, as are lush trees such as palms and eucalyptus. En route are the ruins of Yagúl and other smaller archaeological sites. Striking stone formations sprinkled with greenery are visible in the distance. A burro adjacent to the road carries a vast load of firewood. A goat tender cares for a herd of twelve. Along the stretch immediately preceding the turn off to Mitla is the mezcal district. A conglomeration of mezcal factories populates either side of the highway.

The Orozco Family
Guadalupe Orozco Torres
José Orozco Jiménez
Alejandro Rojas Miguel
Enhancers of Everyday Domestic Life: Woven Cotton Cloth
"We hope consumers will recognize work of superior quality."

See Family Tree #13, "The Orozco Family," in Appendix on page 179.

Guadalupe Orozco Torres, her paternal uncle José Orozco Jiménez, and her husband Alejandro Rojas Miguel make up one of several outstanding weaving families in the hilly Xochimilco section of the city of Oaxaca. In this primarily residential area, a 10-15 minute walk from the center of town and beginning just across the Pan American Highway, the click clack of shuttle looms can be heard emanating from a number of home workshops. This family produces handsome and durable cotton fabric from which table cloths and bedspreads of all sizes, table napkins, tortilla napkins, towels, and place mats are created. Their cloth can also be purchased by the yard to be used for curtains, upholstery and other home decorations. The Orozco family has a sizeable showroom of ready-made pieces, but special orders are welcomed.

Guadalupe is a methodical, no-nonsense business woman who was "born into" the art of weaving patterned cloth. She is the only one of her siblings to perpetuate their family's tradition. For this reason she and her husband and elderly paternal uncle have hired several assistants to work in their home workshop.

Guadalupe, who feels that many artesanías (crafts) are being lost, underlined the importance of increased governmental support to sustain them. She hopes that work of superior quality will be brought to the attention of consumers to facilitate the preservation of important folk art and craft traditions.

Biography
Guadalupe grew up learning to card and spin cotton thread in her family from an early age, as did all of her siblings. At ten years of age she began to do her own work, making napkins and small tablecloths. Her family is responsible for the creation of many woven designs. However, it is difficult to preserve ownership of these patterns, since other artisans with ready access to them in the market can produce copies. When her father died, Guadalupe was the only one of his many children who chose to continue the business, and she has served as boss ever since.

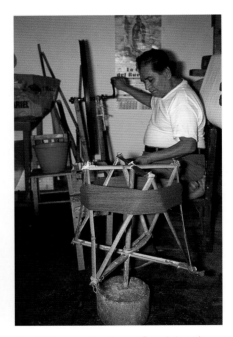

Guadalupe and her husband Alfredo holding their pieces. Table centerpiece, 16" x 71", $4
Small tablecloth, 31.5" x 27.5", $15

José Orozco Jiménez (Guadalupe's uncle) preparing cotton

Technique
The process of weaving begins with buying crude cotton, which is washed to remove impurities. It is then carded, spun into thread and placed on spools to be used on large weaving looms. The cotton thread is subsequently dyed with chemical dyes, generally a twelve-hour process.

The amount of time necessary for weaving depends upon the style to be carried out: the design and the size desired. Guadalupe estimates that production of a

José Orozco Jiménez (Guadalupe's uncle) weaving

tablecloth of three feet by eight feet with a "greca" design (based on the geometric patterns of the ruins of Mitla) takes approximately eight hours on the loom, and two and one-half days from start to finish. A bedspread requires an additional day.

Address:
Santo Tomás #214
Xochimilco
Oaxaca
C.P. 68040
Telephone: 01 (95151) 52332

Tablecloth with napkins, 79" x 53", $35

Bedspread, 110" x 86.5", $50

Gildardo Juárez Sosa
Accomplished Weaver in Cotton
"We make the most traditional cotton clothing in honor of our ancestors."

See Family Tree # 14, "Family of Gildardo Juárez Sosa," in Appendix on page 180.

On the far side of the fascinating ruins of Mitla, Gildardo Juárez Sosa weaves excellent quality cotton fabric on huge wooden, hand-operated looms. His teenage son Juan Carlos is already proficient in this handicraft as well. Many patterns incorporate Zapotec designs (such as the geometric stepped fret design known as "grecas") that derive from the ruins of Mitla. Gildardo's wife, Ofelia González García, and mother, Natalia Sosa Méndez, assist in assembling, sewing and adding finishing touches - such as embroidery and crocheted and ribbon trim - to the garments and other pieces produced from this weaving. Adjacent to the family's looms is a well-appointed and airy shop displaying the many items for which their cloth is used. These include bedspreads and tablecloths, dresses of many varieties for all ages (young children up to adults), matching shorts and blouses, shirts, pants and shawls ("rebozos").

A close-knit traditional family, they speak the indigenous Zapotec language among themselves, although they know a sufficient degree of Spanish to conduct their business. The number of shops in Mitla selling clothing and other woven goods is dizzying. However, most re-sell the work of the few weavers in this pueblo, making it worth the effort to reach workshops such as Gildardo's.

Biography
Gildardo began to weave at 13 years of age, taught by a neighbor with whom his family was close. At first he earned very little, helping to spin thread and fill the spools used on looms. Because his father had left the family when Gildardo was young, as the eldest he had to help support his mother and siblings. "Rebozos" were the first pieces he wove. A few years later he bought his own loom and started a small business, weaving shirts and "rebozos" in cotton only.

Family portrait (left to right) with dresses in background
Back row: Eduardo, Luis, Juan Carlos
Front row: Ofelia, Saúl, Gildardo, Natalia

When he married at age 25 Gildardo and Ofelia enlarged this business, and diversified the items made from the woven cloth. Prior to her marriage she had learned about sewing, embroidering and crocheting from her family, also weavers.

Technique

Wider looms are used for tablecloths and bedspreads, compared with the narrower ones for dresses, shirts and shorts sets. Gildardo buys thread that has already been prepared with chemical dyes. To create dresses with "grecas," he begins by creating a piece of weaving approximately 275 yards long. His weaving has built-in dividers at the point where the fabric for one dress ends and another begins. Such a woven piece takes between 20 and 30 days, depending upon the complexity of the pattern and number of colors. Once the weaving is completed, Ofelia cuts each piece and creates dresses. She estimates that the simpler ones require approximately two hours, while the more complex ones that have crocheted and/or embroidered portions take up to six hours. Gildardo's mother also helps with the embroidery.

Address:
Camino Nacional #24
Mitla
Oaxaca
C.P. 70430
Telephone: 01 (95156) 80361

Tablecloth, 9' x 6', $20
Twin-sized bedspread, $25
Queen-sized bedspread, $30

Cotton dresses (left to right):
White $20
Blue $10
White with red trim $15
Beige $20

Gildardo at work

Juan Carlos at work

(Left to right):
Black and white acrylic rebozo $6
Green bermuda set, $17
Blue cotton rebozo, $9

Arturo Hernández Quero
High Quality Weaver of Rebozos
"We invite the new generations to learn this art so that we will not run the risk of its disappearance."

See Family Tree #15, "Family of Arturo Hernández Quero," in Appendix on page 181.

Deeply committed to producing weaving of high quality and enterprising in spirit, Arturo Hernández Quero and his wife Marta Luis Marcos have recently built an expansive open dwelling in a picturesque spot adjacent to fields that back up into gentle mountains. There they produce "rebozos" and blouses, dying and carding the cotton and weaving on three prominent looms. Their "rebozos" are of many styles: multi-colored stripes, two types of solid-colored open work, and geometric woven patterns inspired by the archaeological site of Mitla. All are trimmed with hand-tied fringes. Arturo and Marta plan to add a restaurant in this appealing roadside location.

Arturo is concerned that many young people today are disinterested in their craft because it is laborious and not highly profitable. However, he urges them to learn its satisfactions, as his children have done, and to insure that it does not die out.

Biography
Arturo began to weave at the age of eight as an employee in the house of neighbors. Neither of his parents were weavers, his father a farmer and his mother a homemaker. At the time of their marriage he and his wife began to work together and to form their own factory. Arturo was 25 years old and Marta was 22. She had learned to dye and prepare wool from her mother.

Technique
This couple's work is primarily in cotton and less often wool, with very occasional use of acrylic fiber. After buying thread from the state of Puebla, Marta dyes it with both natural and chemical substances. Fifty skeins of one color are treated in one day, and then dried in the air, out of the direct sunlight to prevent fading. The wool or cotton thread is then spun on a droll-looking device incorporating bicycle wheels. A roll is created that is attached to a large wooden, pedal-operated loom.

Once the arrangement of threads is designed, the weaver works with a shuttle principle. A handle is pulled, setting in motion the shuttle that glides back and forth across the threads. After several such passages, a "comb" built into the loom is used to pack the threads tightly. Striped or solid color "rebozos" are made with an even rhythm of the four pedals, each foot directing two pedals. However, when a geometric pattern is woven into the fabric, each foot must alternate between its two pedals. Tassels are formed by hand.

The fabric for many "rebozos" is created within the same piece. One hundred and forty "rebozos" can be made from the same roll once it is completed. Arturo and Marta estimate that 15 are completed in one day's weaving.

Arturo weaving

Address:
Carretera International S/N (without number)
Paraje Roobias
Mitla
Oaxaca
C.P. 70430
Marta dying wool

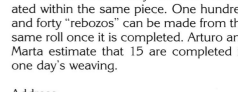

Family (left to right): Arturo, Martín, Marta, Arturo, Jr.

Plain stripe rebozo, $6
Open work pattern rebozo, $12

Blouse, $6
Rebozo, $5

Open work rebozo, $10

Additional weavers of tablecloths, bedspreads, unfinished yard goods and cotton clothing
In Oaxaca City:
José Leyva (Bolaños Cacho #206 in Xochimilco)
Joaquin Prieto Saavedra in the shop M.A.R.O, A.C. (5 de Mayo #204)
In Mitla:
Doña Julia in her shop "Lad Naa" (Hidalgo #10)
Artesanos en Solidaridad en Mitla (Hidalgo #37)

Embroidery
of San Antonino Castillo Velasco and San Juan Chilateca

Here we feature artists whose major art is delicate hand embroidery, primarily on clothing. Many types of embroidery can be found in Oaxaca, on both garments and domestic items, complementing patterns and colors that are woven into the fabric from which they are made. San Antonino Castillo Velasco, and its neighbor San Juan Chilateca, are the main pueblos within our geographical radius where this type of embroidery is created. We feature one artist family in San Antonino Castillo Velasco and another in San Juan Chilateca.

The garments for which these pueblos are best known are called "wedding dresses." Generally made from white cotton, they are flowing (unwaisted) dresses (or blouses) with elaborately embroidered decoration on the yolk, short (occasionally long) sleeves and front segments. In addition to embroidery, these garments have crocheted portions around the arm section and neckline, and "hazme si puedes" (literally translated as "make me if you can"). This term refers to the horizontal row of human figures embroidered in the smocked segment of the garment, just under the yolk

Artists range in quality from the most outstanding – those who produce merely a few elaborately-embroidered dresses or blouses per year – to more commercial artisans whose decoration is far simpler, even omitting some of the elements considered crucial by the finer embroiderers. One clear indication of quality is the degree of delicacy and clarity of the "hazme si puedes." Prices vary widely according to the excellence of this and other portions of the work.

San Antonino Castillo Velasco
(more commonly called San Antonino)

San Antonino, approximately 30 kilometers (40 minutes) from Oaxaca, is situated on the same highway that one travels to Ocotlán de Morelos (see page 50 in Chapter One). A right turn off the highway takes the visitor into a pueblo not noteworthy for its beauty. Nevertheless the pride of its dwellers is evident in their custom of artfully trimming the trees that border its main cement-surfaced street. A sign announces the pueblo's most prominent types of folk art: "ropa bordado y flor inmortal" (embroidered clothing and dried flowers, see Chapter Nine for dried flowers).

Virginia Sánchez de Cornelio and her Five Daughters
A Close-Knit Clan of Embroiderers
"We hope the younger generation will continue our art."

See Family Tree #16, "Family of Virginia Sánchez de Cornelio," in Appendix on page 181.

After walking through prominent metal doors to enter a lush courtyard with flowering trees, you find a well-appointed house. It has many bedrooms and an elaborately decorated living room, replete with television and other signs of material success. There a talented and feisty woman, Virginia Sánchez de Cornelio, works with her five daughters - Reina, Silvia, Antonina, Carmen and María de la Luz (from eldest to youngest) - to create fine hand-embroidered blouses and dresses for which their pueblo, San Antonino Castillo Velasco, has long been known. In addition to the traditional "wedding dresses" and blouses (decorated in the same style), the members of the Sánchez family have introduced more contemporary items, such as embroidered shorts sets, skirts, and everyday dresses for adults and children.

There is an atmosphere of joy, warmth and pensiveness in this family's collaboration. Although each member makes her own pieces, they sit together, talking, consulting and listening to music. Companionship is crucial to their ability to carry out the various demanding stages of their creative process. Silvia and Carmen live with their mother, and the other three sisters live nearby.

The Sánchez's are one of the few remaining families who perpetuate their pueblo's embroidery tradition. At present there are not enough women trained to carry on the work. Many have moved to the north, especially to the United States, in search of a better living. The Sánchez family's greatest hope is that their tradition will not be lost, that the younger generation will perpetuate their art. They enthusi-astically welcome visitors to their home where they are happy to share their original work: its process and products.

Biography

Virginia started working actively when she was 20, often embroidering by candle-light into the wee hours of the morning. This was a quiet time after the responsibilities of her children and household chores were completed. As a child she was taught to embroider by her mother, Florentina. Although a tortilla maker for a living, she herself enjoyed embroidering in her free time.

Times have changed dramatically. Twenty years ago there were ten to 15 families who created this distinctive work. At that time Virginia administered the production of 200 dresses per week, farming out various stages to many workers once they were designed. In addition, she and some of her daughters contributed their own high quality pieces.

Sisters at work (left to right): Silvia, Carmen, Antonina

Wedding blouse for 6 year old, $60

Family (left to right): Reina, Silvia, Virginia, [Anya Rothstein], Carmen, Antonina (in front) Luz Clarita

Technique

The process of creation of embroidered blouses and dresses is multi-faceted and laborious. Virginia estimates that the most complex pieces can take up to five months to complete. The members of the Sánchez family begin by buying fabric (either cotton or silk) in their pueblo and cutting it to dimensions for blouses or dresses. Next they create a sketched design. This is typically a resplendent array of flowers and birds that fill the front and back of the yolk, and spill onto the capped sleeves. One sister, María de la Luz, has a special talent for drawing with pen on fabric the designs to be transformed into vibrant and ornate displays, often in glorious colors. Her talents were recognized when she was a small girl; at the age of eight, she began to contribute sketches to the family effort.

The most outstanding garments encompass three types of needlework. First there is the main pattern, usually a combination of pansies and other flowers and foliage along with birds. It is embroidered in varied combinations of colors, most frequently a lively medley, but sometimes in primarily monochromatic displays with contrasting small details. At the juncture of the yolk and sleeve is an area of open crocheted work (called "el deshilado"). This is an art form in itself. There are two varieties, one finer in quality than the other. Some garments consist of a larger and more elaborate segment of this type of work. Finally, there is the renowned "hazme si puedes" (literally translated "make me if you can"). This is the humorous name given to the exceedingly challenging band of small human figures stitched across the bottom of the yoke. It is the smock work from which the flowing plain fabric of the body of the blouse or dress emanates.

Each of these segments is created separately and sewn together later. Not all garments are equally complex and detailed. They may vary in the quality, and even the presence, of the crocheted portion, the "hazme si puedes" and the embroidery itself.

Address:
Libertad #1
San Antonino Castillo Velasco
Ocotlán
Oaxaca
C.P. 71520
Telephone: 01 (95157) 10092

Wedding dress with long sleeves, $135

Detail of yolk in preparation for wedding dress

Blouse and skirt set, $55
Small tablecloth, 20" x 20", $35

San Juan Chilateca

San Juan Chilateca, approximately 33 kilometers (slightly over 40 minutes) from Oaxaca, is also on the highway to Ocotlán de Morelos, and on the right just beyond San Antonino. It is located in a lovely valley that affords picturesque views of farmers cultivating corn and beans using oxen-drawn ploughs of olden times rather than tractors.

The Sumano Family

See Family Tree #17, "The Sumano Family," in Appendix on page 182.

The Sumano sisters are two of the remaining artists who produce outstanding embroidered dresses and blouses, in the longstanding tradition of San Antonino. They live in the neighboring pueblo of San Juan Chilateca to which San Antonino's influence has extended.

Faustina Sumano García
Virtuoso of Creative Blends of Embroidered Design and Color
"It is never possible to receive enough money for this difficult work. I do it out of love."

Faustina Sumano García is a master of gloriously detailed and colorful embroidery in the traditional "wedding dress" style. Her remarkable work has been featured in many books on Mexican folk art and recognized in multiple contests.

The array of pieces she showed us was breathtaking, both in its range of design elements and color combinations. One dress was made of black silk with a mandarin collar, on which she embroidered stunning, multi-colored pansies and other flowers. Another consisted of white embroidery on white cotton, while yet another featured primarily pale blue embroidery on white cloth.

Faustina's daughters, who embroider well, do not do so for a living. However, they may occasionally help her if a commissioned piece needs to be completed quickly. They have not been specifically taught by Faustina, but have grown up watching her embroider all their lives. One daughter, a doctor with her own infant daughter,

Faustina embroidering a black silk wedding dress with mandarin collar and long sleeves, $1000

showed us her nearly completed embroidery of a wedding dress. This is a piece she has undertaken for her personal pleasure.

Biography

Faustina began to embroider at the age of six, as did all girls in the school she attended. She sold her first piece, a pillow with a "muñeca" (doll-like figure) in Louis XV dress, at the market. Her mother did not do this type of work for a living. However, she occasionally decorated an excessively plain tablecloth or napkin. Faustina, who loved to embroider right from the start, continued making pillow cases, napkins, tablecloths, men's shirts with embroidered cuffs, pockets and shoulders, conventional dresses and wedding dresses.

She created her first wedding dress when she was 27 years old. It was important to her at that time, and continues to be equally important, to carry out all parts of the process herself. She cuts the fabric, designs the figures, embroiders, and sews the dress together. She contrasts this with some artists who do not design or cut their pieces, but only embroider.

Technique

Faustina begins a new dress by cutting each part out of the background fabric. She designs the pattern with a pen on cloth, a process that usually takes two days. She has not yet recorded her patterns, but is considering doing so. Recognizing that she will not live forever, and that this is a dying art, she would like to impart her legacy in a more enduring form.

Once the design is completed, Faustina undertakes the embroidery. Some artists assign different parts to different people. Faustina objects to this because work will inevitably vary from individual to individual, compromising the integrity of the piece. She typically embroiders the yolk first, then the sleeves, followed by the portions under the arms and on the abdomen.

Faustina and her daughter Francisca Guillermina

Finally she creates the crocheted portions and the "hazme si puedes." Such a dress takes her three months to complete if she works daily, and four to six months to complete if she works on a less regular basis.

Address:
Cuauhtemoc #11
San Juan Chilateca
Oaxaca
C.P. 71508

Wedding dress with multi-color embroidery, $1100

Detail of its yolk, "hazme si puedes," and crocheted work

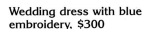

Wedding dress with blue embroidery, $300

Anastasia Sumano García
Master of Contrasting Coloration in Embroidery
"I hope people will learn this art so that when I pass away it will continue."

Anastasia Sumano García, Faustina's older sister, is a peaceful woman who sits contentedly on her screened patio just off the main highway. She embroiders with startling medleys of variegated color. Displaying unequalled imaginativeness and sensitivity, she dips into the palette of her thread box to select the tone with which to stitch her next flower or butterfly.

Anastasia's pieces are actually the product of a mother-daughter collaboration. The fabulous designs she embroiders are created by her extraordinarily talented daughter, María. She lives in the neighboring pueblo of Ocotlán de Morelos with her own family.

At this point in her life, Anastasia completes only a few pieces per year because of the intense visual demands of this work. At her current age Anastasia finishes a dress in five months. The day of our first visit she had no finished blouses or dresses available. However, she showed us an unforgettable yolk that she had completed in preparation for a competition in Mexico City some six months later. The other portions of the dress were in process. By the next day Anastasia brought from her daughter's home several stunning wedding dresses, family heirlooms. Anastasia produces her work for special occasions such as contests or for commissioned projects.

Biography

Like her sister Faustina, Anastasia learned to embroider as a young child from a teacher sent to their pueblo school for six months to instruct all the girls. Much later in her life Anastasia sought further instruction in the neighboring pueblo of San Antonino Castillo Velasco that has long been famous for its embroiderers. There she worked with women in the market to perfect her technique. Her own pueblo of San Juan Chilateca did not have this established tradition.

However, it was not until the age of 51 that she began to produce her work for sale. Her first pieces were blouses in one color: red or blue. At one point she made men's shirts. But because the prices she could command were too low to make this work worthwhile, she reverted to specialization in dresses and blouses alone.

Technique

Anastasia purchases her cotton cloth in Oaxaca City, along with silk thread. She begins by cutting the cloth into the various segments necessary for the dress. Anastasia has never designed her patterns, a phase of the work for which she feels she has little talent. Originally, select women from San Antonino contributed the designs, until her daughter María assumed this role. As she has gotten older, Faustina also accepts the help of a neighbor. Eager to learn Anastasia's art, she assists her by completing only the green leaf and vine portions.

Address:
Carretera Oaxaca-Puerto Ángel #6 (just beyond the marker that reads "Kilometro 27")
San Juan Chilateca
Oaxaca
C.P. 71508

Anastasia embroidering while wearing a wedding dress, $600

Details of yolk and sleeve of wedding dress to be entered in contest

Chapter Three
Woodcarving

Painted woodcarving is a major art form in three pueblos near Oaxaca City: San Antonio Arrazola, San Martín Tilcajete and La Unión Tejalapam. We include several carvers from each pueblo, preceded by a brief description of that pueblo. Unlike weaving and many types of ceramics, woodcarving is a relatively new art. Although unpainted religious masks and small toys for children have long been an important part of the culture, the creation of painted animal, human and fantasy figures for purely decorative purposes is a far later development. Many people have taken to incorrectly referring to this entire class of art as "alebrijes," or monsters. While some artists *do* create monsters, many pieces treat subjects of natural beauty (such as animals or cacti), religious beliefs or fantasy material grounded in myths or cultural traditions (for instance, the "nahuales" also captured in many types of ceramics).

Woodcarving was introduced in the 1950s but gained distinct recognition and popularity only in the 1980s, in response to its soaring demand by American folk art dealers. During the three summers I spent in Oaxaca in the 1960s I was unaware of this type of folk art. Most believe that the pioneering creativity of a single artist, Manuel Jiménez Ramírez (see pages 87 and 88) is responsible for catalyzing this delightful work that has dramatically altered the economic prospects of many of its creators. In the late 1950s Manuel was encouraged to pursue this work by an American living in Oaxaca, Arthur Train. A detailed history of woodcarving is beautifully elaborated in a volume devoted to this purpose (Barbash, 1993).

We begin with Arrazola, the pueblo of Manuel Jiménez Ramírez and many other talented carvers. Then we proceed to San Martín Tilcajete, a pueblo in which artists with prodigious talent reside. Finally we take up La Unión Tejalapam where one can re-capture the spirit of the earliest days of this form of folk art.

San Antonio Arrazola
(more commonly known simply as Arrazola)

San Antonio Arrazola is located approximately 20 kilometers (30 minutes) from Oaxaca. This is the pueblo where Manuel Jiménez Ramírez introduced woodcarving. It is estimated that at present 80 families are currently involved in it, ten of whom produce outstanding work.

En route you see the fabulous archaeological site of Monte Albán at a distance. Turning off on the right side of the highway, there is a stretch of impressive trees that embrace the path below, forming a roof. This enclosure opens up to the rather lengthy road (approximately 5 kilometers) leading into Arrazola proper, through a small pueblo called San Javier Xoxocotlán. The approach to Arrazola features an abandoned hacienda, a small town square with a well-tended gazebo, and a market of "artesanías" (handicrafts) initiated by government officials. This market has not been very successful, since artists fear that others will copy the work they display. The pueblo is quite hilly, offering expansive vistas, including brightly-painted houses and traditional scenes such as oxen bearing cumbersome wooden yolks while pulling carts bursting with produce and supplies.

Manuel Jiménez Ramírez and his sons Angélico and Isaías
King of Woodcarving
"To stop working is to stop the flow of blood in the vessels."

See Family Tree #18, "Family of Manuel Jiménez Ramírez," in Appendix on page 183.

A dignified man in his 80s Manuel Jiménez Ramírez is a person of remarkable achievements for which he demands respect. He is credited as the originator of this genre of folk art and derives great satisfaction from his popularity with collectors all over the world. Manuel and his sons Angélico and Isaías are best known for their animals, angels, shepherds, kings and Christ figures, all of which they regard as their exclusive designs. Their pieces are bold in shape, size and painting style.

The experience of visiting Manuel Jiménez's home is monumental in many senses of the word. This is a place of stature, reflecting Manuel's sense of himself as the reigning king. Contrasted with the simplicity of their studio, the remainder of the family's physical surround clearly announces prosperity. Adjacent to the entrance to their home is the skeleton of an abandoned hacienda perched high on a hill next to cultivated fields. Behind elegant wrought iron doors, a lush shangri-la garden and creative mosaic paths weave through the multiple components of the family's compound.

A sense of love and pride in belonging to this clan, with its small empire, is exuded by all. A swimming pool, a sports utility vehicle and a large tractor are visible. A basketball net and swing are the nidus for spontaneous recreational interludes among the many members of this extended family. A display room is devoted to the family masterworks, as well as t-shirts and sweatshirts commissioned to commemorate father and sons in a logo incorporating one of their pieces. The living room contains velvet-upholstered furniture and a large perpetually operating television.

Family (left to right): Front row: Isaías (holding Eleuterio), Manuel, Angélico holding María del Carmen. Back row: Nicolasa, Roque, Angélico, Jr., Victoria Dolores

Distinguishing himself from the (now innumerable) woodcarvers he regards as imitators of his work is a subject of great concern to Manuel. One approach has been to use a finer wood, cedar, that comes from Guatemala but can be bought in Oaxaca. Prior to this he and his sons worked in "copal," collecting it from the hills near Monte Albán as most carvers do. As an aside Manuel added that cedar also has the advantage of not needing to dry out, since it is softer than "copal," even when dry.

Address:
Álvaro Obregón #1
San Antonio Arrazola
Xoxocotlán
Oaxaca
C.P. 71233
Telephone: 01 (95151) 71293

Angélico painting a rabbit,
9" x 6", $200

Having a philosophical bent, Manuel believes his work to be a "renacimiento" (rebirth), and proudly announces that "to stop working is to stop the flow of blood in the vessels. It makes me sick." He cherishes the idea of his children and grandchildren, not only continuing his artistic tradition, but also insuring future respect for the "rights of the author" of the pieces: "the house of Manuel Jiménez" and his children.

Biography

As a poor eight year old boy, Manuel passed long hours tending sheep in the hills of his pueblo. He developed the habit of occupying himself by carving bits of wood he encountered along the way. His talent and the possibility of earning money by selling his carvings combined to open a distinctly new life path.

Manuel takes pride in having taught himself to carve, creating designs out of his rich imagination. Angélico began to carve at 12 years of age and Isaías at 15 years of age, both learning at their father's side. They continue to work in this way, in their simple but well-appointed and brightly-illuminated indoor studio, seated on modest finished tree stumps.

Technique

Manuel and his sons share all styles, no individual noted for his own specialty. Pieces can be produced in small, medium or large sizes, taking approximately one to two, three or five days, respectively, for the carving alone. Unlike many carvers, Manuel, Angélico and Isaías generally do the painting themselves, their wives rarely contributing to their art. Manuel's favorite colors are yellow and rose, while Angélico favors blue and Isaías prefers a combination of colors.

Isaías painting a cat,
14" x 6", $200

Manuel holding a "nahual,"
17" x 10", $350

Coyote, 15" x 6", $350

Grasshopper, 15" x 6", $350 (the
price of all medium size pieces, all
small pieces are $200 and all large
pieces are $600)

Bull, 10" x 5",
$200

Armando and Moises Jiménez Aragón
Brotherly Environmentalists and Carvers of Distinctive Animals
"We welcome new creative ideas suggested by our visitors."

See Family Tree #19, "Family, of Armando and Moises Jiménez Aragón" in Appendix on page 183.

In the cozy shelter of the natural awning created by wonderfully shady trees, in the corner of a sparklingly-bright courtyard, two brothers, Armando and Moises Jimenéz Aragón, work side by side to create carved and painted wooden figures that make significant statements. Their pieces are prominent, both in size and hue.

Armando and Moises specialize in many varieties of animals. In addition to their traditional rabbits, they exercise their creative spirit to produce animals that do not actually inhabit Oaxaca and its environs, such as flamingos and bears. They are decorated with vibrant colors, two favorites being colonial blue and yellow. Armando and Moises are also receptive to new designs inspired by photographs that prospective clients provide.

While the brothers sit together in their customary chairs, each one produces and signs his individual pieces. As we chatted, Moises's four-year-old daughter joined them, actively working on her own small figure while enjoying the company of her father and uncle. Armando and Moises paint as well. However, when they are absorbed in carving to meet large orders, they rely entirely upon their wives, Antonia Carillo and Oralia Cardenas, to inventively decorate their pieces.

Armando and Moises are quite successful, having begun to achieve recognition in the United States. They have had exhibitions in Washington D.C., Princeton, Phoenix, San Francisco, Los Angeles and San Antonio, during which one or both of them have accompanied their work. Their sincerest hope is to pass their cherished tradition along to their children who will carry it on to another generation.

Biography

Armando and Moises work in the yard of the home originally built during their childhood by their parents, Alejandro Jiménez Hernández and Raquel Aragón. Moises and his wife and child continue to live here, while Armando lives next door with his own wife and child. Although the brothers identify themselves as nephews of the renowned Manuel Jiménez (indicating their father is his brother), they do not regard themselves as direct descendants of his tradition.

Armando and Moises's history is distinct from the more typical custom of learning, from a very young age, at the side of a father who is significantly involved in woodcarving. Alejandro has always been primarily a farmer, only minimally involved in woodcarving. Although he did offer some instruction to his sons, they began their careers rather late, Moises at 15 and Armando at 20 once he had completed school.

Their lovely mother, Raquel, describes several facets of her sons' history. Unlike many men in the pueblo, neither one was obliged to devote his life to this craft. Instead each made this choice out of a natural affinity for creating the beautiful pieces organically inspired by their love. Armando and Moises regard only Sunday as a day of rest, devoting themselves to their beloved artwork the other six days. Raquel is proud that her sons are involved not only in using, but also replenishing, the supply of trees. They do not wish their industry to deplete the environment's bounty.

Family (left to right): Armando, Raquel, Horalia, Moises holding Alejandro, Nancy, Antonia with large cat (painting not quite complete), 30" x 10", $350

Technique

To begin their work Armando and Moises go to the mountains to select suitable pieces of "copal" wood. Having reflected upon the particular designs they intend to make, they search for pieces of the appropriate size and configuration.

Wood is collected only when it is relatively dry because, once drenched, it is more likely to break. Armando and Moises carve with machetes and chisels while the wood is still green (i.e., fresh) and softer to work with.

Once the carving is completed, the pieces are left to dry in the sun. Ultimately they are sanded and painted. The total process, from carving to painting, takes about 15 days for a large piece, six days for a medium size piece and three to four days for a small piece.

Address:
Independencia #1 (at the corner of Tabasco)
San Antonio Arrazola
Xoxocotlán
Oaxaca
C.P. 71233
Telephone: 01 (95151) 71356

Armando (left) and Moises (right) carving

Antonia (wife of Moises) painting

Small cat, 12" x 8", $65 (all pieces in large size, $350, medium size, $100, small size, $65)

Small Frogs, 6" x 6", $65

José (Pepe) Santiago Ibañez
Carver of Lively and Reasonably-Priced Fantasy Figures and Animals
"We would like people to appreciate how much we and our pueblo have advanced since we began to work in woodcarving."

See Family Tree #20, "Family of José Santiago Ibañez," in Appendix on page 184.

In a sparse, narrow courtyard José Santiago Ibañez (nicknamed Pepe), a handsome and modest man from an enormous extended family, carves wooden figures. Pepe and his family specialize in native animals such as armadillos and iguanas, fantasy figures such as winged horses, two-headed serpents ("alebrijes" or monsters, in the true sense of the word) and mermaids. In addition there are masks that derive from the tradition of Pepe's parents, who produced an unpainted vari-

ety. Some of his work leans to the commercial side, including boxes and picture frames. The combination of good quality and reasonable prices provides an alternative to the higher prices of some other artists in this pueblo.

Pepe sits side by side with six other men, in an elevated wooden structure built to provide shade from the intense sun. Surrounded by a thick carpet of wooden shavings, they work as they joke with each other and listen to mariachi music broadcast at a nearly deafening volume. Some of these men are members of the family and others, residents of the pueblo, are hired to help Pepe fill a large order. Behind them is a small but brilliantly painted three-room structure that serves as the family's home and showroom for completed pieces.

Pepe derives a great sense of pride and satisfaction from his participation in the craft of woodcarving. Thanks to this art, his pueblo has progressed a great deal. He wishes to extend a welcome to tourists to visit his workshop.

Biography
Pepe and his wife began their woodcarving business in 1986. Although his parents had done some carving Pepe did not begin until several years into his marriage. Prior to that he worked primarily as a policeman. With only one family member heavily involved in carving, his cousin Miguel Santiago, Pepe taught himself this art form. Observing the work of others, he repeatedly practiced. At first Pepe made many errors and was unable to sell his work. His first pieces were donkeys and dogs. As Pepe's wife recalled this period when no one seemed to help and poverty was near, her eyes filled with emotion. Over time Pepe's work improved and he began to carve panda bears, lions, dogs and mermaids.

Family (left to right):
Front row: Mercedes, Erica Maritza, Malena
Back row: Nicol, Michel

Technique

Once the form is cut out of "copal" with a machete, Pepe places his pieces in the sun to dry for a week. Following this they are sanded and painted with a uniform color that serves as the background. Finer painting is then added by his wife and daughters who work in one of the rooms inside the house. They use exclusively acrylic paints for these purposes. Pepe estimates that it takes eight to ten days to complete one of his medium-size figures.

Address:
Álvaro Obregón #12
San Antonio Arrazola
Xoxocotlán
Oaxaca
C.P. 71233
Telephone: 01 (95151) 71394

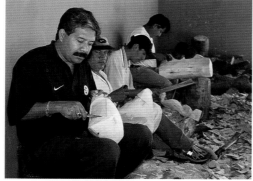

(Left to right): Pepe working with Fernando Morales, Marco, Victor, Hugo (brother)

(Left to right):
Centipede, 5" x 6", $10
Large cactus with hummingbirds, 12" x 6", $14
Small cactus, 5" x 4", $10

Erica Maritza (daughter) painting

Bull masks (left to right): 10" x 10", $40
8" x 8", $35

Dragon, 9" x 7", $25

Additional woodcarvers in Arrazola
Mario Castellanos (Revolución #35)
Narciso González Ramírez and his wife Ruby Hernández Pinos (Venustiano Carranza #26)
José Hernández (Venustiano Carranza #23)
Antonio Mandarín (Alvaro Obregón #20)
Arsenio Morales (Alvaro Obregón #14)
Francisco Ojeda Morales and his wife Lucía Trinidad Santiago (Plan de Ayala #8)
Gerardo Ramírez (Alvaro Obregón #15)

San Martín Tilcajete

San Martín Tilcajete is approximately 26 kilometers (35 minutes) from Oaxaca. The approach by highway consists of a winding road from which you look down upon a wide-open expanse of cultivated fields on the right and up at hills and stupendous land formations on the left.

A newly-created road leads off of the main highway into the pueblo of San Martín Tilcajete. This is a mark of the prosperity of some of its artists. Along this road one sees frequent signs created by some of the more commercial artists, sporting the English words "Wooden Handicrafts." Many of the finer artists live in homes that are more difficult to find, but well worth the adventure. It is estimated that 120 families currently work as woodcarvers in San Martín Tilcajete, 15-20 being of fine quality.

In contrast to the smooth stretch of road leading into its center, most of the streets within San Martín are unpaved and extremely bumpy. Many colorful sights offer themselves along the way. A lazy dog rests in the middle of the road. A herd of cattle meanders along the street. An elderly woman balances a plastic bag full of tomatoes on her head as she returns from market. She is flanked by her daughter who hugs huge bundles of flowers, and her granddaughter carrying a basket teeming with oranges. A wall of cacti provides some measure of privacy and a powerful natural presence in the lives of families whose homes are closely packed.

Isidoro Cruz Hernández
Master Mask Carver and Distinguished Mentor of San Martín Woodcarvers
"I never know in advance what my imagination will create."

See Family Tree #21, "Family of Isidoro Cruz Hernández," in Appendix on page 185.

Isidoro Cruz Hernández, a distinguished-looking man with an energetic, charming and generous disposition and a lively sense of humor, is a renowned carver of wooden masks. Along with Epifanio Fuentes (the next featured artist) he is one of the original woodcarvers of San Martín Tilcajate. However, Isidoro's work has not taken the direction of most of the artists of his village. Rather than the many varieties of animal, human and fantasy figures decorated with acrylic paints typical of his fellow artists, Isidoro creates large dramatic masks, animals, skeletons and devils. He has also developed newer designs: virgins, canes and saints that are painted with natural dyes. Isidoro works from his own imagination, often inspired by nightmarish dreams in which he pictures faces with irregular noses and devils. His pieces are quite valuable, and are widely collected. However, at this stage in his life Isidoro is not willing to sell his favorite creations.

Isidoro also has the distinction of having helped many artists in his pueblo launch or develop their work. This was made possible by the governmental position he was awarded decades ago.

His plantation-like home, with its expansive acreage and inspiring vistas of far off mountain ranges, is also unique in that he raises his own trees. The greatest portion of his forest consists of "zompantle" trees, numbering approximately 1000 at present. Sitting on a low leather chair, looking at his huge expanse of tree-covered property,

Family (left to right): Blanca Nayeli (Isidoro's daughter), Margarita (Isidoro's wife), Isidoro

Isidoro carving

Isidoro is a contented man. The beauties of nature never fail to impress him. During our visit one of his farmers handed him a newly discovered beehive dripping with honeycomb. Thrilled, Isidoro paused to admire this natural wonder and to share his sense of awe with us.

Isidoro hopes that his children will continue his craft, although at this time only his daughter, Blanca Nayeli, is involved. He enthusiastically receives visitors to see his studio and to buy his work, which he considers a good investment as well as a source of current pleasure.

Biography

Isidoro taught himself to carve in wood. Knowledge of woodcarving was not in his family tradition, nor was it practiced in San Martín in his childhood. He began working at the age of ten, out of necessity. Being from a poor family, he tended animals for his father, a farmer. As he did so with a friend, they talked about how to earn more money and amused themselves by making toys. Using pieces of sugar cane, they cut out faces and legs. They also made bows and arrows out of branches, which they used for hunting birds. During a year-long serious illness when he was 14 Isidoro occupied himself by creating small toys of wood. His mother sold them for five "centavos" each in town.

By 18 Isidoro was making masks for carnivals. Some years later, he created wooden toys specifically intended for sale in a folk art shop in the city of Oaxaca. In 1970 Isidoro had achieved a significant degree of success. He was sent to Los Angeles on a government mission to demonstrate his work, along with that of other Mexican artists. He was also invited to exhibit his work in Mexico City.

The contacts Isidoro developed later enabled him to become a mentor and facilitator of the work of many artists in his own pueblo. When, in 1980, one of the people from the artistic mission he joined was offered a prominent position in the government, he selected Isidoro to stimulate the work of artisans in several areas.

Technique

"Zompantle" is one of the major types of wood Isidoro uses for his carving. Others are "sabino" and cedar, rather than the "copal" employed by most carvers.

After cutting the wood, Isidoro dries it for approximately 15 days before carving so that it does not crack. Before carving the features of the mask, he hollows out the basic form. His design depends upon his imagination, and often emerges differently from what he anticipates. Only when Isidoro takes orders to reproduce one of his already-created pieces does he know in advance what he will carve.

When the carving is completed, Isidoro sands his mask and decorates it in any one of a variety of ways. He may use aniline paints, or natural-dyed substances created from materials such as "cochineal" (small insects found in a particular type of cactus). Once completed, the decoration is preserved with a coat of lacquer. An individual mask may take from three weeks to a number of months to complele, depending upon the degree of detail and size.

Address:
Domicilio Privada del Olvido #1
San Martín Tilcajete
Oaxaca
C.P.71506

Isidoro in his "zompantle" grove

Bull mask, 20" x 13", $625

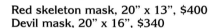

Red skeleton mask, 20" x 13", $400
Devil mask, 20" x 16", $340

Picture frame for 4" x 6" photos by Blanca Nayeli, $12

The Fuentes Family
Carvers Who Delight in Creative Industry

See Family Tree #22, "Family of Epifanio Fuentes Vázquez," in Appendix on page 186.

Behind massive iron doors an expansive courtyard is surrounded by the multiple dwellings that house this prolific family. The external and internal walls are a rich and cheerful shade of purple that reflects the contented feeling one encounters in visiting this productive family. Three generations, soon to be four, are at work in this extended family home. Epifanio Fuentes, his wife Laurencia Santiago Hernández and their three eldest sons, Zeni, Efraín and Iván, are actively at work, at the height of their productivity. Epifanio's father, Zenén Fuentes Méndez, who works primarily as a farmer, also still produces some carved pieces.

Epifanio's children carry out his designs, both their form and decorative painting style, but are also developing their own styles. In fact Zeni and Efraín, fine carvers in their own right, have begun to sign their own pieces and to establish their own reputations. This tradition continues, evident as Epifanio's youngest son, four-year-old José Alberto, learns to carve at his father's side. Now there are several infant grandchildren who will no doubt occupy a place at their father's and, with good fortune, their grandfather's (or even great grandfather's) side within a few years.

Epifanio Fuentes is the head of this remarkably talented, prolific family of woodcarvers. (In this exceptional case we place his father last, since he is not as actively engaged in this artform.) As we approach their home, a lazy dog resting in the middle of the road begrudgingly relinquishes its place to make way for our vehicle. Up ahead a herd of cattle slowly meanders up the path.

Epifanio Fuentes Vázquez
Inspired Carver of Angels and Maestro of his Craft
"What is important is quality, not quantity."

Epifanio Fuentes Vázquez is one of the original and most successful carvers in San Martín. He is best known for the charming angels he introduced in 1971. His wife Laurencia paints most of his pieces, originally taught by Epifanio just after their marriage. She, in turn, has taught their daughters how to paint. During our visit their five-year-old daughter, Lucerito, sat rapt in attention at her mother's side, applying paint with her small brush. Following tradition, Zeni, Epifanio and Laurencia's eldest son will teach his wife to paint.

Epifanio's growing reputation in the United States is deeply important to him, both because it enhances his financial prospects and because of his great satisfaction in teaching others about his work. He is especially gratified by invitations to instruct children in woodcarving. Epifanio proudly shared with us a notebook recently sent to him documenting his trip to a school in Philadelphia, where he and Laurencia were invited to teach elementary school children to carve and paint. The children wrote individual thank you notes detailing the Fuentes's educational influence. Epifanio has also demonstrated his work in San Antonio, Phoenix, Santa Fe and Boston.

Biography

Epifanio and his brother learned to carve from their father, who worked in wood as a supplement to his primary role as a farmer. He continues to work today, living in the same home with Epifanio, making his characteristic pieces: masks and animals. Earlier in his adult life Epifanio sought work as a migrant harvester, ending up in jail a number of times in his failed attempts to cross the American border.

Technique

Epifanio works in several types of wood, including "copal", cedar and "zompantle." Currently he purchases his wood from pueblos, such as Ejutla, that are up to four or five hours away. However, earlier in his career he collected pieces from the mountains surrounding his village. Epifanio underlined the importance of environmental conservation, especially the replenishment of trees cut down by woodcarvers.

The piece Epifanio chooses to carve depends either upon the nature of his creative idea or the shape of the wood. He begins with a machete, and then a chisel and other finer tools, to create his forms and their details. Once finished with the carving, Epifanio dries his pieces for approximately three days, following which he sands them. His wife creates the painting, first applying a white sealer, then a solid background and, finally, the details.

Epifanio and his three eldest sons at work (left to right): Zeni, Iván, Efraín, Epifanio

Family (left to right): Front row: Fatima (granddaughter), José Alberto (son), Lucerito (daughter). Back row: Zenén (father), Magali (daughter), Reyna (daughter-in-law), Zeni (son) holding Laura (granddaughter), Angélica (daughter), Laurencia (wife), Epifanio

Epifanio carving with José Alberto (his youngest son)

Margarita (Epifanio's wife) painting with Lucerito (their daughter)

Zeni Fuentes Santiago
(son of Epifanio)
Charismatic Carver
"I hope the art of my family is never forgotten and that my children choose the same work."

Zeni, Epifanio and Laurencia's eldest son, is a talented carver in his own right. His favorite pieces are lions, armadillos and giraffes that he both carves and paints. Decorative painting is extremely important to him, a portion of the creative process with which his wife sometimes assists. He has also developed a reputation as an instructor of woodcarving, especially for children. The combination of his talents, his commanding personality, and his proficiency in English has led to many invitations to cities in the United States. In addition, an instructional video has been produced in the United States featuring his work.

Biography

Zeni initially worked in woodcarving at the age of seven, helping his father sand and prepare his pieces. Only slightly later he began to use a machete, carving his own first pieces: ducks and panda bears.

As early as 14 years of age Zeni was invited to Arizona to demonstrate his carving. Since then he has traveled to cities such as Kansas City, Los Angeles, and Chicago to present his techniques and to instruct children in his methods.

Zapata, 24" x 8", $440

Mother nursing child, 15" x 4", $135

Zeni at work

Armadillos with books, 9" x 7", $35 each

(From left to right):
Cat, 19" x 13", $40
Zebra, 12" x 5", $60
Bear anteater, 16" x 5", $140

Efraín Fuentes Santiago
(son of Epifanio)
Carver of Fantasies
"I love my work and to develop new styles."

Efraín is a cheerful young man who delights in his carved creations. Cats are his favorites, although armadillos bearing their young and mermaids run a close second. He is also known for his angels, witches and skeletons.

Biography
Efraín also began to carve at seven years of age, learning at his father's side. With the dual advantages of belonging to a well-known carving family, and being extremely talented in his own right, he spent time in the United States beginning as early as 13 years of age. More recently he made an extended visit of three months to the Jackolope Gallery in Santa Fe where he demonstrated his techniques.

Technique
Using primarily the same techniques as other family members, Efraín has recently begun to carve in cedar as well as "copal." In addition to carving he repairs antique pieces made of cedar, such as saints and sculptures.

Technique
Zeni begins a piece by cutting out the segment he will use and creating the basic form with a machete. The natural form of the wood dictates the piece he creates. Then he dries it in the sun for a week. Following this he sands the figure and washes it before painting. He finds properly preparing the carved product far more demanding than doing the carving itself.

Lion, 13" x 17", $90

Efraín carving

Armadillo with family, 20" x 19", $170

Mermaid on tortoise,
12" x 11", $120

Angels (left to right):
18" x 16", $120
21" x 14", $150

Zenén Fuentes Méndez
(father of Epifanio)
Dignified Farmer/Carver
"My work is more primitive than my son's."

Although his main identity is that of a farmer, Zenén creates prominent carved pieces that parallel his dignified physical presence. He regards his angels as his most important pieces, but cautions that his work is far more primitive than that of his son, Epifanio. He also makes striking cowboys and saints.

Biography
Zenén began to carve in 1955 at the age of 31, making children's toys. Primarily a farmer he was inspired by the animals he saw in the fields - bulls, cows and sheep - and thought to recreate them in wood.

Address:
Hidalgo #38
San Martín Tilcajete
Oaxaca
C.P. 71506
Telephone: 01 (95154) 82637

Iván Fuentes Santiago
(son of Epifanio)
Young Specialist in Carved Animals
"*Anteaters are one of my favorites.*"

The newest addition to the talented lineage of carvers in this family, Iván makes a host of animals, including giraffes, cats and coyotes, with facility and dexterity. He is especially partial to anteaters. Iván does his own decorative painting, inspired by colors he visualizes.

Biography
Iván began to carve at the age of seven watching his parents and grandfather. His first pieces were armadillos and small animals. Later his brother Zeni, who creates striking animals, influenced him.

Iván holding his piece, 14" x 10",
$80

Zenén and his pieces
Cat, 15" x 13", $70
San Jodas, 15" x 6", $120

Inocencio Vásquez Melchor
Carver of Animated Figures in Interaction
"I capture the combination of good and bad in life, and old and new technique."

See Family Tree #23, "Family of Inocencio Vásquez Melchor," in Appendix on page 187.

Inocencio Vásquez Melchor is the creator of several distinctive styles of carved and painted wooden pieces. Each has a charming primitive quality. He is best known for his "borrachos" (drunkards) often in the ironic form of angels, his human-like devils and groups of human or "nahual" (human figures with animal faces) musicians. In Inocencio's pueblo it is believed that ordinary people can turn themselves into animals at night, particularly when there is a full moon. (See also his Day of the Dead piece on page 161 of Chapter Ten.)

Many of Inocencio's creations lend themselves to assemblages, such as four drunken angels or four devils seated on chairs around a table (the table and chairs are separate pieces), or skeleton dancing partners. Another is a band composed of four musicians in varied poses, a "marimba" (a popular Mexican instrument resembling a xylophone) and a drum set. Many of Inocencio's figures have articulated joints, one of his signature features. He prides himself most on his jointed devils, his ultimate specialty.

It is clear that Inocencio is deeply satisfied with his work, a spirit he has transmitted to his family members. His sons, Pablo and Esteban, have recently begun to carve as well, specializing in "mariachi" figures and "nahuales."

Marcela, one of Inocencio's sisters who lives with their mother in a house adjacent to his on the same grounds, specializes in carved painted miniatures (she is featured on page 119 in the miniatures portion of Chapter Five). Two of Inocencio's other sisters work in woodcarving as well.

Family portrait (left to right): Marcela (Inocencio's sister), Pablo (son), Inocencio, Lucía (wife), Esteban (son), Juana (mother). Elizabeth (daughter) is in front.

Inocencio painting with son Esteban and wife Lucía

Biography

Inocencio began to carve at 15 years of age as he observed his cousins working. Although they did not explicitly teach him to carve, he admired their work and took note of their technique. Masks and turtles were their primary pieces. Inocencio's own father, who died when he was only 12 years old, did not carve, instead working exclusively as a farmer. Inocencio continued in his own fashion, producing individual skeletons and pyramids of skeletons that derived from images in his own mind. He also created devils and animals. At that time he left his pieces in their state of unpainted natural wood. He only began to use painted decoration after he married, collaborating with his wife.

Technique

Father and sons use "copal" wood. Inocencio goes to the mountain to cut pieces of wood that lend themselves to the images in his mind. He estimates that the process of carving a devil takes approximately six to seven hours, as he works in parts: the head, body, arms, and legs.

At present painting is done by many family members, including Inocencio himself, his wife, his mother, his two sons and his daughter. Multiple family members can be seen working side by side at one of many painting stations arranged at the oblong table on their patio. It is customary for Inocencio to sign the pieces.

Address:
Allende #1
San Martín Tilcajete
Oaxaca
C.P. 71506
Telephone: 01 (95157) 15390

Inocencio carving, surrounded by devil, animal and "muertos" pieces, ranging from $25-45

Jacobo Ángeles Ojeda
A Young Wise Man Who Incorporates Native American Decorative Elements
"A woodcarver's art is limited only by his imagination."

See Family Tree #24, "Jacobo Ángeles Ojeda," in Appendix on page 188.

A special thrill awaits the visitor who enters this family's large courtyard, the home of Jacobo Ángeles Ojeda and his extended family. Jacobo and his wife, María del Carmen Mendoza, are a dynamic couple with a developing reputation for their distinctive painting style, reminiscent of the fine brushwork of Native American ceramists. They collaborate in creating pieces, primarily animals, that are remarkable both in dimension and in their finely detailed decoration.

Jacobo is an extremely talented and reflective young woodcarver whose wisdom and artistic sophistication extend well beyond his years. At exhibitions, Jacobo has had the disappointing experience of not being taken as seriously as the more senior members of his community, merely because of his young age. His current work reflects his belief that every person resembles an animal in some respects. This is a variant of the "nahual," the belief in his pueblo that humans transform into animal spirits at night. According to Jacobo a woodcarver's work is limited only by his imagination, as exemplified by one of his recent designs: an armadillo with a human face.

Jacobo aspires to have his own work, as well as that of other fine artists, appreciated as true art: the imaginative creation of an individual, with its corresponding respect and value. He has taken to assigning a name to each type of piece. In addition, he numbers each individual edition of that piece, no two of which are identical.

Animal musicians, 11" x 3", $23 per piece

Drunken angels with chairs and table, each of the four angels with chair, 10" x 7.5" and table, 6" x 4", $60 for the set

Family (left to right): Noemí (sister-in-law), Dionisio (brother), Jacobo, María (wife), María and Jacobo's son Ricardo in front, Gerardo (brother)

Woodcarving is a deep source of satisfaction for Jacobo, who also loves to farm, even though this is not a source of income. He and María are pleased to receive visitors to see them working, and to convey their way of life in a broader sense. Jacobo especially enjoys opportunities to teach children through his work. Recently he was invited to visit a school in Pennsylvania, a scrapbook of which he proudly shared with us. In addition, his pieces have been exhibited in Phoenix, and he participated in a fundraiser for diabetes at the University of Southern California with two well-known Oaxacan painters, Rodolfo Morales and Alfonso Castillo. There he demonstrated his carving and painting for art students, culminating in a television series about his process of creating a coyote, one of his signature pieces.

Biography
Jacobo's maturity was stimulated by necessity. The eldest child in his family, he was propelled into adult responsibilities early in his life by his father's death when Jacobo was only 12 years old. Having just graduated from primary school, he immediately assumed a major role in contributing to the family's living.

Fortunately Jacobo had developed some proficiency as a woodcarver at his father's side, as he watched him make angels and musical bands (Jacobo considers these "old designs") and armadillos, iguanas and devils (these were his father's own, that is "new," designs). Jacobo decorated them with aniline paints, now infrequently used in San Martín. In retrospect, he now regards the pieces he produced at that time as crude. In those days tourists did not visit the pueblos as frequently as they do today. Therefore, Jacobo had to rely upon selling his pieces to folk art shops in the city of Oaxaca. His first sale, a fox, was to one of the better-known shops, Fonart.

As the eldest male child Jacobo also naturally assumed the fatherly role of teaching his younger brothers to carve. The continuity of their family tradition is concretized in their custom of working today on the same table at which their father worked 25 years ago. Their mother creates embroidered garments that are displayed on the patio, alongside completed pieces of woodcarving.

María, Jacobo's wife, already knew how to paint, having learned to do so in her family of origin, well-known carvers. However, she has further developed her expertise in the special style of Native American painting for which Jacobo is currently developing a reputation.

Technique
Jacobo's inspiration to make a particular design derives from the characteristics of the individual piece of wood that he possesses. Originally he collected wood in the mountains, generally using whole pieces to make large figures. He regards branches with twists as the best, because they facilitate the communication of expressive movement.

Jacobo takes pride in creating especially fine pieces that often require a month's time to produce. This is due to the combination of their size, their delicate painting and his practice of drying them in the sun for an unusually long period of time. He believes this is the best protection against infestation by insects.

Address:
Callejón del Olvido #9
San Martín Tilcajete
Oaxaca
C.P. 71506
Telephone: 01 (95154) 85153

Family members painting at their father's table

Jacobo carving

Coyote, 25" x 25", $500

Armadillo, 12" x 8", $170

Tiger, 23" x 8", $115

Turkey, 9" x 5", $110

María Jiménez Ojeda and her Four Brothers
Master of Painted "Embroidery"
"We hope clients always search for quality, not quantity."

See Family Tree #25, "Family of María Jiménez Ojeda," in Appendix on page 189.

María Jiménez Ojeda creates enchanting and original painted designs for pieces carved by her four brothers: Aarón, Miguel, Cándido, and Alberto. She is best known for her delicate butterflies, doves, and rabbits, patterns that derive from her earlier work in embroidery. Not only the painting, but also the carved forms, of many of the pieces produced by this family are unique. These include sleek animals in graceful poses (such as a toucan with an exaggerated beak, and an elongated dog with an exaggeratedly arched back) and a Virgin of Soledad. María regards carved angels with dramatically spread wings as her own special design, the carving of which is generally executed by her brother Aarón.

The family's practice of artistic attribution is unique to the woodcarving tradition, in which the male carver traditionally signs a piece regardless of who has decorated it. In this family María paints some pieces, while her sisters-in-law or her brothers decorate others. The family custom is that María signs the pieces she paints, and the carver signs when he or his wife creates the decoration. Her soaring reputation notwithstanding, María's magnanimous spirit is evident. As we photographed individual works, she insisted that one piece attributed to each brother be included, to prevent overshadowing them with attention to her productions alone.

María and her brothers invite collectors to visit their home, especially if they seek work of the best quality. She cautions that in shops one finds pieces that

**Family (left to right): Front row: María, Alberto (brother).
Back row: Aarón, Miguel, Cándido (brothers)**

101

reflect merchants' frequent practice of buying woodcarving by known artists, and arranging for painting by people of lesser talent.

Biography

The story of María's initiation into decoration of woodcarving is an interesting one. Up to the age of 20 years, she devoted herself to the art of embroidery, while her brothers learned to carve according to their pueblo's tradition. However, when Aarón, María's eldest brother who carved and painted his own pieces, did not succeed commercially, she experimented with adding her own style of painting. Her technique borrowed heavily from her elegant embroidery patterns. Her work was enthusiastically greeted, and her brother's business began to thrive.

Technique

Today each brother carves using "copal." While others have attempted to copy María's outstanding designs, they do not succeed in reproducing the delicacy of her strokes. Given the unusually ornate quality of her work, the decoration of an individual piece often takes three days. Also original is Maria's practice of combining acrylic paints with "esmalte," a gold-colored substance that provides a dramatic contrast.

Address:
Calle Allende #10
San Martín Tilcajete
Oaxaca
C.P. 71506
Telephone: 044 950 03272

Maria's brothers carving (left to right): **Aarón, Cándido, Miguel, Alberto**

María painting her toucan

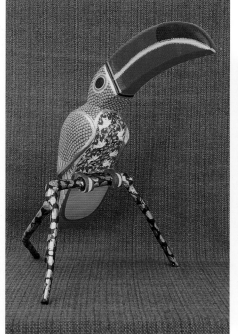

Toucan by María, 11.5" x 7", $40

Angel by María, 15" x 8", $55

Virgin of Soledad by María,
12" x 13", $80

Rabbit by Aarón, 6" x 3", $25

Three Kings and Virgin by Alberto, 10" x 3", $170 for the set

Lions by Cándido, 3" x 4", $17 each piece

Mother pig and piglets by Miguel, 4" x 3" and 2" x 3", $55 for the set

Additional woodcarvers in San Martín
Ventura Fabián (Avenida Hidalgo S/N)
Francisco Hernández Cruz (Amado Nervo #2)
Hipolito López Ortega (Independencia #19)
Martín Melchor (Andrés Portillo #2)
Jesús Sosa Calvo (Progreso #44)
Agustín Vásquez (Avenida Hidalgo #15)

La Unión Tejalapam

The trip to La Unión Tejalapam (more commonly called La Unión), a remote woodcarving pueblo, is fascinating and rewarding but not for the faint of heart. Although only 25 kilometers from Oaxaca City, the highway is so rocky and full of potholes that the journey requires nearly an hour. Despite the fact that this pueblo exceeds our usual 45-minute radius, we have included it because of its many fascinating features. A sports utility vehicle or truck is necessary to negotiate this road. Following a brief stretch of better road surface, the rocky terrain quickly resumes. Obligatory ascents and descents to artists' homes through cornfields require that the visitor be physically sturdy. A guide is essential here, since roads are typically unmarked and correct paths through cornfields are the province of the well-initiated.

Despite these caveats the journey is worth pursuing, both because of the extraordinary artists one finds and the opportunity it affords to recapture the sense of remoteness (and in some respects primitivity) of woodcarving at its inception. Artists in La Unión do not use the now more typical acrylic paints seen in San Martín and Arrazola, but rather the unglossy aniline variety that was customary in those pueblos decades ago. Approximately 18 families work in woodcarving, approximately five producing outstanding works.

This is primarily a farming pueblo. The vistas are stupendous and the tranquility otherworldly. However, it is a hard life in La Unión. Tourists rarely visit and the land is often arid. A valiant octogenarian mounted on horseback straddles two gigantic baskets stuffed with alfalfa. A burro nearly encased in alfalfa follows, its master walking at its side. Two oxen haul a wooden cart.

View of fields of La Unión

View of fields of La Unión

The Santiago Family

See Family Tree #26, "The Santiago Family," in Appendix on page 190.

This family, one of the best known in La Unión, is too large to present comprehensively. For this reason we feature several of its members: three of the four living older brothers – Martín, Quirino, and Plácido - and Martín's son, Jaime, who is recognized as a formidable talent.

Martín Santiago Cruz
Carver of Charming, Primitive Religious Pieces
"We welcome you with open arms."

Martín Santiago Cruz, a warm and welcoming man, lives and works in a remote setting surrounded by his extensive family. Martín's signature pieces are primarily religious in nature: boats reminiscent of Noah's ark, nativity scenes, and virgins and angels (see his Day of the Dead piece on page 162 of Chapter Ten). His figures include highly detailed accessories, such as small bouquets of flowers that are inserted into recesses carved in their hands. As we un-wrapped recent purchases we were charmed by Martín's custom of securely and lovingly placing these bouquets in matchboxes to protect them during travel.

To reach Martín's home, one travels by car only as far as the home of his renowned woodcarver son, Jaime Santiago. From there the rest of the journey must be negotiated on foot through fields, sometimes steep, bypassing goats and crops along the way.

Martín emphasized the artist's need for promotion, commenting that state-run distributors do not help as many artists as they might. He would like people to become familiar with his work and welcomes them "with open arms."

Biography

Martín began carving in 1967 at the relatively late age of 36 to supplement the meager living he made as a farmer. Despite his prodigious talent and productivity as a woodcarver, farming remains his first love and dominant self-image. In his words he is "cien por cien campesino" (100% farmer).

Having seen a piece by Manuel Jiménez, the major historical woodcarving figure of Arrazola (featured on pages 86-88 in this chapter), Martín traveled to the city of Oaxaca to explore the possibility of doing carving himself. He met with Enrique de la Lanza - an important promoter of folk art and owner of Yalalag, the most important folk art store at that time - with whom he began a long and supportive relationship. Martín now fondly remembers him as his "patron." Although Martín did not initially know what type of carving he might undertake, Enrique advised him to buy paints and sandpaper and to get started. Martín feels his early work - small human figures and animals - was badly carved and painted. However, encouraged by Enrique, he persevered and ultimately developed his own designs.

Technique

Martín originally used "copal" for carving but now works in two other types of wood, "jacaranda" and "ocote." They are harder and less receptive to the insects that sometimes lodge in the softer "copal" wood. To make a virgin, one of his original designs, Martín estimates that once the wood is dry, it takes two days for carving and one for painting. His daughters, Benita and Carolina, are primarily responsible for painting his carvings.

Address:
Cañada Cera
La Unión Tejalapam
Etla
Oaxaca
C.P. 68260

Martin at work with his grandchildren and wife (left to right): Víctor Hugo, Martín, Fabiola, Juana

Nativity: figures, 7" x 3", animals, 2.5" x 2", $115 for the 12 pieces

Family portrait (left to right): Front row: Magda, Alicia (nieces), Víctor Hugo (grandson), Fabiola (granddaughter). Back row: Benita (daughter), Martín, Juana (wife), Carolina (daughter)

Small angels, 8" x 3", $15 each

105

Quirino Santiago Cruz
Carver of Charming Primitive Animals
"Oaxaca is a place where people like to work to preserve their traditions. Thanks to artesanías I have a wonderful life."

Quirino Santiago Cruz creates charming animals of all kinds that have a primitive quality: deer, tigers, lions, horses, cows, turtles, frogs, dogs, and armadillos, to name a few. To get to his home a hike from his nephew Jaime's house is required. Traversing cornfields along the way, you pass by the home of his brother Martín. Within view are the houses of another brother, Francisco, who also carves, and his son Felix.

Quirino is a very contented man, surrounded by his large family. His only regret is that some of his fellow residents of La Unión become demoralized and leave because they find it difficult to make a living in woodcarving or farming. By contrast he feels his involvement in woodcarving, which he undertook well into his adult years as a farmer, has greatly improved his life. Quirino sincerely hopes that more people will come to know his work, and that of his family and neighbors, and that this tradition will not be forgotten. He believes "Oaxaca is a place where people like to work to preserve their traditions."

Biography
Along with his brother Martín, Quirino began his work as a woodcarver relatively late, without parental heritage. He was stimulated and supported by several key promoters and sellers of folk art. Foremost was Enrique de la Lanza who also helped his brother Martín. Quirino was 31 when he began, a choice made of necessity. Prior to that he and Martín cut and sold wood for cooking in the pueblo of Atzompa. Unable to make a sufficient living, they began to carve.

Quirino's first pieces were animals that were, in his estimation, very "primitive" and for which there was no market. However, Enrique de la Lanza helped him improve his technique by making suggestions that Quirino implemented. He was also influenced and supported by Nicodemus B. Vázquez who owned one of the other major folk art stores in Oaxaca. He not only bought many of Quirino's pieces for 23 years, but also entered several in contests.

Technique
Quirino goes to the mountain to find wood appropriate to the sizes he requires for his intended pieces. First, he washes and sands them. Then he creates the trunk of his animals, to which he adds the legs, tails, ears, antlers and the like. Limbs and other appendages are either nailed to the trunk, or inserted into recesses created for this purpose. Either Quirino or his wife does the painting, depending upon the volume of orders at any particular time. However, Quirino always carves decorative elements into the painted portions and adds black painted accents. On a very good day, one when he works extremely hard and long, he can complete two pieces.

Address:
Domicilio Conocido (a known residence)
Zona de la Canada Cera S/N (without number)
La Unión Tejalapam
Oaxaca
C.P. 68264

Quirino with his wife Margarita **Quirino carving**

Pieces (left to right):
Deer, 9" x 8", $8
Other animals, 8" x 2", $7

Elephant, coyote and lion,
each 8" x 2", $7

Plácido Arturo Santiago Cruz
Jack of All Trades
"I would like tourists to visit my workshop and my family."

Plácido Arturo Santiago Cruz, Martín and Quirino Santiago Cruz's younger brother, works out of his home along one of the main streets of La Unión. Today his specialty is nativity scenes (small, medium and large), virgins, boats, carts, small devils, rodeos, and figures for the Day of the Dead. He collaborates with his sons who also make small animals such as bulls.

Plácido noted that although he used to sell to Fonart, the national folk art store, he no longer does so. Instead his major source of business is tourist groups who travel to La Unión, or who invite him to display his work at designated locations in the city of Oaxaca. Plácido expressed his hope that this collector's guide will be successful, and that tourists will continue to visit his workshop and his family.

Plácido and his family are jacks of many trades. The outer portion of their home is a small grocery shop where they sell, among other things, the loaves of bread they bake in another of their rooms. When we visited during the week of the Day of the Dead, the aroma of special breads for this holiday permeated the air and the plentiful loaves filled an entire room as well as the adjacent patio.

Biography

Plácido began to carve in 1968, taught by his older brother Martín to make small animal figures such as burros, bulls, wolves and pigs. Initially he worked in "copal" but after many years he began to use "jacaranda" because it is softer when green. After a few years Plácido undertook larger pieces

Family (left to right): Catalina (daughter-in-law) with Eloy, Jr. (grandson), Eloy (son), Alfonsa (wife), Plácido

Technique

Working with his two sons, Hermelindo and Eloy, Plácido buys "jacaranda" branches for carving. Their natural dimensions and configurations determine the figures they create.

Address:
Independencia
La Unión Tejalapam
Etla
Oaxaca
C.P. 68260

Plácido carving

Devils, 8" x 3", $20 each

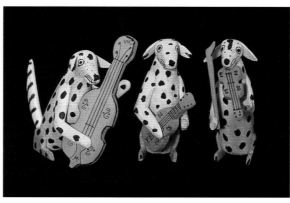

Musician dogs, 3" x 2", $7 each

Jaime Santiago Morales
Carver of Rodeos, Formally Dressed Devils and Agile Elderly Couples
"Our home is open to tourists."

Jaime Santiago Morales, son of Martín Santiago, is one of the best known carvers in La Unión. His signature pieces are well-dressed devils and skeletons, aged couples ("viejos") dancing, and rodeo scenes consisting of a corral and multiple human figures with their horses and processions. Jaime does not sell many of his pieces in the city of Oaxaca, working instead primarily on orders from the United States. Like his father Jaime continues to be heavily invested in his work and identity as a farmer.

Family (left to right): Reina (wife), Francisca Liliana (daughter), Jaime

Biography

Jaime began to work in woodcarving at the age of 13 by helping his father sand and paint his pieces. His first personal pieces, in contrast to his father's animals, were devils. Enrique de la Lanza, the person who helped Jaime's father launch his career, was equally encouraging and constructively critical of Jaime's early work. "Since everyone makes red devils, why not make something different?" he queried Jaime. This stimulated his imagination to create devils attired in ties, vests and jackets. By 18 years of age Jaime's career was well launched, and he began to sign his pieces.

The recognition his work earned in many contests has contributed to Jaime's custom of signing his pieces. He won third place in a national contest in Guanajuato, and Fonart (the national store that used to promote many better folk artists) arranged an exhibition of his work.

In recent years Jaime has especially enjoyed visits by groups of students arranged by the Institute of Culture in Oaxaca, where many young people come to study Spanish and Oaxacan culture.

Jaime carving

Technique

Jaime begins by going to the mountain to search for pieces of "copal" wood that lend themselves to his intended designs. At the same time the configurations of wood he finds inspire specific ideas. Green wood must be left to dry for approximately two to three days. Jaime then cuts the basic shape with a machete and subsequently carves more detailed portions of his figure with smaller knives. His wife does the majority of the painting, Jaime adding the finishing touches. They use a combination of aniline and acrylic paints, depending upon his customer's desires.

Jaime estimates that he creates ten pieces in the course of an average week's work, although weather conditions may radically affect his productivity. For example, "copal," although thoroughly dried, can easily become moistened in rain even when kept indoors. Conversely hot weather facilitates his work.

Address:
Domicilio Conocido (a known residence)
La Unión Tejalapam
Oaxaca
C.P. 68264

Skeletons and devil, 10" x 2", $12 each
Tiger, 6" x 1.5", $4

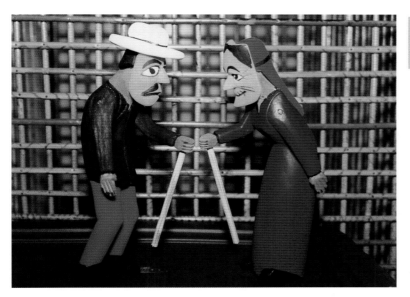

"Viejos" (old couple), 10" x 2", $12 each

Jaime and his son and daughter with two rodeo scenes, each consisting of fences plus 8 additional pieces (cowboys, band figures, cattle), approximately 12" x 3", $120 for the scene

Gabino Reyes López
Carver of Elegant Detail in Surprising Places
"I am very proud of my work and hope my children will continue this tradition."

See Family Tree #27, "Family of Gabino Reyes López," in Appendix on page 190.

Gabino Reyes López is a most unexpected find in the pueblo of La Unión with its typical charmingly primitive style. The first time we visited his home we expected to find work similar to that of his fellow carvers. We gasped with surprise as we turned over a rather simple but friendly black and white cow to make a discovery. On its belly was an extraordinarily elegant and finely detailed carving of the Virgin of Guadalupe, replete with a bouquet of delicately colored flowers. Below the Virgin was a table whose legs doubled as teats for the calf that accompanied its mother.

Gabino enjoys the expansiveness of his imagination. It is his intention to surprise his visitors with this unexpected design element, initially out of sight. He plans soon to introduce animals bearing the Virgin of Soledad, the most revered religious figure in Oaxaca. His other favorite pieces are crocodiles carrying their young on their back, angels and Virgins of Guadalupe surrounded by natural elements such as cacti.

Family (left to right): Jhovani (son), Gabino, Areli (wife), Uriel (son)

Biography

Gabino began to carve wood at 23 years of age. Prior to that he helped to cultivate the land. He learned about carving from his brother-in-law, Santiago Cruz Reyes, to whom he gives credit for motivating him. Gabino might easily have become discouraged by the difficulty he experienced in his first attempts at woodcarving, had he not had the benefit of Santiago's support and patience.

109

Gabino's first pieces were armadillos, deer and giraffes that were quite different from the more rustic pieces of his mentor. He discovered in himself a very active imagination when he tried to depict his image of the animals he observed in the fields. Gabino introduced one of his signature pieces in 1995, a baby animal with its mother who bears the Virgin of Guadalupe on her belly.

Technique

Gabino searches for needed pieces of "copal" or "jacaranda" in the mountains around La Unión. He uses "jacaranda" for his animal mothers and "copal" for their babies. His animal figures are made in one piece, the limbs or other extensions carved from branches emerging from the portion used for the animal's trunk. Therefore, he searches for branches that lend themselves to creating feet, methodically measuring them as he goes.

Gabino does all the highly detailed carving of his pieces, while his wife does the majority of the painting. He also creates the mane and alfalfa portions that his animals chew by wedging crevices into their backs and mouths. In these he painstakingly inserts and secures small bits of "ixtle" (a bristly fiber from the maguey plant). Gabino estimates that it takes him approximately three days to complete a pair of animals, such as the mother cow bearing the Virgin of Guadalupe and her calf.

Address:
Domicilio Conocido
La Unión Tejalapam
Oaxaca
C.P. 68264

Gabino painting

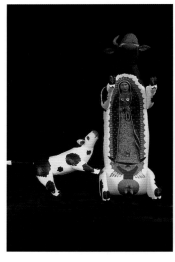

Cow with Virgin of Guadalupe and its calf (front and bottom views), 9" x 4" and 3.5" x 4", $115 for the pair

Virgin of Guadalupe, 12" x 6", $90

Donkey with Virgin of Guadalupe and its baby (side and bottom views), 10" x 6" and 3" x 5", $225 for the pair

Additional Woodcarvers in La Unión
Ángel Cruz Solis (Zona del Arroyo S/N)
Sergio Santos (Zona del Arroyo S/N)

Chapter Four
Metal Work

Tin Work
of Oaxaca City

Tin work, or "hojalata," dates back to the 16th century. It is primarily produced in the Xochimilco section of the city of Oaxaca. The best artisans create a wide range of pieces, most of them decorated with bright colors in lacquer. Some examples are Christmas decorations, mirrors, lamps, trees of life, candleholders, and lanterns.

The Leyva Family

Alfonso Santiago Leyva
A "Gefe" (Leader) in Tin
"We would like the visitor to distinguish between true art and work of an inferior quality."

See Family Tree #28, "The Leyva Family," in Appendix on page 191.

Alfonso Santiago Leyva, a colorful and philosophical man, is one of the foremost artists in "hojalata," or tin pieces for decorative and utilitarian use. He was one of the first artists to decorate tin pieces with assorted colors. Alfonso produces a wide array of designs, depending upon the requests of his customers. However, soldiers, candleabras and mirrors in the shape of stars are among those he considers most significant. Another is a type of mirror with filigree border that he introduced 20 years ago. He has entitled this "German style" because many such pieces have been sold to Germans.

Alfonso collaborates with several of his children, most notably his son Tomás, in the workshop in their current (and his former) home in the Xochimilco section of the city of Oaxaca. Alfonso derives great pleasure from his work and loves the freedom of being his own boss. He commutes from the nearby town of Santa María El Tule, beginning his workday unusually early. This arrangement leaves him time to enjoy his other interests such as baseball.

The family workshop consists of one large room and a smaller area in which completed pieces are displayed. An expansive table also serves as a major workspace for initially cutting the pieces of metal that will later be assembled and engraved. Large sheets of metal, as well as residual fragments, are strewn everywhere, conveying the industry of this family.

Family (left to right): First row: Miriam, Ricardo, Edgar, Magdalena. Second row: Alicia, Alfonso, Violeta, Matilde. Third row: Esteban holding Erik, Jerónimo holding Cesar, Belen, Raquel, Tomás

Reflecting upon his life's work Alfonso has noted a diminishing number of clients, although increasing prices have largely compensated for this decline in quantity. However, Alfonso is concerned that his cherished form of folk art may be threatened by tourists' lack of awareness of the variable quality of "hojalata." There is a distinct range from fine to commercial. Alfonso would like people to differentiate between those who are true artists, and others who produce work of the inferior variety often seen in markets. According to Alfonso, past directors of government-owned stores and private shops featured artisans who produced work of superior quality. However, today this is not always the case. Alfonso has promoted his own work with a stamp bearing his name, insuring that his pieces can be identified.

Biography

Alfonso began to work in tin at 12 years of age, taught by a number of people outside of his family. His own father had not engaged in this craft. Initially Alfonso worked for four years with Rafael González, a neighbor in Xochimilco, in his workshop in the center of town. Then he established a formal working relationship with

José Velasco that lasted for ten to 11 years. Following this he began his own business at the age of 30.

His son, Tomás, began to work in tin at ten, taught by his father. He carries out Alfonso's (the "gefe's," that is, the director's) patterns to this day. In Alfonso's view the work of father and son cuts the same. So is that of men and women. In his family both male and female members of the family cut the tin *and* paint.

Technique

The technical process Alfonso employs differs to some degree with the type of piece he is creating. He invariably begins by forming patterns in flat sheets of tin by tracing around a template with a pointed tool. Then he cuts the metal with powerful shears. Some pieces require tooling, while others do not. Alfonso originally used aniline paints, but ultimately developed a preference for automobile paints.

Address:
Río Pedregal #211
Colonia la Cascada
Xochimilco
Oaxaca
Oaxaca
C.P. 68040
Telephone: 01 (95151) 52609

Family members with pieces (left to right):
Jerónimo with mirror, 12" x 16", $20
Jaime with rooster, 16" x 10", $25
Alfonso with soldier, 21" x 6", $15
Violeta with angel, 13" x 9", $7
Matilde with mermaid, 12" x 10", $8
Raquel with Santa Claus, 12" x 9", $13

Alfonso holding a lantern, 13" x 6", $30

Alfonso and son Tomás cutting tin

**Hen, 20" x 13", $25
Soldiers, 13" x 6", $8 each**

Víctor Rubén Hernández Leyva
Dedicated "Hojalatero" (Tinmaker)
"Better quality tin work should not be missed."

Víctor Rubén Hernández Leyva, a somewhat reserved man whose dedication to his craft is clear, creates a variety of tin objects of excellent quality. Some of Víctor's specialties are elaborate tin boxes, made either in pure tin or with glass inlay, and ornate mirrors. However, he is happy to produce a wide array of pieces depending upon customers' preferences.

Víctor, his son Juan, and his wife's brother, Miguel Montes, work in a small studio in Víctor's home in the Xochimilco section of the city of Oaxaca. This is not far from where his older cousin, Alfonso Santiago Leyva, (their mothers are sisters) and his family engage in their tin work. The women in the family do not contribute to Víctor's work.

Like his cousin, Víctor emphasizes that artists require more support from the government and secretary of tourism. It would be helpful for them both to promote the work, and to better enable tourists to differentiate pieces of quality from those that are inferior and purely commercial. Unless they visit workshops such as his own, or are directed to shops in town where their pieces are displayed, visitors may never see better quality work.

Biography
Víctor began to work in "hojalata" at ten years of age. Initially he was taught by his prominent older cousin Alfonso Santiago Leyva. This arrangement extended for decades, from 1962-1985, when Víctor opened his own business in his current location.

Family with pieces (left to right):
Bricia (daughter-in-law) with round eclipse mirror, 15" diameter, $10
Víctor with rectangular mirror, 17" x 14", $13
Juan de Dios (grandson, in front) with sun design mirror, 15" diameter, $10
Juan de Dios (son) with jewelry box, 10" x 8", $14

Technique
Víctor begins each piece by marking the sheet of tin from which it will eventually be cut. Then he forms the indentations and, finally, cuts the piece. Some pieces have a series of parts, requiring a more laborious process. Víctor's largest pieces, such as grand mirrors, take three days to make.

Address:
Río Pedregal #112
Colonia la Cascada
Xochimilco
Oaxaca
Oaxaca
C.P. 68040
Telephone: 01 (95151) 35267

Víctor working

Víctor with mask, 16" x 10", $50

Pieces:
Box, 9" x 12", $20
Angel, 12" x 5", $9
Small tree, 9" x 6", $5
Medium tree, 12" x 7", $7
Large tree, 16" x 9", $10
Elephant, 7" x 5", $3
Soldier, 12" x 3", $9

Miguel Ángel Aguero Pacheco
Poet of Tin
"Only art and music express the soul."

See Family Tree #29, "Family of Miguel Ángel Aguero Pacheco," in Appendix on page 192.

Miguel Ángel Aguero Pacheco, a poetic and thoughtful man, creates expressive tin pieces in his home workshop, also in the Xochimilco section of the city of Oaxaca. Miguel works with several of his sons and a son-in-law to make special pieces such as trees of life, lamps, and skeletons engaged in human activities, the latter in honor of the Day of the Dead.

Proud of his recognition, he pointed out the section devoted to his work in a recent Mexican book, *Senderos Oaxaqueños*, featuring the artisans of Xochimilco. He is also included in a forthcoming American book, *Country Art*.

With intense emotion, Miguel related his belief that "only art and music express the soul." He has a vision of people helping one another and of the unification of the world, without national boundaries, political disputes, or divisions between the disadvantaged and the wealthy.

Biography

Miguel's father died when he was young, a loss that shaped his life in many ways. Most importantly, he assumed major responsibilities at a relatively early age. As the eldest child, he spent a great deal of time taking care of his siblings. Miguel was taught to work in "hojalata" by his mother beginning at age seven. She had learned this handicraft from her husband before his death. Since her major designs were saints, these were the first pieces Miguel produced. His aunt, Serafina Pacheco, introduced additional designs such as soldiers, Santa Claus, cars, and stars, inspired by her work in a toy store. At 13 years of age Miguel began to work with his first cousin, Aarón Velasco Pacheco, another well-known "hojalatero" (tin maker).

Miguel began his own tin business at the early age of 18, working with some of his brothers until they married and established their own workshops. Originally he specialized in objects like those of his aunt: soldiers, toys and Christmas objects such as nativity scenes. Within several years he also began to create some of his own original designs, such as trees of life, "muertos" (skeletons engaged in human activities in celebration of the major holiday, Day of the Dead) and lamps. These were sold at one of Oaxaca's well-known folk art shops, El Arte Oaxaqueño, owned by Nicodemus B. Vázquez.

Family (left to right): First row: Mónica, Yazmín (granddaughter), Cecilia (granddaughter), Miriám. Second row: Miguel Ángel, Miguel, Jr. (son) holding Margarita (granddaughter), Artemia (wife), María (daughter), José Luis (son-in-law). Third row: Xochitl, Adriana (daughters)

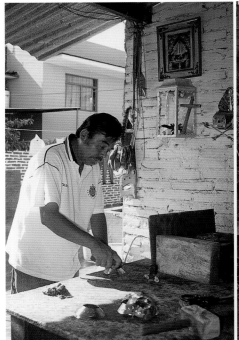

Miguel working

Miguel with his pieces:
Mirror: large size, 36" x 20", $85
medium size, 28" x 15", $55
small size, 12" x 9", $12
Tree of life, 12" x 9", $12

Technique

After designing a piece, Miguel traces it on a sheet of tin. Then he cuts out the outline and hammers the elevated elements of the piece. The tree of life is created in segments that are subsequently assembled. Finally they are decorated with aniline paints. Miguel estimates that it takes approximately one day to make a tree of life, although three can be produced at the same time.

Address:
Santo Tomás #118
Xochimilco
Oaxaca
Oaxaca
C.P. 68040
Telephone: 01 (95151) 59405

Medium candleabra, 16" x 12", $20 (large size, 36" x 20", $85)
Tree of life, 12" x 9", $12

Additional tinmaker
Aarón Velasco Pacheco (Calz. Heroes de Chapultepec #213)

Cutlery and Swords
of *Ocotlán* and *Oaxaca City*

The production of cutlery and swords is far more than a utilitarian endeavor. It represents a blend of artistry and an appreciation of historical tradition. Techniques date back to the Spanish conquest of Mexico when weapons and knives were important. Today there are several families, primarily in Ocotlán de Morelos (the pueblo also known for its painted red ceramics, see pages 50-60 in Chapter One) and in Oaxaca City, whose outstanding work has been transmitted for many generations. Knives can also be purchased in some folk art shops in Oaxaca City, as well as in many of the markets in Oaxaca and its surrounding pueblos.

In addition to swords and machetes, knives for hunting and fishing, kitchen ware and other domestic utensils (letter openers, cake servers and the like) are created. These are attractively, and often elaborately, decorated and protected in tooled leather cases.

Apolinar Aguilar Velasco
Master Cutlery and Sword Maker
"Que he hecho yo, por ti Ocotlán. Aqui el más fuerte, es el creador, no el Capitalista." (That which I have made is for you, Ocotlán. Here what is stronger is the creator, not the capitalist.")

See Family Tree #30, "Family of Apolinar Aguilar Velasco," in Appendix on page 193.

Apolinar Aguilar Velasco creates museum quality cutlery and swords that also serve utilitarian purposes. He prides himself on making replicas of antique knives and swords seen in museums or photography books, rather than the more commercial pieces produced in the many knife workshops found in the city of Oaxaca. Apolinar's pieces range from kitchenware (place settings, cooking and carving utensils), to knives for camping and fishing, and swords for martial arts, films and bullfights. Some serve multiple functions such as cutting food and opening bottles. His reproductions of medieval swords are particularly spectacular and fascinating.

Knife handles are decorated with innumerable natural, and often exotic, materials: tropical wood; bronze; amber; coral; elephant tusks; bull, buffalo, reindeer, elk

Apolinar working

and deer horns; deer feet; and snake, iguana, and bird skins. Many of these decorative substances are imported from Canada and Alaska during hunting season.

Biography

Apolinar began to learn to make knives from an uncle, the husband of his mother's sister at the age of six. Coming from a family of 16 children, his financial contributions were necessary even at that young age. Until his death a few years ago Apolinar worked closely with his brother Ángel. Ángel's involvement in this art began at 16, and that of another brother, Jesús (also deceased), began at eight. Jesús is particularly proud that the knives he and his brothers crafted were exported in World War II.

Apolinar's first individual piece was a short knife with a horse's face. This was followed by a long knife with a handle bearing wolves.

A master of his trade, Apolinar has taught and given demonstrations of his methods in several cities in the United States (mostly in Texas), Guadalajara and Oaxaca. Students are often sent to him to be trained in his methods.

Technique

Apolinar uses an open oven, constructed in stone and clay, in which charcoal is burned. The fire is stimulated by a large hand operated bellows. After the fire reaches a steady level, recycled steel from car parts (such as pistons and springs) are melted and cut into long narrow strips. These are further heated and hammered into the desired form. Once completed, the knife is polished on a motorized device combining cotton, cardboard and the polishing substance emery. No chrome or nickel is used.

A kitchen knife takes approximately one day to make, while a sword may take up to 15 days. In all Apolinar typically makes 20 pieces per week.

Address:
Callejón Victoria S/N (without number)
Ocotlán de Morelos
Oaxaca
C.P. 71510
Telephone: 01 (95157) 10784

Cutlery artisans in Oaxaca City
Guillermo Aragón Guzman (in Casa Aragón, J.P. García #503)
Hermanos Zavaleta (Benito Juarez market stalls 272-273 as well as in the pueblo of Xoxocotlán, Pipila #120)

Medieval swords:
50" x 3", $1100
42" x 3", $615

(left to right): Hunting knife, 13" x 2", $25
Letter opener 7" x 3", $13
Fishing knife with bottle opener, 10" x 2", $25

Serving pieces, knives and fork, 13" x 2", $67 per piece

Chapter Five
Miniatures and Toys

The love of miniatures and other types of toys in Oaxaca (and Mexico in general) reflects the culture's strong investment in children and family. Nearly all types of folk art are made in miniature: ceramics, woodcarving, baskets, and tin work, to name a few. Rather than being confined to particular pueblos, creators of miniatures can usually be found wherever folk artists work. Some artists specialize in this medium, while others produce miniatures along with pieces of larger dimensions. We feature ceramists and woodcarvers for whom this is a specialty.

A great variety of ceramic human and animal figures and domestic pieces (pots, cups and saucers, jugs, and the like) are created in natural and glazed finishes. Oaxacan artists are also known for many varieties of wooden toys. They range from tiny carved and painted human and animal figures, to carved wooden hand coordination games (such as "baleros," cylinders with recessed portions that must be caught on a handle to which they are tethered by string), to elaborately carved and painted carousels and ferris wheels.

Corn husk toys (and decorative objects) are a relatively new form of folk art, referred to as "totomoxtle." Many types of doll-size figures are produced, some engaged in everyday activities such as cooking or selling their wares, while others are dressed in regional costumes or other types of finery. "Totomoxtle" artists also make glorious flowers of all varieties, Christmas ornaments, decorated baskets and many other objects. Artists who work in this medium are in their first generation. While knowledge of most types of folk art is passed from generation to generation, dissemination of "totomoxtle" techniques is usually in the form of instruction offered in pueblos or city schools.

In addition to miniature baskets and tin objects, there are also lead figures, much like the toy soldiers of old. Although we do not feature the artisans who make them (the most recognized one being Alberto Vázquez Sánchez whose pieces are sold in shops and parks in Oaxaca City), we call attention to their striking celebration of religious, historical and cultural themes.

Woodcarved and Ceramic Miniatures
San Martín, Arrazola, Atzompa, and Coyotepec

Justo Xuana Luis
Carver of Whimsical Miniature Animals in Human Activity
"I like progress. I do not like to rest on my achievements of the past."

See Family Tree # 31, "Family of Justo Xuana Luis," in Appendix on page 194.

Justo Xuana Luis is known for his whimsical miniatures, work he began in 1995. A mother giraffe seated on an armchair reads a story to her attentive baby giraffe, while a band composed of a lively upright wolf, dog and anteater play the trumpet. Justo also specializes in nativity scenes, priding himself on his carving of the faces of the Three Kings. These can be ordered as miniatures, as well as in an array of larger sizes.

Justo takes great pleasure in creating new pieces. He is a man to whom progress is deeply important. Averse to repeating the same kind of work, he does not rest on the achievements of his past alone. He lives with his wife and four children. Departing from the tradition of many artisan families, Justo and his two brothers, also well known carvers in San Martín Tilcajete, have separate homes in which they reside with their spouses and children.

Display box containing Oaxacan miniatures in ceramics, basketry, and wood, designed by Arden Rothstein

Biography

Justo began carving at the age of 17. He was inspired by the work of Isidoro Cruz (featured on pages 92-93 in Chapter Three), one of the original woodcarvers of San Martín Tilcajete, who invited him to initiate this work. Justo was also influenced by his paternal grandmother who made Christ figures from sugar cane. He and his brothers started together, carving simple figures such as frogs, armadillos and mice. Later they undertook to make horses wearing hats and then pyramids of "muertos" (skeletons engaged in human activity in honor of the Day of the Dead).

Justo's eldest son Edilberto began to carve at six years of age (see his Day of the Dead piece on page 162 of Chapter Ten). Unlike the vast majority of woodcarving families in which females do not carve, one of Justo's daughters, Silvia, is developing her own line of work. In addition to assisting her father in his designs, she specializes in picture frames.

Justo, Silvia and Feliza carving and painting

Giraffe mother reading to her baby, 7" x 3" and 3" x 1", $17

Family (left to right): Justo, Feliza (his wife), Justina (daughter), Silvia (daughter)

Technique

Justo uses in two types of wood, "copal" and "zompantle." He explained that in making nativity scenes he prefers straight branches. It takes approximately three days for him to complete such an assemblage, which can comprise nine, 12, or even 14 pieces, depending upon the collector's wishes. Both Justo and his wife paint the pieces he carves. Although they began with aniline paints alone, they now use both aniline and acrylic paints.

Address:
Avenida Galeana #6
San Martín Tilcajete
Oaxaca
C.P. 71506

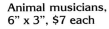 **Animal musicians, 6" x 3", $7 each**

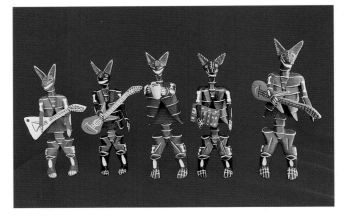

Coyote, armadillo and toucan musicians, 3" x 1", $4 each

Marcela Vásquez Melchor
Woodcarving Animal Miniaturist
"I work from my heart. When tourists share my love for my pieces, even kissing them sometimes, I am rewarded."

Marcela Vásquez Melchor is one of the very few women to assume the role of carver, rather than the more typical custom of women painting the carved pieces of male members of the family. An attractive, modest woman who confidently creates tiny animal figures and decoratively paints them with delicate detail, she lives with her mother in a separate house on the same grounds as her woodcarving brother, Inocencio Vásquez (see pages 98-99 in Chapter Three). Marcela's favorite animals are cats, rabbits, and dogs. However, she also loves her armadillos, pigs, elephants and lions. She prides herself on working purely from her imagination, never copying or relying upon others to carry out portions of her work. The only exception is her mother's occasional contribution to sanding her tiny pieces before she paints them.

Biography
Marcela began her work in woodcarving at the age of ten, helping her brother to sand and paint his pieces. When she tried her hand at carving she found it very difficult to produce large or even medium size pieces. This prompted her to attempt small pieces such as pregnant women and other human figures. Ultimately at the age of 18 she found greatest satisfaction in producing animal miniatures, work she has continued ever since.

Technique
From "copal" branches Marcela cuts the small pieces she needs for her miniatures. First she removes the bark. The animal to be created depends in large part upon the shape of the wood selected. Marcela is also an able painter, working with tiny brushes and a wide array of lively colors and patterns. She estimates that carving each figure requires approximately two hours, but creating the piece from start to finish occupies the better part of half a day.

Address:
Allende #1
San Martín Tilcajete
Oaxaca
C.P. 71506
Telephone: 01 (95157) 15390

Marcela decorating a carved piece

Miniature dogs and cat, 1-2" x 1-2', $3 each

Assorted animal miniatures, 1-2" x 1-2", $3 each

Antonio Aragón Ramírez and his brothers Saúl and Sergio
Carver of Animal Miniatures in Natural Movement
"We love our work and are very proud of it. We wouldn't do anything else."

See Family Tree # 32, "Family of Antonio Aragon Ramírez," in Appendix on page 195.

Antonio Aragón Ramírez and his two brothers, Saúl and Sergio, work together with their wives to carve and paint fabulous miniature animals in graceful, natural movement. They live and work in Arrazola, the pueblo heavily influenced by the tradition of Manuel Jiménez (see pages 86-88 in Chapter Three) who initiated carving of decorative pieces. At one end of a spacious yard, a small building houses the workshop for all six members of the family. A neat white cloth covers the display table on which two dozen charming, cheerfully painted miniature animals strike a wide variety of poses. Unlike many artists who make miniatures in addition to other pieces, miniatures are the centerpiece of the creative life of the Aragón brothers.

Although the range of their work is always growing, they estimate that they currently make 30 animals. An abbreviated list is coyotes, giraffes, deer, goats, cows, burros, rabbits, several types of bears, dogs, "tepeizcuintles" (stylized mountain dogs appearing in work of the pre-Hispanic era) and fantastic monsters. In recent years the Aragón brothers have improved their pieces by introducing colors and movements that are more realistic. Antonio feels extremely grateful to all who have offered their opinions about his work: what they like and what they do not like. He and his brothers always profit from this feedback, and are happy to create new figures suggested by visitors.

Biography

Antonio did not begin to carve until he was 19, and had completed his secondary school education. His uncle, José Hernández, was a carver of large animals, as was Antonio's older brother Ramiro. While assisting Ramiro by sanding and carving the feet for his figures, Antonio experienced a great deal of difficulty, frequently cutting himself. As a result the two brothers came up with the idea of Antonio's making miniatures, work in which he has been involved ever since the age of 20. When he married at 19, Antonio and his wife, Beatríz Arreola Robles, established their own home. Antonio, in turn, mentored the two younger brothers with whom he now works very closely.

The outstanding work of Antonio, Sergio and Saúl is gaining recognition, as witnessed by the many invitations they have received to demonstrate their art in the United States and Canada. Between 1994 and 1999 Antonio visited Los Angeles, Long Beach, Santa Barbara, San Francisco, Phoenix, Woodstock, and Montreal.

Technique

Antonio, Saúl and Sergio begin by going to the mountains to select segments of "copal" that lend themselves to the pieces they intend to create. After removing the bark, they carve with machetes and then smaller knives to form the more detailed portions of their figures. They work from images in their mind, not drawings. Once the carving is completed, the pieces are dried in the sun for approximately three days. Sanding and decorating with acrylic paint follow. For the most part, the wives of Antonio, Saúl and Sergio paint the background colors and the men add decorative details, following which their wives provide the finishing touches. Some pieces incorporate other natural materials, such as "ixtle" (a fiber from the maguey plant) for manes or tails.

From start to finish Antonio estimates that easier pieces require six hours and more difficult ones require one to two days. Some figures are single pieces of wood and others have segments that are inserted. In all, the family produces approximately 12 to 15 pieces per week.

Address:
Álvaro Obregón #24
Arrazola
Xoxocotlán
C.P. 71233
Telephone: 01 (95151) 72393

Family (left to right): Front row: Kevin, Rubén, Paula, Ariel (all nieces and nephews). Middle row: Beatríz (wife), Antonio holding Shobany (daughter). Back row: Sergio (brother), Martha (sister-in-law), Alma (sister-in-law), Saúl (brother)

Antonio carving the initial stage of a miniature

Giraffe, 7" x 3", $10
Gazelle, 5"x 2", $10
Deer, 3" x 2", $8

Rabbit, 3" x 4", $8
Cow, 2" x 3", $8

Blue coyote, 6" x 2", $8
Goat, 3" x 2", $8
Green coyote, 6" x 2", $8

Joel Velasco Lara and his wife Manuela Villanueva Vázquez
Versatile Creators of Ceramic Miniatures and Unique Filigree
"We are delighted when people like our work."

See Family Tree #33, "Family of Joel Velasco Lara," in Appendix on page 196.

Joel Velasco Lara, a modest and somewhat retiring man, and his wife Manuela Villanueva Vázquez are unusually versatile miniaturists. Their work encompasses multiple styles and materials. They create dishware (cups and saucers, teapots, dishes, bowls, serving pieces) in the traditional green glazed finish of Atzompa (to which they also add blue and gold glaze), as well as in plain terra cotta and terra cotta with intricate filigree decoration. In addition, they make charming terra cotta animals, both in natural poses and elaborated as musicians. Joel and Manuela also produce tiny, delicately filigreed two-tone boxes and crosses. They apply their unique filigree decoration to larger pieces, such as "muñecas" (doll-size human figures), bowls and crosses as well.

Joel and Manuela live with their seven children, all of whom work in clay, as does one of Joel's brothers and a niece, Isabel Velasco Lara, who is also an excellent miniaturist. Joel and Manuela welcome visitors to their home to see their process of creation.

Biography
Joel began to work in clay at the age of six, learning at the sides of his parents. His mother produced everyday items such as flat terra cotta plates ("comales") for making tortillas. Both his father and grandfather made miniatures, a longstanding tradition in the green glazed and terra cotta work of their pueblo, Santa María Atzompa. However, Joel's filigree style of decoration is his innovation, one he introduced approximately 15 years ago.

Joel and his wife have worked together closely during their 26 years of marriage. Until two years ago Manuela was primarily engaged in producing the commercial pottery she learned in her family. At that time, Joel began to teach her to do the more creative and original work that he has developed, in part out of the necessity created by his medical problems.

Technique
Miniature dishware and musical figures are created entirely by hand, while small boxes are initially formed with the assistance of molds. Filigree decoration is a detailed process. Joel begins by drawing the desired pattern on the wet background of the figure to be decorated. He uses a sharp object, such as a needle or the antennae of a transistor radio. Then tiny pieces of clay are applied by hand to create the filigree effect. This clay is of a different color than that used to create the background figure. Joel estimates that it takes him three and one-half hours to decorate a small box and two and one-half hours to decorate a set of miniature dishes. The creation and decoration of dishes in terra cotta ("natural") or glazed finish is not as laborious. Joel can make 300 such pieces in eight hours.

To complete a large filigree "muñeca" typically takes four days, the figure being made in parts. A large filigree cross takes approximately two and one-half hours. Unlike many of the creators of pottery in this book, Joel works both by hand and on a potter's wheel when producing round objects, such as the skirt portion of his "muñecas."

Address:
Avenida Juárez #100
Santa María Atzompa
Oaxaca
C.P. 71220

Family (left to right): Front row: Lisia (daughter), Manuel with arms around Beatríz (daughter), Manuel behind Rocio (son). Back row: Joel, Jr., José (sons)

Joel working on his potter's wheel

Terra cotta dishware with filigree decoration, approximately .5" x 1", $1.50 per piece or $12 for a 15-piece tea set

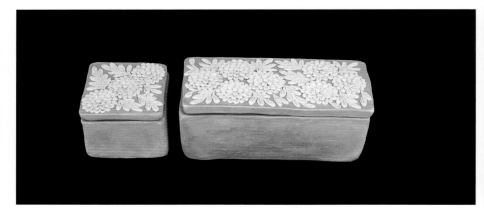

Terra cotta animal musicians, 1.75-2" x .75-1", $1.50 per piece

Filigree boxes, 2" x 1.5", $11 4.5" x 2", $20

Glazed dishware, 1-1.25" x .75-1", $.50 per piece

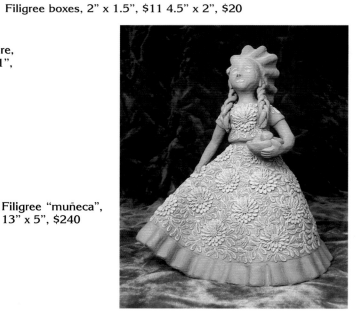

Filigree "muñeca", 13" x 5", $240

Floriberta Reyes Gómez and her husband Andrés Cruz Hernández
Designer of Exquisite Miniature Kitchen and Household Vessels in Black Pottery
*"I hope this work does not go out of style. Few make miniatures. I want
my children, grandchildren, nieces and nephews to learn this detailed work."*

See Family Tree #34, "Family of Floriberta Reyes Gómez," in Appendix on page 197.

Floriberta Reyes Gómez and her husband, Andrés Cruz Hernández, work together with their two children, Carlos and Érica, to create wonderful miniature jugs and pots in black pottery. Their versatility and delicacy is unequalled. At present they produce 20 varieties, including jugs, pots, pitchers, vessels for making chocolate, flower pots, and vases. Customers rarely visit their home, although they are welcome to do so. It is located in a heavenly spot, adjacent to glorious open fields at the end of a long, little traveled road. Instead the family typically sells to fellow artisans in the local market who in turn sell to the public.

Biography
Floriberta learned to work in clay from her mother who made only utilitarian jugs. Finding it difficult to create the larger pieces because of their weight, Floriberta turned to making small pots at the age of 12. She began to make miniatures at 15, experimenting with these forms by herself.

Prior to meeting his wife, Andrés had made only bottles for mezcal starting at the age of 16. He did not come from a ceramic family, but rather a purely farming family. When they married Andrés left this work, joining his wife in her specialty of miniatures.

Family (left to right): Carlos (son), Floriberta, Andrés (husband), Érica (daughter)

Technique
Floriberta forms the main portion of her miniature jugs one day, adding the lips the next day. The third day she decorates them. In one week the family typically creates 500 pieces, firing them all at once for five hours. Andrés takes special pleasure in decorating the miniatures.

Address:
Independencia #2
San Bartolo Coyotepec
Oaxaca
C.P. 71296
Telephone: 01 (95155)
10067

Family at work

Domestic miniatures, 1.75-2" x 1.75-1.5", $1.25 each

Eustolia González Mateos
Miniaturist of Animal and Human Figures in Black Pottery
"My children got me started by asking, 'Mom, why don't you make little pieces?'"

See Family Tree # 35, "Family of Eustolia González Mateos," in Appendix on page 197.

Eustolia creates a spectrum of well-formed and decorated miniature animals and human figures. Her repertoire includes armadillos, turtles, frogs, dolphins, whales, elephants, pigs, burros and giraffes. In addition, she makes small female figures. Some miniatures are prepared with metal loops to be turned into earrings. Little known by the public in her own right, Eustolia typically sells her pieces for resale to merchants with stands in the local market. She and her daughter Nancy collaborate in this work.

Biography
Eustolia began to work in clay at the age of ten, watching her mother make the small birds traditionally strung together to form necklaces in her pueblo, San Bartolo Coyotepec. By 15 she was making small animals such as turtles and frogs. However, it was not until she was 22 that Eustolia began to produce miniatures. This was prompted by her children who questioned, "Mom, why don't you make little pieces?"

Technique
Eustolia begins with a small ball of clay in which she creates a hole. She forms the head, feet and shell of a turtle. She then uses a knife to smooth its surface and to decorate it with scales. Working in this manner she is able to create approximately 20 pieces in a day, which must be fired in the oven for three hours.

Address:
Zaragoza #4
San Bartolo Coyotepec
Oaxaca
C.P. 71296

Nancy (daughter) and Eustolia working

Animal and human miniatures, 1-1.75" x .5-2", $1.50 per piece

Family (left to right): María (mother), Uriel (son), Nancy (daughter), Eustolia

Carousels and Ferris Wheels
from the environs of Oaxaca City

Antonio Villafañe Acevedo
Woodcarver of Carousels and Ferris Wheels
"Life offers a lot of surprises. Thanks to God who gave me a satisfaction that allows me to feed and dress my family. I owe everything to 'artesanías' (handicrafts)."

See Family Tree #36, "Family of Antonio Villafañe Acevedo," in Appendix on page 198.

Antonio Villafañe Acevedo and his large family work together closely to produce outstandingly imaginative and whimsical wood-carved carousels and ferris wheels. Combinations of animals, human figures and skeletons ride spirited horses. Antonio and his family are extremely versatile, ready and able to produce any type of wooden pieces, toys and otherwise, that a client desires.

They sell their pieces and take direct orders (which they are extremely personable in filling) from their home and workshop in the Barrio del Progreso, a section of Oaxaca about ten minutes by car from the center. Be forewarned that reaching the Villafañe family requires an unforgettable climb up a sheer incline. However, they will deliver (within the city of Oaxaca) pieces that are ordered. A philosophical and practical man, Antonio and his family take their art and business very seriously. Several of his aphorisms are illustrative: "The person who makes bad things will never keep a client," and "Humility is the 'don' of intelligence."

Although we feature their toys, Antonio and his family make many other wonderful pieces in wood. These include "retablos" (three-dimensional scenes, reli-gious and otherwise, constructed within boxes that are mounted behind doors, resembling a cabinet configuration) and freestanding nativity scenes. Antonio boasts that his family has so many designs that there is not enough time to create them all. Some pieces are produced only at particular periods, such as those celebrating the Day of the Dead (see a Day of the Dead carousel on page 162 of Chapter Ten).

Biography
Antonio began his career in woodcarving at the age of 13, helping his father sell the "retablos." By the age of 17 he contributed to the production of these pieces, carving the goats that they incorporated. Antonio began to work in this art for real when his father became severely ill and was known to be dying. He spent the last two years of his father's life learning everything he could. Being the eldest of many siblings, Antonio was expected to assume major responsibility for the support of his family. He admits to having aspired to be a carpenter, and to not having liked "artesanías." However, he had no choice under the circumstances.

Antonio's talents were immediately evident to the owners of the major folk art shops in Oaxaca at that time. Casa Cervantes and Yalalag, owned by Enrique de la Lanza, offered a great deal of encouragement. When the state-run store ARIPO opened its doors, they bought all the pieces he had at the time. Soon Antonio began to win contests, including second prize in a national competition in 1965, second prize in a nativity contest in 1983 and fifth place in another nativity contest in 1999. Antonio grew to love his work and to appreciate the opportunities it offered him.

His wooden carousels and ferris wheels resulted from the creative collaboration of many family members who introduced this novel design in 1970.

Technique
Antonio estimates that it takes three days to make a carousel. The process begins with selection of the necessary pieces of "copal" from a supplier. First the animal or human figures are cut, their trunks and then their hands, face, and feet. Antonio believes that the full moon is the perfect time for cutting the wood, cautioning, "If you don't learn to respect nature, it will destroy you."

Many members of the Villafañe family contribute to the creation of these pieces. Some are especially adept at producing the carousel's base, and others its roof. Pieces are assembled with glue; nails are not used. All members of the family decorate with acrylic paint.

Address:
Donají #104
San Juan Chapultepec
Barrio del Progreso
Oaxaca
C.P. 68150

Antonio holding a small "retablo," 17" x 13", $145 (right) and his son Marco holding a small carousel, 16" x 9", $110 (left)

Antonio painting a carousel

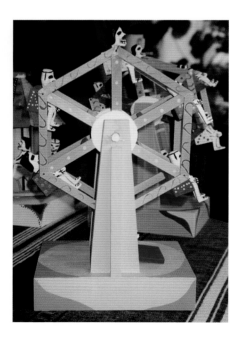

Virgin of Guadalupe "retablo"
(opened and closed).
Large size, "35 x 22", $550
Medium size, 30" x 22", $330
Small size, 23" x 16", $170

Carousel:
Large size, 20" x 13", $165
Medium size, 18" x 11", $135
Small size, 16" x 9", $110

Ferris wheel:
Large size, 27" x 20", $200
Medium size, 23" x 16", $175
Small size, 18" x 13", $135

Corn Husk Figures
from the environs of Oaxaca City

Unlike most of the folk art and handicrafts of Oaxaca, corn husk toys ("totomoxtle") were introduced within the last decades. Artisans who work in this type of craft also typically create flowers and other decorative objects.

Cornhusk flower display in Mercado de los Abastos

"Totomoxtle" (corn husk) pieces found in markets and folk art shops in Oaxaca City, ranging in price from $4-15 each. (left) Female figure, 8" x 5.5" (right) Female figure, 12" x 7"

Woman making tamales, 7" x 4.5" and woman selling beans, 6" x 6"

Mónica Bernardino Martínez
Valiant Creator and Teacher of the Art of Corn Husk Figures
"A lot of people don't know they have ability. They need to practice to discover this."

See Family Tree #37, "Family of Mónica Bernardino Martinez," in Appendix on page 199.

Mónica Bernardino Martínez creates fabulously detailed and imaginative corn husk dolls in brilliant colors. Extremely versatile in her repertoire, she seems to especially love the figures she dresses in traditional costumes of the state of Oaxaca. In addition, she creates many other types of work, such as baskets decorated with glorious flowers, centerpieces, and bouquets.

Mónica has offered courses to a vast number of women in many pueblos, helping them to launch their careers in this handicraft (the next featured artist is one of her former students). She takes great pride in enabling them to discover their talents, and transcend their self-doubts.

Monica's small and hard-to-find house is in a sublime

Mónica at work

setting, at the end of an unpaved road. This spot affords glorious vistas of the mountains, including a distant view of the ancient Zapotec ruins of Monte Albán.

Biography

Mónica grew up in Mexico City until 18 years of age. During her secondary school years she took a course in decoration of various types, an experience that she drew upon later. She later came to Oaxaca to study law. When visiting her father's family, residents of Santa Cruz Papalutla (see page 139 in Chapter Eight) she fell in love with their pueblo. Upon graduation Mónica practiced law for approximately five years. However, when her husband had an accident that left him quadriplegic three or four years after marriage, she was faced with finding both a means of support and a diversion that would allow her to be at his side.

Serendipitously a cousin asked Mónica to help her develop ideas for decoration, especially in "totomoxtle" at her "quinceaños" (15th birthday celebration, roughly the equivalent of a Sweet Sixteen). Monica enjoyed brainstorming, and came up with designs for centerpieces and party favors. Within 15 days of the party, she began to receive orders from those who had attended the event or heard about it. This was the beginning of her business, in which she has been deeply involved ever since.

As Mónica's reputation developed, a congressman asked that she offer courses to women in many pueblos. Her first was in 1999 in San Jacinto Amilpas where she taught for a year. This was followed by Etla, Tlacolula, and Ejutla, to name a few. Mónica's greatest satisfaction was in Etla where a woman with cancer worked with her in "totomoxtle" to get her mind off her problems. Not only did she survive her cancer, but she began her own workshop. To Mónica this represents "vive de totomoxtle" (living from "totomoxtle"). Mónica has also stimulated her mother, as well as her sister and grandmother, to undertake this handicraft.

Technique

Mónica cited two classes of "totomoxtle." In one the corn husks are dyed with a special type of paint that is long-lasting. When the paint, added to water, reaches a boil, the husks are immersed in this solution. The longer the period of time for which they are cooked, the deeper the color. When the desired

"Totomoxtle" figures in regional costume:
Man in traditional costume of Danza de la Pluma, 12" x 4", $30
Woman from Isthmus of Tehuantepec, 10" x 4", $12

color is achieved, the husks are placed in cold water that removes the excess. They are then dried in the shade for half a day.

The other type consists of mixing the same paint with alcohol. This solution is applied with a brush when uniform color is not desired, such as in creating flowers that have multi-color petals. The limitation of this simpler technique is that colors are not as firm.

Depending upon the piece to be created, corn husks need to be dry or wet. For example, to form the classical "alcatraz" (callas lily), the husk must be wet to permit folding it over. On the contrary, husks for the rose can be neither very wet, nor completely dry. If they are too wet the petals cannot be shaped properly. Cotton thread is used to attach the necessary pieces to one another.

Address:
Privada de Vicente Guerrero #1
Barrio de San Antonio
Tlalixtac de Cabrera
Oaxaca
C.P. 68720

Fruit basket decorated with assorted "totomoxtle" flowers, 14" x 10", $20

Basket decorated with "totomoxtle" daisies, callas lilies and gardenias, 14" x 12". $25

Hilaria Zárate Hernández
Creators of Lively Corn Husk Figures and Flowers
"A woman's participation in the economy of her family and community is deeply satisfying."

See Family Tree #38, "Family of Hilaria Zárate Hernández," in Appendix on page 199.

Hilaria Zárate Hernández currently works closely with her 18-year-old daughter, Graciela Morales Zárate. They produce male figures, female figures in regional costumes (such as Tehuanas and China Oaxaqueñas, see the map of regional costumes on page 12), and a host of flowers (roses, "alcatrazes," sunflowers, tulips and "bougainvilleas"). Hilaria's favorite pieces are male figures with painted faces and sombreros, while Graciela's are tulips. They also produce tortilla baskets, napkin holders, baskets with flowers, Christmas wreaths and reindeer, fans, hats and table decorations.

Hilaria is one of many participants in a woman's cooperative in the center of Oaxaca City, where every type of folk art and craft is represented. Only artisans of outstanding quality are invited to join. Since this is a celebration of the competence of women, nearly all members are female.

Female figures, 10" x 3", $10

Hilaria and her daughter Graciela with "totomoxtle" flowers and decorated basket, 8" x 6", $13

Biography
Five years ago Hilaria and two of her daughters, Ana Marcela and Graciela, signed up for a four month course offered to women in their community. When the teacher for their intended course did not arrive, another who offered instruction in "totomoxtle" was substituted. This serendipitously resulted in Hilaria's and Ana Marcela's current livelihood. Their teacher was none other than Mónica Bernardino Martínez (the previously featured artist). At first Hilaria felt awkward in her efforts to create these pieces. However, her teacher's patience and strong encouragement enabled her to persist. Today she feels immense gratitude to this woman, who allowed her to reach her current level of proficiency.

Technique
The process of creating corn husk figures begins with selecting the best materials at market. Once bushels of corn husks are purchased, they must be examined closely, since only 30 to 40 percent lend themselves to this work. Long pieces are necessary for many of the figures, and only clean pieces will do. In addition, those that are durable and do not break easily when bent are most desirable. Most of the local corn is inadequate for both these reasons, with the exception of the area surrounding the pueblo of Ocotlán. Produce from the isthmus of Tehuantepec is usually preferable.

Husks come in natural white and brown colors, and are purchased when already dry. They may be used as such, or painted with aniline paints. Painting is done before assembling the pieces, with the exception of water paints that are sometimes added for final decorative touches. As pieces are shaped into desired configurations various types of glue are used to secure them in place. Hilaria estimates that it takes her half a day to create a clown figure or female figure.

Address:
Mujeres Artesanas de las Regiones de Oaxaca A.C. (commonly called MARO A.C.)
5 de Mayo #204
Oaxaca
Oaxaca
C.P. 68000
Telephone: 01 (95151) 60670

Christmas ornaments: Reindeer, 10" x 7", $10
Wreath, 15" x 15", $14

Clowns, 10" x 4", $10

Chapter Six
Jewelry

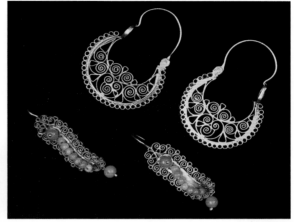

Gold filigree hoops, $145
Elongated gold filigree earrings decorated with coral, $95
Both sold in Tere, Oaxaca City

Oaxaca offers an abundance of distinctive jewelry, much of it at very affordable prices. Many styles are produced in Oaxaca City, where the visitor can also find pieces created in other parts of Mexico, especially the silver of Taxco.

We focus on the array of jewelry that originates in Oaxaca. One particularly famous type is ornate filigree that is often decorated with pearls, coral or semi-precious stones. This is variously produced in gold, gold-plate, silver and "chapa de oro" (an inexpensive metal with gold tone). The basic techniques were introduced by the Spaniards who were influenced by the Arabs. Reproductions of the ancient Mixtec and Zapotec jewelry designs discovered in the archaeological site of Monte Albán are produced most often in gold, but also in silver. There is also jewelry from the Spanish colonial period, composed of small stones (so called "white sapphires") mounted in silver that is soldered onto gold bases. In addition, large silver Yalalag crosses, from which smaller crosses dangle, are worn on prominent silver chains. Tiny ceramic animals and beads made in the pueblos of Santa Maria Atzompa and San Bartolo Coyotepec are strung together to create necklaces.

To provide a mere sample of the beauty of this type of art work, we feature one very well-known family that produces three types of jewelry: gold filigree, colonial style and Monte Albán reproductions

Silver filigree earrings, $20

Yalalag and Mitla crosses in 14 karat gold (Yalalag crossesalso made in silver)
Courtesy of Alberto Rojas, Oro de Monte Albán
(Clockwise from bottom):
Large Yalalag pendant alone, $440 in gold, $40 in silver
32.5" chain and large pendant, $1750 in gold, $235 in silver
Mitla crosses (gold only):
Small, $35
Medium, $65
Large, $85
Yalalag cross earrings, $275 in gold, $40 in silver

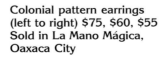

Colonial pattern earrings
(left to right) $75, $60, $55
Sold in La Mano Mágica, Oaxaca City

The Rojas Calvo Family
Developers and Pioneers of Fine Hand-Made Traditional and Ancient Reproduction Jewelry

See Family Tree #39, "The Rojas Calvo Family," in Appendix on page 200.

The Rojas Calvo family has improved or pioneered many of the major styles of fine traditional or ancient reproduction jewelry found in the city of Oaxaca. Tere Calvo Quevedo's mother and Alberto Rojas Calvo's grandmother, Rosa (known as Rosita during her lifetime), opened the very first jewelry shop in town in 1946. Currently Tere and her son Alberto have eight stores in all: six in the center of town, one of which accompanies their workshop, one at the site of the ruins of Monte Albán and the last in the distant Oaxacan coastal city of Puerto Escondido. Tere runs the two that specialize in gold filigree and colonial style pieces (a mixture of silver, gold and tiny diamonds), while Alberto and his wife Inés manage the shops primarily dedicated to gold reproductions of pre-Columbian jewelry discovered in 1932 in Monte Albán.

It was to Maestro José Ortiz, who used to manufacture jewelry for Rosita, that the famous pieces discovered by archaeologist Alfonso Caso in Monte Albán's Tomb 7 were brought for cleaning and restoration. Because of the trust placed in both Rosita and Maestro Ortiz, and the quality of their work, they were later granted sole rights to make reproductions. The two established a workshop devoted to this purpose beginning in 1937.

Today all three types of jewelry are produced in the family's workshop near the church of Santo Domingo. It is accompanied by a small display of completed pieces for sale. The family extends a warm invitation to visitors to see all phases of production, exemplifying their dedication to preserving the basics of the old principles. The interest of tourists enhances the craftsmen's belief in the importance of their work.

Family (left to right): Tere, Alberto, Inés (Alberto's wife)

Tere Calvo Quevedo
Guardian of Treasures in Gold Filigree and Colonial Style Jewelry
"Our work is an art, finishing the pieces beautifully. We love the work and believe in it and would like others to value it too."

Tere is a lively, elegant and yet down to earth woman who lives in an exquisite colonial mansion near the church of Santo Domingo. She can often be found at "Tere," the shop bearing her name that is located near the zocalo. In addition she runs another shop, Xipe, just across from the Camino Real Hotel on 5 de Mayo.

Biography
At age 11 Tere began to assist her mother in finishing pieces of filigree jewelry, for example, selecting the needed pearls or pieces of coral. But because she was seriously involved in her studies she did not dedicate herself to this work until many years later.

Tere never made jewelry but rather supervised its production. However, her personal participation in every aspect of the process enables her to appreciate what is involved. At the time when she began to devote herself to the jewelry business, there were only two types of jewelry: gold filigree and colonial style, the latter introduced by the Spaniards.

Technique
Tiny raw diamonds are set on top of silver that is mounted on a backing of gold. At times pearls are suspended from these pieces as well. The filigree style can be produced in both silver and gold. However, Tere, like Rosita before her, strongly favors gold pieces.

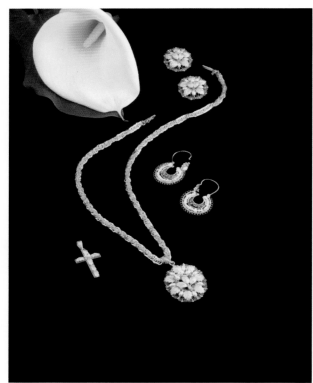

14 karat gold filigree pieces. *Courtesy of Alberto Rojas, Oro de Monte Albán* **(Clockwise beginning at the upper right corner):**
Earrings, $300
Earrings, $155
Pendant, $230;
and with 16" chain, $470
Cross, $78

Colonial style pieces. *Courtesy of Alberto Rojas, Oro de Monte Albán* (Clockwise beginning at the upper left corner):
Pendant, $40
Necklace, $250
Earrings #2120, $90
Ring, $195
Pendant, $135

Alberto Rojas Calvo
A Blend of Modern Technical Expertise and Respect for Tradition
"Making money is easy but preserving our cultural heritage and convincing people to do it well is difficult. It is our responsibility. We are probably the last ones."

Alberto Rojas Calvo is deeply dedicated to his work, preserving its tradition and facilitating its improvement. He studied processes of jewelry production in Dallas, Texas (thus his fluency in English) to enhance his family's mission. His goal was to preserve technical principles, while increasing productivity.

Biography

Alberto jokes that his involvement in the creation of jewelry began early, amidst his family's excitement. "I grew up behind my mom's jewelry cases, running to the workshop." His desire to contribute to the family endeavor culminated in his studying for a Masters degree in Business Administration at the Universidad Iberoamericana in Mexico City. Following this he returned to the family workshop in Oaxaca. There he married his wife Ines with whom he collaborates in business and shares their two children, 20-year-old Eduardo and 18-year-old Ileana.

Technique

Filigree work is based on natural materials such as leaves and flowers. The artisan begins with a solid rod of gold that is made thinner and thinner until it is of the desired dimensions. It is then put through a pair of rollers to flatten the wire. Filigree forms are created by hand, based on old designs. Pieces of wire are twisted with pliers, then put in charcoal and pressed inside. The artisan's work is like a jigsaw puzzle, requiring that he assemble pieces until the figure is completed. Solder is then applied to the silver or gold forms. Once soldered the pieces are taken out of the charcoal, and decoration is applied. Leaves, made separately, may be attached to the filigree work. These are cut and hammered to create domed shapes, and then engraved by hand.

Colonial designs are similarly drawn from natural sources such as leaves and flowers. Many also derive from colonial iron work seen on windows and doors in houses and churches. Silver is used to create the basic foundation to which decorative elements are attached, and a matching gold shape is soldered onto the back. Finally the stones are set.

Monte Albán reproductions are created with the "lost wax process." A metal mold is vulcanized in a special type of rubber. Pieces are placed on top and on bottom, and wax is injected into the cavity. A small wax tree is formed, around which metal cylinders are placed. The wax inside is surrounded by cement made of a mixture of powder and water. Once dried and solidified, the metal cylinder is placed in the oven where the wax melts, leaving the cavity empty, thus the "lost wax." Gold, subjected to centrifugal force, occupies the cavity.

Molds for "lost wax technique" used in making Monte Albán reproductions

Artisan firing in workshop

133

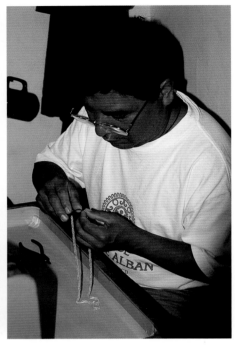

Gold wire being put through rollers to be flattened for filigree jewelry

Artisan assembling pieces in the workshop

Addresses:
(In the center of Oaxaca City)
Oro de Monte Albán (workshop and shop)
Calle Adolfo C Gurrión S/N (without number)
Telephone 01 (95151) 64528

Oro de Monte Albán (shops)
Calle Alcalá #307, 403 and 503

Tere
Calle Avenida Hidalgo #600 W

Xipe
Calle 5 de Mayo #315

(At the site of the ruins of Monte Albán)
Oro de Monte Albán

(Puerto Escondido)
Oro de Monte Albán (juncture of Pérez Gasga and Marina Nacional Street)

Monte Albán reproduction jewelry in gold. *Courtesy of Alberto Rojas, Oro de Monte Albán* **(Clockwise beginning at the upper left corner): Necklace, $700
Pins or pendants (clockwise from upper left):
medium, $390
large, $590
small, $165
Charm or pendant, $100
Bracelet, $140
Earrings with posts, $210
Hanging earrings, $225**

Chapter Seven
Candles

Candles are an important part of pueblo life. They are used for a variety of religious and other celebrations such as weddings, confirmations and "quinceaños," the Mexican equivalent of Sweet Sixteen that takes place at 15 years of age. The finer candle makers create graceful, elaborate configurations incorporating natural elements such as glorious flowers and birds in a wide array of sizes. Candlemakers create wonderful wax palettes, encompassing a range of subtle and brilliant colors, sometimes accented with flowers of paper and tinsel.

The great majority of candles are made in Teotitlán del Valle, the same pueblo known for rugs and wall hangings (see Chapter Two, page 61 for our description). Here the creation of ceremonial candles to be placed before altars is in keeping with the pueblo's persistent religious and cultural Zapotec influence. This is evident in the older generation's traditional dress, their greater familiarity with the Zapotec language than with Spanish, and the bi-lingualism of many of its younger citizens.

Viviana Alavéz Hipólito
Master Candlemaker
"I hope people come and visit to appreciate this beautiful 'artesanía' (handicraft). You don't have to feel obligated to buy. We are happy to have people come to visit and know us."

See Family Tree #40, "Family of Viviana Alavéz Hipólito," in Appendix on page 200.

An elegant and friendly woman, Viviana Alavéz Hipólito creates delicately elaborated candles with a velvet touch. Her son José and daughter-in-law Petra work closely with her. Assemblages of glorious flowers such as roses and "alcatrazes" (callas liles), fruit such as apples, pomegranates and limes, and birds envelop the dignified, slender candles she creates entirely by hand. They range in size from table decorations to those nearly a yard high for use in religious processions. Colors may be single tone or multi-tone.

Earlier in Viviana's life candles were not valued to the degree they are now. As they have come to command more respect, many fellow dwellers in Teotitlán have chosen to study with master candle maker Viviana.

Biography
Viviana was orphaned at the age of three. She was raised by her maternal aunt, and separated from her brother who was taken into the home of a member of their father's family. María Pablo, her mother's sister, was a candle maker who taught her niece this craft from the time Viviana was eight. By the time she married at 14 Viviana was sufficiently competent to work independently. She added to her aunt's custom of decorating only the front of the candle, her own style of decorating the rear portion as well.

By 22 years of age Viviana had established her own clientele. Interested in improving her designs and the quality of her work she introduced roses. For this purpose she grew a rose plant to study the flower's form, and developed an original, extremely full design. In relating this history Viviana laughed at the idea dominant in her youth that, were a girl to be unmarried by the age of 22, she would be left behind.

Before marrying José, Petra had never made a candle. However, once married and working with her mother-in-law she discovered her great talents for this art.

Family portrait (left to right): Viviana, José (son), Petra (daughter-in-law)

Technique

Wax is purchased in a large tan-colored block. It is placed in a tub to be melted with lime and herbs. When this mixture is brought to a boil impurities are deposited on the bottom. Then the flame is lowered, and the mixture cools off gradually. It is put in a special receptacle overnight until it becomes solid again. The next step is cleaning the wax, washing it and drying it in the sun. In this way its water content is eliminated. The resulting substance is a golden yellow color. When white wax is desired, the substance is placed in the sun for 30 days to bleach the wax's natural golden yellow color.

White wax is also used for colored portions. Cheaper colored candles are produced with aniline paints, the color of which lasts only two to five days. Better candles for special occasions are made with natural substances, such as "cochineal." These last for one to four years.

The body of the candle is produced by initially suspending string (wicks) from a wrought iron rack. Liquid wax is poured over the wick in many layers. An hour must be left between pourings. This process, at one time called "baño María" (María's bath), can take the better part of several days.

The creation of flower decorations is begun with a "mold." This is actually a hand-made process. The bottom half of a small jug is momentarily dipped into a pot of hot melted wax, and immediately immersed in a pot of cold water. The resulting hemisphere is removed from the jug, thus the "mold." This piece is variously cut with a scissor to form the beginnings of petals that are further shaped by hand. One layer is placed inside another to replicate the configuration of a flower. Some candles have paper portions that are also created by the artisan. Viviana creates approximately eight large candles and six or seven small candles per week.

Address:
Abasolo #7
Teotitlán del Valle
Oaxaca
C.P. 70420
Telephone: 01 (95152) 44309

Viviana and Petra creating decorative flowers

Decorated candle in front of wrought iron rack used for pourings, 47" x 19", $20

A variety of candles:
green & pink candles, 10" x 3", $12
Small red candle, 3" x 2", $4
Sunflower and pink candles, 7" x 2", $7
Callas lily candle, 5" x 2", $5

Sofía Ruíz Lorenzo
Young Creative Candlemaker
"I hope you come to visit. For me this is a very beautiful place with a lot of traditions and 'artesanías' that reflect our culture."

See Family Tree #41, "Sofía Ruíz Lorenzo," in Appendix on page 201.

Sofía is a delightful young woman whose creativity is boundless. Her candlemaking repertoire is extraordinarily diverse, including ornate designs and others that are simple and elegant. She lives with her very traditional Zapotec parents at the top of a hill in Teotitlán del Valle.

Biography

Sofía learned to make candles beginning at the age of 6, at her paternal grandmother's side. Her great-grandmother had taught her grandmother in turn. Sofía also studied with Viviana Alavéz Hipólito for many years. When her grandmother died Sofía, who was nine, inherited her clients: local people and others who came from the pueblo of Tlacolula to buy for "fiestas." By the age of 18 Sofía started to work for herself. Initially she made candles similar to those of her grandmother with simple flowers, birds, and fruit. However, she added far bolder roses to these designs.

Sofía traced the evolution of her many original contributions to this "artesanía" (handicraft) with delight. The range of her work is truly astonishing. By 13 she introduced dahlias, a type of flower. Following this she made wedding candles that are entirely white. At 15 she began to create carnations, her favorite flowers. Following this were "alcatrazes" (callas lilies), marigolds, "flowers of the night," sunflowers, and gladiolas.

Technique

Sofía paints with "cochineal," a natural substance, emphasizing the importance of using non-toxic materials. When candles are completed it is essential to lick them to enhance their sheen. Doing so with unnatural substances would be bad for her health.

Sofía's most ornate candles (for example those surrounded by sunflowers on one side, and other types of flowers with tinsel on the other) can take up to three months to make, from start to finish. Two hundred and twenty individual pourings over the wick are necessary to make the largest size candles.

Address:
Belizario Dominquez #7
Teotitlán del Valle
Oaxaca
C.P. 70420
Telephone: 01 (95152) 44199

Sofía forming a rose

Family (left to right): Francisca (mother), Sara (sister), Sofía, Enrique (father)

Rose and lily candle, 23" x 9", $40

Sunflower candle (front and back views), 14" x 7", $50

Additional candlemakers
Jacinto Lazo and his wife Rosa Hernández (Prolongación de Avenida Juárez)
Mercedes Montaño (Avenida Jurez S/N [without number])

Chapter Eight
Basketry

Baskets of innumerable types are sold in abundance in all indigenous markets and in shops. There are rigid laundry baskets with tops ("canastos"), rigid open baskets with handles used for marketing ("canastas"), bird cages, flexible round wastebaskets, and cases for eyeglasses and for money, that are made of palm. Many, however, come from distant pueblos well beyond the geographical radius we consider, for example, from the Isthmus of Tehuantepec and the Mixteca (in the northwestern portion of the state of Oaxaca).

The pueblos relatively close to Oaxaca City in which baskets are produced are Santa Cruz Papalutla, San Juan Guelavía and Magdalena Teitipac, all to the southeast. These are rarely visited by tourists and are off the beaten path. We feature one especially noteworthy artist in Santa Cruz Papalutla to provide a sample of the beauty of this type of work.

Basket vendors in the market of Tlacolula

Basket stand in 20 de Noviembre market of Oaxaca City

Woman from La Mixteca region making and selling palm baskets in 20 de Noviembre market of Oaxaca City

Close-up of three completed palm baskets from the La Mixteca region

Miniature baskets sold in 20 de Noviembre market of Oaxaca City

 below caption:
Family (left to right): Front row: Francisca (Amador's mother) and Rufina (Amador's sister) in front holding lamp base with metal decoration (10" x 6", $10), José and Guadalupe (the children to the right). Back row: José Manuel, Lidia (Amador's daughter), Amador, Felicitas (Amador's wife), Robí, Carmela (Amador's sister)

Santa Cruz Papalutla

Santa Cruz Papalutla, a remote pueblo 27 kilometers (approximately 35 minutes) from Oaxaca, lies along the same highway that leads to Teotitlán del Valle, the archaeological site of Yagúl, the memorable Sunday market of Tlacolula and the ruins and weaving town of Mitla. After turning off the highway to the right, a journey of 11 kilometers remains on frequently unpaved streets through small, little-known pueblos heavily populated with cornfields: Lachigoló and San Sebastián Abasolo. This is a route rarely traveled by tourists. Along this road a father and son haul a huge bundle of alfalfa on their burro. Another father and son ride in a wooden cart pulled by oxen. Finally, a large stone edifice with a red roof, followed by three crosses, announces your arrival in Santa Cruz Papalutla.

Amador Martínez Antonio
Master Basket Weaver, Student of Chinese Basketry and Generous Teacher
"I love to teach what I have learned. I won't take my knowledge to the grave."

See Family Tree #42, "Family of Amador Martínez Antonio," in Appendix on page 202.

Amador Martínez Antonio is a warm, generous man who delights in weaving bamboo baskets used primarily for utilitarian purposes. He explained that in the marketplace staples, such as grain and corn, are measured by the size of the client's basket rather than by weight. For this reason ownership of baskets of various sizes is crucial to pueblo life, comparable to our need for a measuring cup. Baskets are also used for carrying and displaying produce, as well as for storage of dirty laundry.

Amador's baskets range in size and strength, lending themselves to these different purposes. He also creates woven bamboo lamps, some laced with decorative, enameled metal segments.

Amador has a scholarly bent. Having won an award to study basketry in China, he is methodical in his craft and takes great pleasure in generously disseminating what he knows to other indigenous pueblo dwellers. As he put it, "I won't take my knowledge to the grave." In this spirit he invites all artisans to transmit their experiences to the next generation.

Currently Amador is engaged in founding a place for artisans - those from more distant pueblos in the state of Oaxaca - to exhibit their work closer to the capital city. This will enable them to profit from tourist trade and to become better known.

The bountiful spirit of Amador's family was also evident during our visit. In preparation for a nephew's confirmation, approximately 20 members of the extended family worked together in their communal courtyard preparing delicacies and arranging the space. Ten young children joyously romped through a nearby room and played on the grounds. In an adjacent area a huge pig nursed her ten new offspring and, in a more remote area, a large collection of family livestock - burros, horses and bulls - were being fed.

Biography

Amador remembers playing with bamboo from two to three years of age, as both his parents and his paternal grandfather wove baskets. Sitting with his family, he routinely cleaned bamboo at first, and later wove small saucer-like baskets. As Amador reminisced about this, he pointed to his nephews who, while sitting with us, similarly cleaned a new piece of bamboo and began to carve it.

Beginning in 1980 Amador evolved from making more rustic baskets to finer ones. He has enjoyed participating in contests in the state of Oaxaca since 1981, winning first, second, and third prizes. The change in his style was precipitated by "a sad but real story." One day he made a group of baskets that came out too large. His wife, who attempted to sell them, was rejected in her efforts. Amador, with a deep feeling of having failed her, stayed up all night not only to make baskets of the right size but to create ones of better quality. Thanks to her, he feels, he was spurred to improve his work.

Since his trip to China in 1985, where his work was further enhanced, Amador has become an important teacher of basketry, an art form he loves. He has introduced artisans in many pueblos, such as San Juan Guelavía, Magdalena Teitipac and Santo Domingo Jalieza, to the finer techniques he learned in China. He also prides himself on having taught courses in basketry to prisoners in the pueblos of Pochutla, Ejutla, Jamiltepec, and Ocotlán. This training contributes to rehabilitation, enabling the prisoner to leave prison with a means of self-support. Amador is extremely proud if his student is launched on a profitable career, and does not have to suffer the sense of inadequacy he did earlier in his life.

Technique

Amador works with both "carrizo" (a reed from Antilla introduced in Spanish times) and bamboo (more recently introduced in Morelos, Mexico, from Asia). He imports some of his bamboo from Japan, and other portions from the state of Morelos. "Carrizo" of three ages is used for different types of baskets. The body of a basket is constructed with bamboo aged six months to one year. The base is best created with bamboo of two to two and one-half months, since it is more flexible. The handle requires bamboo of one and one-half to two months since it is the most flexible. After removing the outer layer of the bamboo, Amador runs it through his feet to separate various fronds.

He divides his work into two types, the more traditional baskets used for all types of practical purposes and stronger baskets needed to carry very heavy things. "Carrizo" of anywhere from one year to three years is best to make the stronger baskets, since it is most durable. The other type is the "Chinese technique" in which bamboo is passed through a fire to remove moisture. Since the workmanship and materials used in this type are finer, the pieces produced are more expensive.

Address:
Avenida Hidalgo #19
Santa Cruz Papalutla
Tlacolula
Oaxaca
C.P. 70456
Telephone: 01 (95155) 38125

Amador preparing bamboo

Classic basket with handle,
14" x 13", $17

Chinese style round
basket, 23" x 18", $9

Assorted small baskets,
3" x 5" to 5" x 7", $3-5

Chapter Nine
Dried Flower Crafts
of San Antonino

A mere handful of artisans continue to create the beautiful, natural handicraft referred to as "flores inmortales" (literally immortal flowers). The objects fashioned from these vibrantly colored dried flowers are central to many aspects of Oaxacan culture. They are used year-round as toys, placards in religious and other celebratory processions ("calendas"), and decorations. They are also designed to commemorate the Night of the Radishes, a holiday on December 21st that is part of the Christmas celebration. On this occasion radishes are artistically carved in countless variations, and many types of decorative objects are created from "flores inmortales." San Antonino Castillo Velasco (described in the section of Chapter Two on embroidery, page 80) is home to the few remaining artists who produce this folk art.

Pieces by Delfino Gómez (deceased) and his brother Timoteo Gómez of San Antonino del Castillo Velasco

Manuel Raymundo Córdoba (father of Israel Raymundo Cornelio) at his daily stand at the entrance to the Benito Juárez market in Oaxaca City

Israel Raymundo Cornelio and Liliana Sánchez Mateos
Close Collaborators in the Creation of Dried Flower Pieces
"We worry that this work carried out with great effort and love will not be sustained by the next generation."

See Family Tree #43, "Israel Raymundo Cornelio," in Appendix on page 203.

Israel Raymundo Cornelio, his wife Liliana Sánchez Mateos and their children collaborate to produce a great variety of delicate decorative pieces made of dried flowers ("flores inmortales"). Huge placards of religious images such as the Virgin of Soledad and the Virgin of Juquila are mounted on the walls on their patio, while others bearing the name of specific pueblos are secured in large baskets to be carried on the heads of pueblo women participating in a procession. "Muñecas" bearing regional costumes are adorned with accessories. Two such figures strike poses of dances of the "Guelaguetza" (an annual indigenous dance festival): the "Jarabe Mixteco" and "Danza de la Pluma." Large baskets and small baskets are also produced.

The Cornelio family typically enters some of their pieces in contests for these forms of celebratory folk art held around the Night of the Radishes, a celebration just before Christmas. They begin their preparations two months in advance.

Few artisans perpetuate this type of folk art. Indeed a concerted effort was necessary to find this family, whose craftsmanship is impeccable and guaranteed for five years. Although flowers may begin to tatter by three years, their bamboo base and background of bamboo shavings endures. If the client brings these pieces back, the family will replace the flowers. We can attest to the durability of their products since we had (unknowingly) purchased two of their pieces, a small basket and wreath, three years before. The man seated at the entrance to the Benito Juárez market in Oaxaca City from whom we bought them turns out to have been Israel's father, Manuel Raymundo Córdoba. He travels daily to this market with some of the family's products.

Israel and Liliana extend a warm welcome to those interested in their techniques and appreciative of the value of their art.

Biography
Israel began to work with dried flowers as a young child, taught by his parents who had in turn learned this craft from their parents. By the age of ten he made his first pieces: doves, harps, daisies, and small baskets. Israel married Liliana at 21 and proceeded to teach her this art form. The two have, in turn, passed their techniques along to their six children. Although his parents, who live just across the street, do not continue to produce much of this laborious work in their old age, they collaborate in marketing the pieces made by Israel's family.

Technique
Frames are constructed for each piece out of bamboo. This is the only step in the process that Israel carries out exclusively. Then bamboo shavings and dried leaves are used to form a background on which the flowers are mounted. The pattern to be created with flowers is designed on this background with aniline paints. All members of the family go to the countryside to pick flowers that are preserved with their natural colors. While the flowers are still fresh, metal threads are inserted. These eventually serve as anchors to the background.

Address:
Independencia S/N (without number)
San Antonino Castillo Velasco
Ocotlán
Oaxaca
C.P. 71520

Family portrait (left to right): Juanita (daughter), Israel, Sergio (son), Maricela (daughter), Lidia (wife)

143

Israel attaching flowers
to a small basket

Placard for celebration in pueblo of San
Antonino del Castillo Velasco, 30" x 26",
$135

Dried flower figures:
Female figure, 13" x 9", $23
Male figure, 17" x 9", $20
Female figure with large skirt,
18" x 18", $30

Virgin of Soledad,
23" x 20", $115

Chapter Ten
The Day of the Dead

The Day (or more accurately Days) of the Dead is a major stimulus for Oaxacan folk art and handicrafts, both year-round and during the months immediately preceding this most important celebration of the year. It is based on a derivative of the ancient idea that death is part of the process of life. Spirits of deceased members of the family, of both recent times and long ago, are believed to rejoin their families and friends for one day each year to share with them the pleasures of the living in the home in which they resided. Departed relatives' possessions and preferred types of food, objects and toys (in the case of children who meet an early death) are offered with love.

Stands displaying an array of celebratory objects in Mercado de los Abastos in Oaxaca City just before the Day of the Dead

There is nothing morose or frightening about this occasion. Instead it is an affectionate, and in some respects humorous, celebration of the memories of those who have died, and of the loving bonds their descendants sustain with them. The comforting unity of family, and an appreciation of each living person's part in the magical circle of life and death, is experienced. As Andrade (1996) puts it, "During this celebration death is transformed into a friend and companion with whom we share good times (p. 37)." The Day of the Dead simultaneously offers the community an opportunity to publicly mock and defy death, a devastating experience that many pueblo dwellers have come to know all too well. Performances or processions are sometimes put on for this purpose.

Pre-Hispanic elements are blended with the Roman Catholic customs of All Saints' Day and All Souls' Day, when ancestors are honored. More recently a touch of Halloween is evident as well. The events of this celebration generally extend from October 31st through November 2nd, traditions varying from pueblo to pueblo. In many (but not all) villages, October 31st is the day on which those who died as children are honored. November 1st is All Saints Day, and November 2nd is the day of departure of those who died as adults.

Since this is the most significant indigenous holiday of the year, nearly all folk artists create pieces in its honor. This is especially true of those who work in ceramics and woodcarving throughout the year. In addition, there are objects made specifically for this occasion, for placement on home altars and gravesites. These include decorated sugar skulls and miniature tables bearing bottles and food offerings for "muertos" (the souls who return for one day to visit their families). There are also clay and wire figures of skeletons in every human pose imaginable (getting married, having and performing dental work, riding a bicycle, dancing, and fishing, to name a few), pullstring skeletons that pop up within their coffins, and display boxes containing detailed scenes of this event.

Miniature offering table ("ofrenda")

Manifestations of this holiday are everywhere. For at least one week prior, and most especially in the days immediately preceding the celebration, Oaxacan markets (the Mercado de los Abastos being the prime example in the city of Oaxaca) are flooded with all types of goods. These include breads baked specifically for this occasion ("pan de muertos," bread of the departed souls) in distinctive shapes with decorations such as skulls and flowers, and bunches of traditional flowers: yellow gold "cempasuchil" (a relative of marigold) and deep red "cresta de gallo" (cockscomb). Endless fields of "cempasuchil" that blossom for about two weeks at this time of year are visible on trips to the pueblos surrounding Oaxaca. Flowers are used for decorations and offerings and their petals are plucked to create paths that point the returning spirits in the right direction. Brightly decorated skulls made of sugar, often bearing names of members of the family, line table after table. Ingredients for special dishes and mezcal are purchased, as are varieties of incense and candles that light the way for the souls' journey to and from earth. All varieties of "moles" (sauces for chicken and beef including chocolate, chilies, almonds, sesame seeds and innumerable other spices), corn-based dishes (such as tamales and tortillas), and fruit are offered. Candles, pictures, sand paintings, small figures and tissue paper cut-outs may be added to the display.

All is preparatory to creation of the altar, usually on October 31st, on which the offerings ("ofrendas") are placed. Bamboo or sugar cane support the altar that is constructed on a table covered with a white cloth. Families also decorate gravesites. Decorative styles for home altars and gravesites range from simple to extraordinarily lavish. Fabulous sand paintings, some of subtle and others of brilliant hues, can be seen at gravesites and inside shops in town. Some shops have other types of decorative pieces, often of a humorous type. The City Council of Oaxaca de Juárez sponsors an altar decoration contest in San Miguel's cemetery, where outstanding altars and sand paintings may be viewed.

Clay and wire "muerto"

In some pueblos, after sunset, families with folding beach chairs sit together keeping an all-night vigil at candlelit gravesites. They eat and chat as they wait for the souls to join them and take pleasure in their generous offerings. Children play and romp, while adults exchange memories and sing. At home, members of extended families visit one another, bringing food and flowers to add to their relatives' altars. The spirits are believed to consume only the aroma of the edibles offered. Their substance is eaten by the surviving relatives at a later time, often in the cemetery, much like a picnic.

Display boxes of "muertos"

Breads for the Day of the Dead ("Pan de Muertos") displayed in the markets of Oaxaca City

"Cempasuchil" (a relative of marigolds) and cockscomb sold in the markets of Oaxaca

"Cempasuchil" blooming in the countryside during the Day of the Dead

Decorative flower arrangements
using "cempasuchil" and cockscomb

149

A gravesite decorated with "cempasuchil" and cockscomb

Displays of decorative skulls, baskets, sheep, coffins and other items made from sugar

Woman in Mercado de los Abastos selling incense for Day of the Dead

Woman selling oranges for Day of the Dead altars

Market stand of candles for Day of the Dead

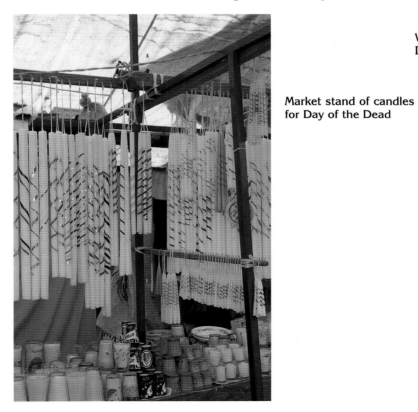

Muertos fruit bowl. *Courtesy of Casa Panchita*

Clay and wire "muertos"

A family's home altar in Teotitlán del Valle

Detail of the bottom portion of this family altar, showing the miniature offering for a deceased child

Altars for Day of the Dead displayed in shops and at the altar contest in Oaxaca City

Altars for Day of the Dead displayed in shops and at the altar contest in Oaxaca City

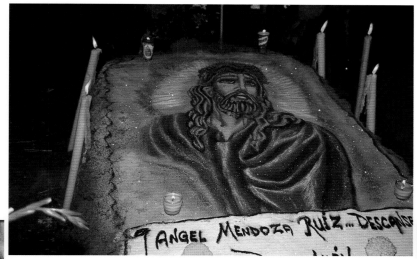

Illuminated sand paintings in the cemetery of
Xoxocotlán on the first night of the Day of the Dead

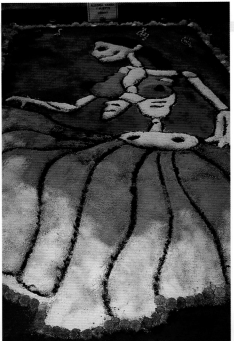

Sand paintings displayed in shops and at the altar contest in Oaxaca City during the Day of the Dead

A "muertos" display in the woman's cooperative in Oaxaca City

María Esperanza Arizmendi Bazán
Humorous and Sophisticated Celebrator of the Day of the Dead
"Women in all environments can triumph when united."

See Family Tree #44, "Family of María Esperanza Arizmendi Bazán," in Appendix on page 203.

María Esperanza Arizmendi Bazán (she prefers to be called Esperanza) creates a wide array of imaginative and humorous pieces celebrating the Day of the Dead. Some are ornately-elaborated display boxes, usually encased in glass, containing altars and tables ("ofrendas") bearing the favorite foods and drink of the deceased who purportedly return once a year to join their families. Esperanza also makes skeleton figures outfitted in every type of dress, and engaged in every imaginable activity. Several examples are Frida Kahlo and Diego Rivera, an elegant lady wearing a formal gown and plumed hat, a bride and groom, a bicyclist, and a couple showering. The humor, imaginativeness and sophistication with which she renders these figures are boundless.

Esperanza also produces another type of work: pre-Columbian reproductions, many of which relate to the Day of the Dead. She proudly celebrates the value of tradition, both Mexican and world-wide, in re-creating what belonged to our ancestors. "They are part of our race and our culture."

In addition to her cultural heritage, Esperanza celebrates the capabilities of women. She is a central member of the largest women's cooperative in Oaxaca City that encompasses nearly all types of folk art and handicrafts. One of its rooms is almost exclusively devoted to her pieces. Esperanza believes that women in all environments can triumph if they are united, and that they must learn to survive by themselves: "In this house, our cooperative, there is the opportunity to demonstrate our work."

Biography
Esperanza began to create an array of primarily ceramic pieces to commemorate the Day of the Dead in the mid-1980s. Prior to that she made candy skeletons for the occasion. After taking a course offered by the Museum of Anthropology in Mexico City in which such pieces can be found, she has dedicated herself to this work. Enchanted by pre-Hispanic culture, its beliefs and communion with nature, she enrolled in an additional course in reproduction of pre-Hispanic ceramics.

Esperanza has had a number of exhibits featuring her work in galleries in Oaxaca beginning in 1997 and in Mexico City in 1994. The local galleries repeatedly showing her pieces are Galería Miguel Cabrera and Galería Rodolfo Morales.

Technique
To create figures that stand alone, as well as those incorporated in display boxes, Esperanza begins by softening and moistening the clay she has purchased. After she models the desired figure, time is necessary for it to dry. Some pieces are painted first and then fired later, while others are fired first and painted only after-

Esperanza assembling a Day of the Dead display box

Maria Elena (Esperanza's cousin) and Esperanza holding their pieces

Day of the Dead figures (from left to right): Diego and Frida, 5" x 1.5 ", $7
Small male figures, 2.5" x 1.5", $2.50 each
Large female figures, 4-5" x 1.5", $3

ward. There is no limit to her decorative motifs, executed with materials such as paint, feathers, and glitter. Figures generally require two days to complete.

Display boxes are constructed in various sizes, ranging from miniscule to nearly a foot in length. Esperanza then elaborately fills and decorates them with small twigs, palm leaves, fabric, miniature bottles, cardboard, tissue paper, feathers, and miniature pictures of saints and virgins, to name only a few possibilities. In one dedicated to the revered figure Frida Kahlo, glitter surrounds two images of her that are affixed to the wall. A long table bears her favorite items. Also attached to the walls are miniature pieces of pottery. When her decorative work is finished, Esperanza seals the boxes with rectangular pieces of glass on the top, side, and front. These permit viewing from multiple angles. From start to finish Esperanza estimates that it takes her 15 days to complete one of the larger display boxes.

Pre-Columbian reproductions are created in stages. First the base is formed and then the other elements. Using the "pastillaje" technique of attaching clay to the main form, decorative effects are created. Once the clay has dried, Esperanza paints the piece prior to firing it. Her multi-faced mask takes 15 to 20 days to create. When making pre-Columbian reproductions the artist is required to respect the original work by never creating an exact reproduction. The size must be altered (it must be either smaller or larger), as must the tone of the paint. In preparation for reproducing a piece, Esperanza goes to the museum to study the original, usually taking photographs.

Address:
Mujeres Artesanas de las Regiones de Oaxaca (M.A.R.O., for short) A.C.
5 de Mayo #204
Oaxaca
Oaxaca
C.P. 68000
Telephone: 01 (95151) 60670

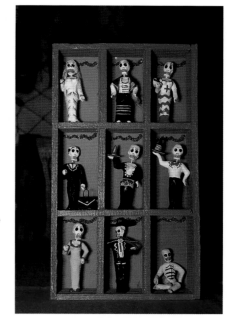

Figures in display box, 11" x 6", $20

Large display box, 14" x 7", $25

Reproduction of pre-Colombian figure of three masks, 15" x 9", $40

DAY OF THE DEAD FOLK ART BY FEATURED ARTISTS

Many of the finest artists - most frequently those who are ceramists and woodcarvers -
create outstanding pieces inspired by the profound significance of the Day of the Dead.
We present a sampler of their work.

Guillermina Aguilar, Muertos female
figures making tortillas and selling
fruit, 9" x 6", $45 and 12" x 5", $35

Jesús Aguilar, Muertos figure with
serpent and cactus, 10" x 6", $15

Josefina Aguilar, Muñeca,
30" x 20", $280

Concepción Aguilar, "Catrinas",
15" x 6", $35

Carlomagno Pedro,
"Catrina", 10" x 4", $200

Magdalena Pedro, "Catrina",
17" x 7", $225

Demetrio Garcia Aguilar, "Muñeca"
with "cempasuchil" (marigolds),
23" x 13", $200

Inocencio Vásquez, "Muertos" mariachi band, 9" x 4", $23 each

Martín Santiago, Parade of skeletons, 5" x 3", $10 each

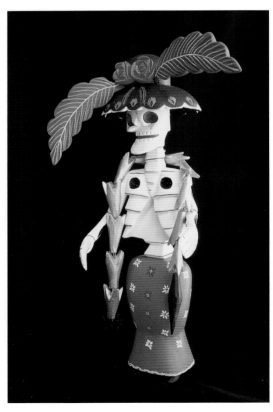

Justo Xuana's son, Edilberto Xuana, "Catrina," 14: x 4.5", $20

Antonio Villafañe, Carousel of "muertos", 18" x 10", $75

Appendix
Family Trees

Family Tree #1, The Blanco Family

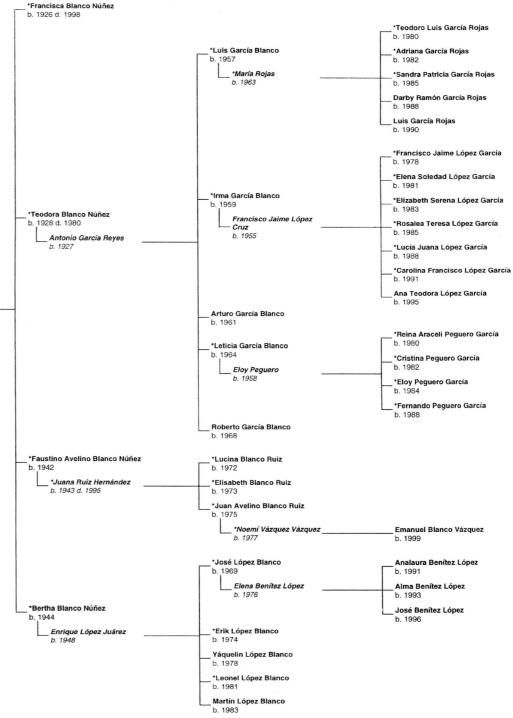

*Carmen Núñez Ramírez
b. 1900 d. 1985
   Amado Blanco Ruiz
   b. 1900 d. 1954

*Francisca Blanco Núñez
b. 1926 d. 1998

*Teodora Blanco Núñez
b. 1928 d. 1980
   Antonio García Reyes
   b. 1927

*Luis García Blanco
b. 1957
   *María Rojas
   b. 1963

*Teodoro Luis García Rojas
b. 1980

*Adriana García Rojas
b. 1982

*Sandra Patricia García Rojas
b. 1985

Darby Ramón García Rojas
b. 1988

Luis García Rojas
b. 1990

*Irma García Blanco
b. 1959
   Francisco Jaime López Cruz
   b. 1955

*Francisco Jaime López García
b. 1978

*Elena Soledad López García
b. 1981

*Elizabeth Serena López García
b. 1983

*Rosalea Teresa López García
b. 1985

*Lucía Juana López García
b. 1988

*Carolina Francisco López García
b. 1991

Ana Teodora López García
b. 1995

Arturo García Blanco
b. 1961

*Leticia García Blanco
b. 1964
   Eloy Peguero
   b. 1958

*Reina Araceli Peguero García
b. 1980

*Cristina Peguero García
b. 1982

*Eloy Peguero García
b. 1984

*Fernando Peguero García
b. 1988

Roberto García Blanco
b. 1968

*Faustino Avelino Blanco Núñez
b. 1942
   *Juana Ruiz Hernández
   b. 1943 d. 1995

*Lucina Blanco Ruiz
b. 1972

*Elisabeth Blanco Ruiz
b. 1973

*Juan Avelino Blanco Ruiz
b. 1975
   *Noemí Vázquez Vázquez
   b. 1977

Emanuel Blanco Vázquez
b. 1999

*Bertha Blanco Núñez
b. 1944
   Enrique López Juárez
   b. 1948

*José López Blanco
b. 1969
   Elena Benítez López
   b. 1976

Analaura Benítez López
b. 1991

Alma Benítez López
b. 1993

José Benítez López
b. 1996

*Erik López Blanco
b. 1974

Yáquelin López Blanco
b. 1978

*Leonel López Blanco
b. 1981

Martín López Blanco
b. 1983

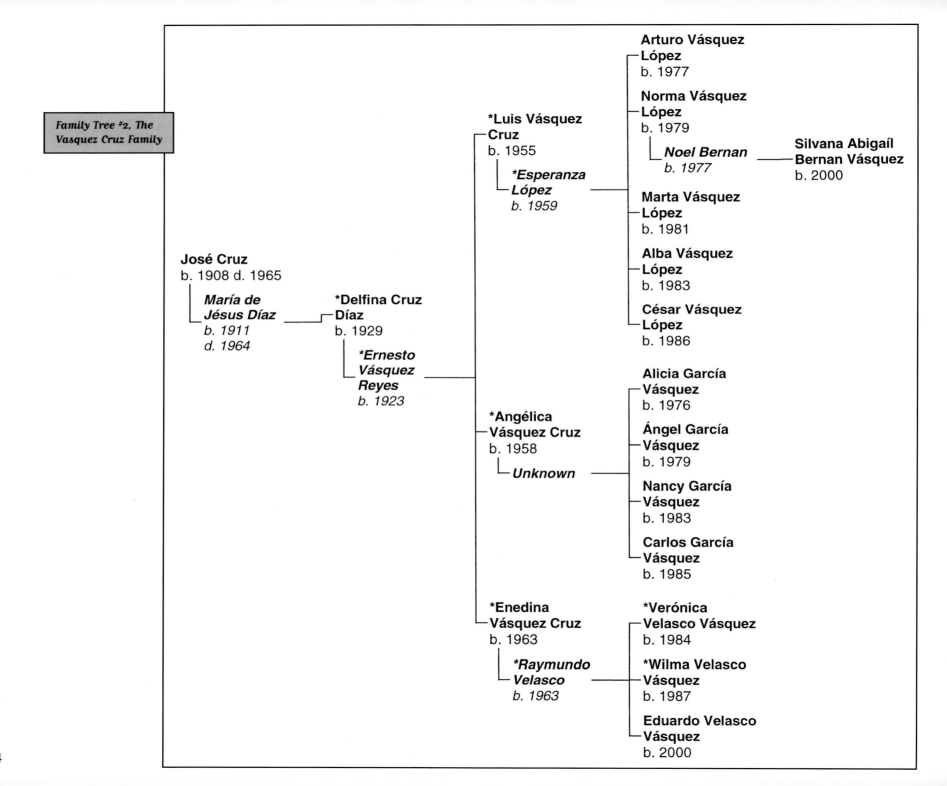

Family Tree #2, The
Vasquez Cruz Family

José Cruz
b. 1908 d. 1965

María de
Jésus Díaz
b. 1911
d. 1964

*Delfina Cruz
Díaz
b. 1929

*Ernesto
Vásquez
Reyes
b. 1923

*Luis Vásquez
Cruz
b. 1955

*Esperanza
López
b. 1959

Arturo Vásquez
López
b. 1977

Norma Vásquez
López
b. 1979

Noel Bernan
b. 1977

Silvana Abigaíl
Bernan Vásquez
b. 2000

Marta Vásquez
López
b. 1981

Alba Vásquez
López
b. 1983

César Vásquez
López
b. 1986

*Angélica
Vásquez Cruz
b. 1958

Unknown

Alicia García
Vásquez
b. 1976

Ángel García
Vásquez
b. 1979

Nancy García
Vásquez
b. 1983

Carlos García
Vásquez
b. 1985

*Enedina
Vásquez Cruz
b. 1963

*Raymundo
Velasco
b. 1963

*Verónica
Velasco Vásquez
b. 1984

*Wilma Velasco
Vásquez
b. 1987

Eduardo Velasco
Vásquez
b. 2000

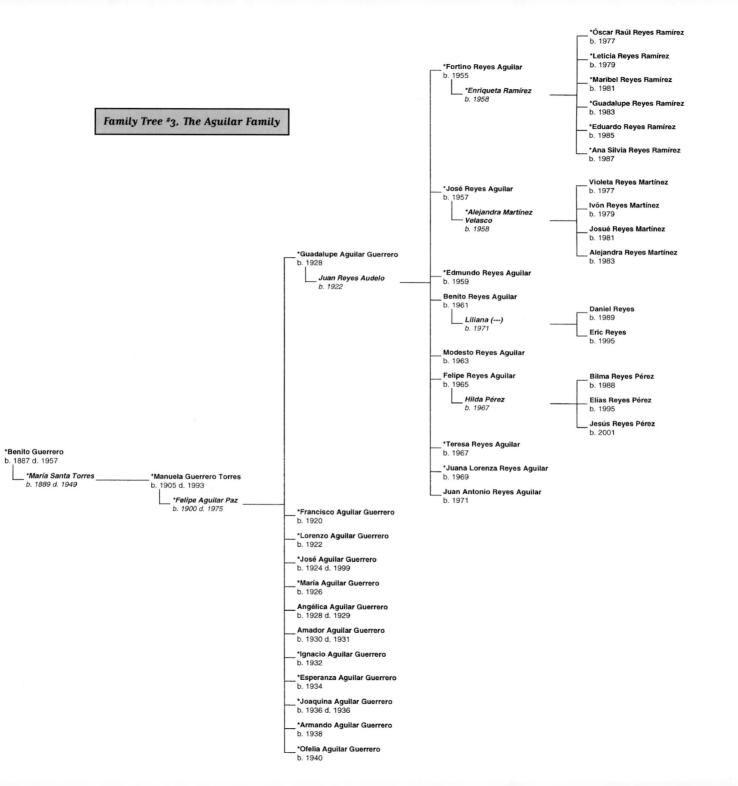

Family Tree #3, The Aguilar Family

*Óscar Raúl Reyes Ramírez
b. 1977

*Leticia Reyes Ramírez
b. 1979

*Maribel Reyes Ramírez
b. 1981

*Guadalupe Reyes Ramírez
b. 1983

*Eduardo Reyes Ramírez
b. 1985

*Ana Silvia Reyes Ramírez
b. 1987

*Fortino Reyes Aguilar
b. 1955

*Enriqueta Ramírez
b. 1958

Violeta Reyes Martínez
b. 1977

Ivón Reyes Martínez
b. 1979

Josué Reyes Martínez
b. 1981

Alejandra Reyes Martínez
b. 1983

*José Reyes Aguilar
b. 1957

*Alejandra Martínez Velasco
b. 1958

*Guadalupe Aguilar Guerrero
b. 1928

Juan Reyes Audelo
b. 1922

*Edmundo Reyes Aguilar
b. 1959

Benito Reyes Aguilar
b. 1961

Liliana (---)
b. 1971

Daniel Reyes
b. 1989

Eric Reyes
b. 1995

Modesto Reyes Aguilar
b. 1963

Felipe Reyes Aguilar
b. 1965

Hilda Pérez
b. 1967

Bilma Reyes Pérez
b. 1988

Elías Reyes Pérez
b. 1995

Jesús Reyes Pérez
b. 2001

*Teresa Reyes Aguilar
b. 1967

*Juana Lorenza Reyes Aguilar
b. 1969

Juan Antonio Reyes Aguilar
b. 1971

*Benito Guerrero
b. 1887 d. 1957

*María Santa Torres
b. 1889 d. 1949

*Manuela Guerrero Torres
b. 1905 d. 1993

*Felipe Aguilar Paz
b. 1900 d. 1975

*Francisco Aguilar Guerrero
b. 1920

*Lorenzo Aguilar Guerrero
b. 1922

*José Aguilar Guerrero
b. 1924 d. 1999

*María Aguilar Guerrero
b. 1926

Angélica Aguilar Guerrero
b. 1928 d. 1929

Amador Aguilar Guerrero
b. 1930 d. 1931

*Ignacio Aguilar Guerrero
b. 1932

*Esperanza Aguilar Guerrero
b. 1934

*Joaquina Aguilar Guerrero
b. 1936 d. 1936

*Armando Aguilar Guerrero
b. 1938

*Ofelia Aguilar Guerrero
b. 1940

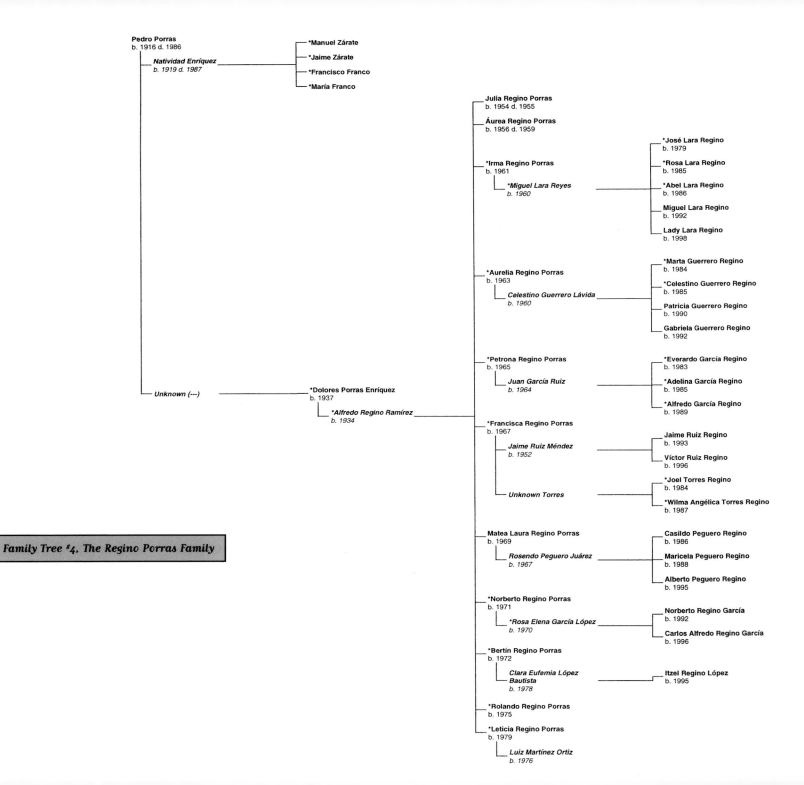

Pedro Porras
b. 1916 d. 1986

Natividad Enríquez
b. 1919 d. 1987

— *Manuel Zárate
— *Jaime Zárate
— *Francisco Franco
— *María Franco

Julia Regino Porras
b. 1954 d. 1955

Áurea Regino Porras
b. 1956 d. 1959

*Irma Regino Porras
b. 1961

Miguel Lara Reyes
b. 1960

— *José Lara Regino
b. 1979
— *Rosa Lara Regino
b. 1985
— *Abel Lara Regino
b. 1986
— Miguel Lara Regino
b. 1992
— Lady Lara Regino
b. 1998

*Aurelia Regino Porras
b. 1963

Celestino Guerrero Lávida
b. 1960

— *Marta Guerrero Regino
b. 1984
— *Celestino Guerrero Regino
b. 1985
— Patricia Guerrero Regino
b. 1990
— Gabriela Guerrero Regino
b. 1992

*Petrona Regino Porras
b. 1965

Juan García Ruiz
b. 1964

— *Everardo García Regino
b. 1983
— *Adelina García Regino
b. 1985
— *Alfredo García Regino
b. 1989

— *Unknown* (---)

*Dolores Porras Enríquez
b. 1937

Alfredo Regino Ramírez
b. 1934

*Francisca Regino Porras
b. 1967

Jaime Ruiz Méndez
b. 1952

— Jaime Ruiz Regino
b. 1993
— Víctor Ruiz Regino
b. 1996

Unknown Torres

— *Joel Torres Regino
b. 1984
— *Wilma Angélica Torres Regino
b. 1987

Matea Laura Regino Porras
b. 1969

Rosendo Peguero Juárez
b. 1967

— Casildo Peguero Regino
b. 1986
— Maricela Peguero Regino
b. 1988
— Alberto Peguero Regino
b. 1995

*Norberto Regino Porras
b. 1971

Rosa Elena García López
b. 1970

— Norberto Regino García
b. 1992
— Carlos Alfredo Regino García
b. 1996

*Bertín Regino Porras
b. 1972

*Clara Eufemia López
Bautista*
b. 1978

— Itzel Regino López
b. 1995

*Rolando Regino Porras
b. 1975

*Leticia Regino Porras
b. 1979

Luiz Martínez Ortiz
b. 1976

Family Tree #4, The Regino Porras Family

166

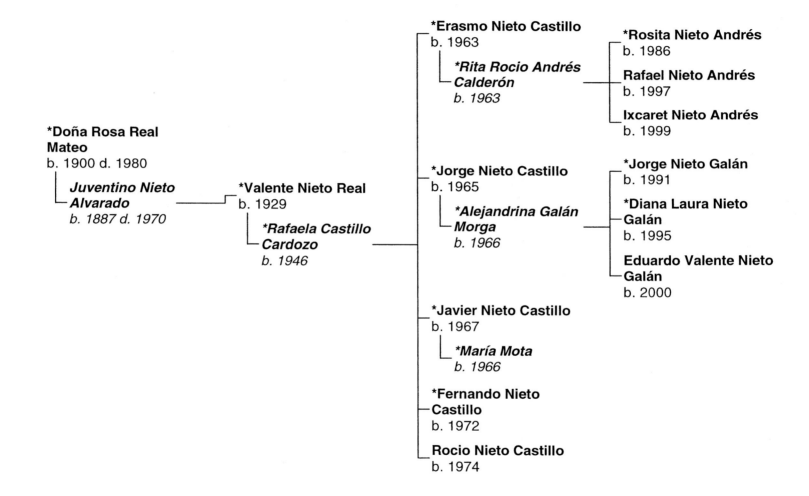

*Doña Rosa Real Mateo
b. 1900 d. 1980

Juventino Nieto Alvarado
b. 1887 d. 1970

*Valente Nieto Real
b. 1929

*Rafaela Castillo Cardozo
b. 1946

*Erasmo Nieto Castillo
b. 1963

*Rita Rocio Andrés Calderón
b. 1963

*Rosita Nieto Andrés
b. 1986

Rafael Nieto Andrés
b. 1997

Ixcaret Nieto Andrés
b. 1999

*Jorge Nieto Castillo
b. 1965

*Alejandrina Galán Morga
b. 1966

*Jorge Nieto Galán
b. 1991

*Diana Laura Nieto Galán
b. 1995

Eduardo Valente Nieto Galán
b. 2000

*Javier Nieto Castillo
b. 1967

*María Mota
b. 1966

*Fernando Nieto Castillo
b. 1972

Rocio Nieto Castillo
b. 1974

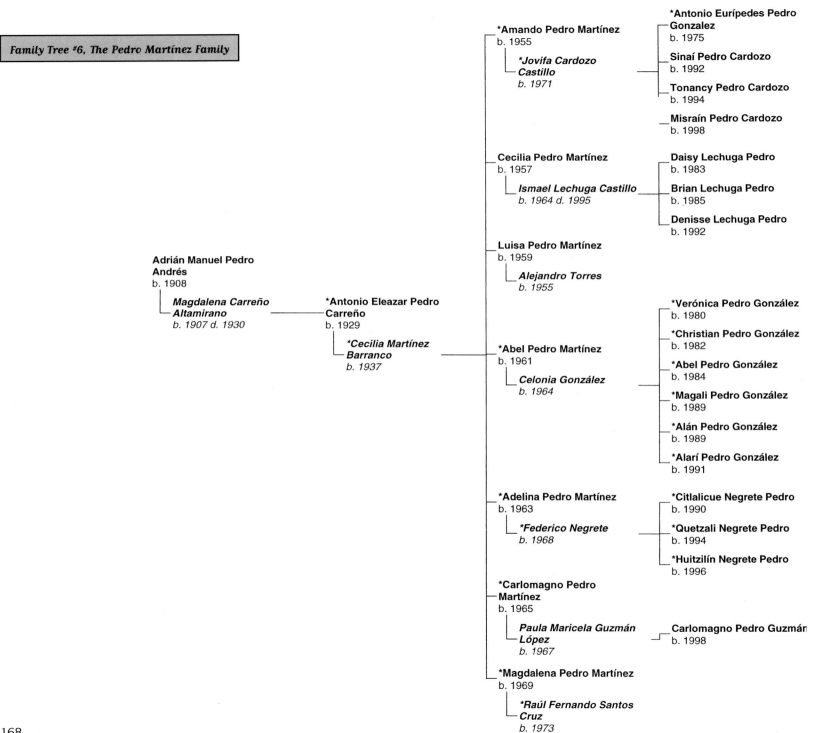

Adrián Manuel Pedro Andrés
b. 1908

Magdalena Carreño Altamirano
b. 1907 d. 1930

*Antonio Eleazar Pedro Carreño
b. 1929

Cecilia Martínez Barranco
b. 1937

*Amando Pedro Martínez
b. 1955

Jovita Cardozo Castillo
b. 1971

*Antonio Eurípedes Pedro Gonzalez
b. 1975

Sinaí Pedro Cardozo
b. 1992

Tonancy Pedro Cardozo
b. 1994

Misraín Pedro Cardozo
b. 1998

Cecilia Pedro Martínez
b. 1957

Ismael Lechuga Castillo
b. 1964 d. 1995

Daisy Lechuga Pedro
b. 1983

Brian Lechuga Pedro
b. 1985

Denisse Lechuga Pedro
b. 1992

Luisa Pedro Martínez
b. 1959

Alejandro Torres
b. 1955

*Abel Pedro Martínez
b. 1961

Celonia González
b. 1964

*Verónica Pedro González
b. 1980

*Christian Pedro González
b. 1982

*Abel Pedro González
b. 1984

*Magali Pedro González
b. 1989

*Alán Pedro González
b. 1989

*Alarí Pedro González
b. 1991

*Adelina Pedro Martínez
b. 1963

Federico Negrete
b. 1968

*Citlalicue Negrete Pedro
b. 1990

*Quetzali Negrete Pedro
b. 1994

*Huitzilín Negrete Pedro
b. 1996

*Carlomagno Pedro Martínez
b. 1965

Paula Maricela Guzmán López
b. 1967

Carlomagno Pedro Guzmán
b. 1998

*Magdalena Pedro Martínez
b. 1969

Raúl Fernando Santos Cruz
b. 1973

168

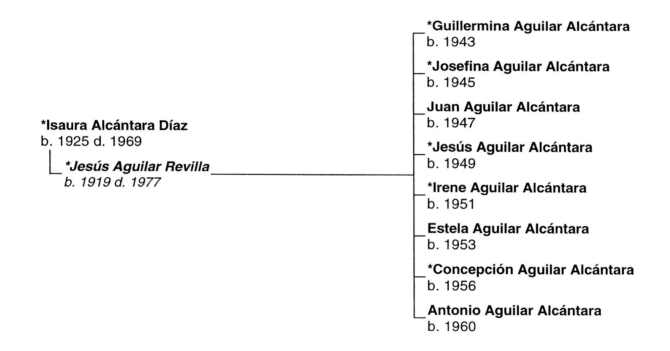

*Guillermina Aguilar Alcántara
b. 1943

*Josefina Aguilar Alcántara
b. 1945

Juan Aguilar Alcántara
b. 1947

*Jesús Aguilar Alcántara
b. 1949

*Irene Aguilar Alcántara
b. 1951

Estela Aguilar Alcántara
b. 1953

*Concepción Aguilar Alcántara
b. 1956

Antonio Aguilar Alcántara
b. 1960

*Isaura Alcántara Díaz
b. 1925 d. 1969

*Jesús Aguilar Revilla
b. 1919 d. 1977

Family Tree #7-A, Family of Guillermina Aguilar Alcántara

*Silvia García Aguilar
b. 1960
  Antonio Cruz Mendoza
  b. 1950 — **Esmeralda Cruz García** b. 2000

*Juan García Aguilar
b. 1962
  *Gabriela Sarmiento
  b. 1980
    Karina García Sarmiento b. 1998
    Ricardo García Sarmiento b. 2000

*Alejandro García Aguilar
b. 1963
  *Alejandra San Juan
  b. 1963
    Imelda Sacorro García San Juan b. 1986
    Roberto García San Juan b. 1988

*Fidel García Aguilar
b. 1964
  *Guadalupe Martínez Díaz
  b. 1971
    Cristina García Martínez b. 1992
    Mercedes García Martínez b. 1993
    Ángela García Martínez b. 1997
    Frank García Martínez b. 2000

*Maximina García Aguilar
b. 1965
  Luis García
  b. 1953
    Alba García García b. 1987
    Pedro García García b. 1989
    Juliana García García b. 1991

*Julián García Aguilar
b. 1966
  Matilde Rosario
  b. 1971
    Jesús García Rosario b. 1990
    Julio García Rosario b. 1991
    Estefana García Rosario b. 1994
    Martín García Rosario b. 1997
    Roxana García Rosario b. 2000

*Isabel García Aguilar
b. 1968
  Arnulfo Badilla Pérez
  b. 1973 — **Rosario Badilla García** b. 1997

*Guadalupe García Aguilar
b. 1978
  Mauro González Vázquez
  b. 1980 — **Jaime González García** b. 1999

*Polo García Aguilar
b. 1980

*Guillermina Aguilar Alcántara
b. 1943
  *Leopoldo García Cruz
  b. 1939

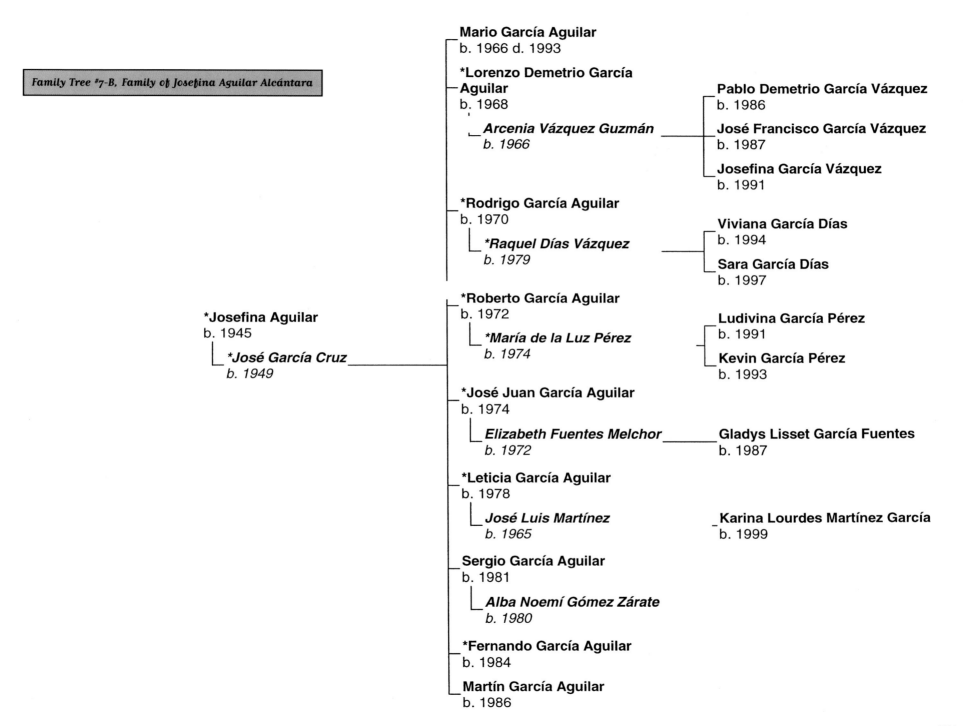

Mario García Aguilar
b. 1966 d. 1993

*Lorenzo Demetrio García Aguilar
b. 1968

    Arcenia Vázquez Guzmán
    b. 1966

Pablo Demetrio García Vázquez
b. 1986

José Francisco García Vázquez
b. 1987

Josefina García Vázquez
b. 1991

*Rodrigo García Aguilar
b. 1970

    *Raquel Días Vázquez
    b. 1979

Viviana García Días
b. 1994

Sara García Días
b. 1997

*Josefina Aguilar
b. 1945

    *José García Cruz
    b. 1949

*Roberto García Aguilar
b. 1972

    *María de la Luz Pérez
    b. 1974

Ludivina García Pérez
b. 1991

Kevin García Pérez
b. 1993

*José Juan García Aguilar
b. 1974

    Elizabeth Fuentes Melchor
    b. 1972

Gladys Lisset García Fuentes
b. 1987

*Leticia García Aguilar
b. 1978

    José Luis Martínez
    b. 1965

Karina Lourdes Martínez García
b. 1999

Sergio García Aguilar
b. 1981

    Alba Noemí Gómez Zárate
    b. 1980

*Fernando García Aguilar
b. 1984

Martín García Aguilar
b. 1986

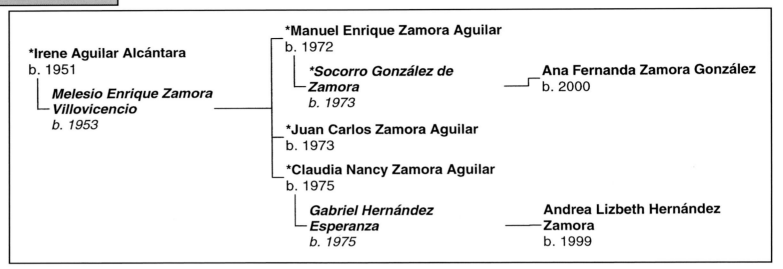

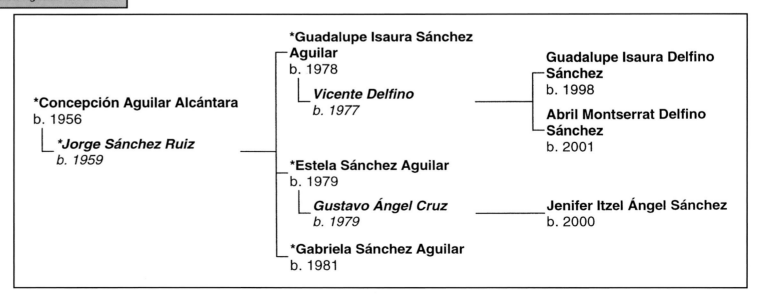

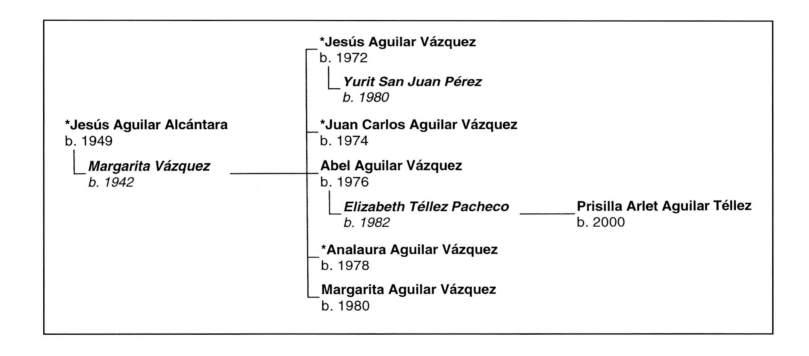

*Jesús Aguilar Alcántara
b. 1949

Margarita Vázquez
b. 1942

*Jesús Aguilar Vázquez
b. 1972

Yurit San Juan Pérez
b. 1980

*Juan Carlos Aguilar Vázquez
b. 1974

Abel Aguilar Vázquez
b. 1976

Elizabeth Téllez Pacheco
b. 1982

Prisilla Arlet Aguilar Téllez
b. 2000

*Analaura Aguilar Vázquez
b. 1978

Margarita Aguilar Vázquez
b. 1980

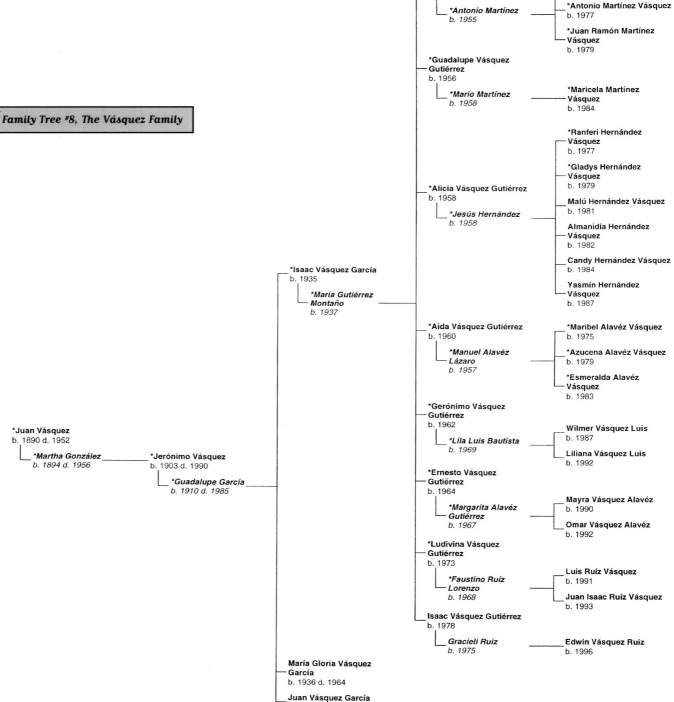

Family Tree #8, The Vásquez Family

*Juan Vásquez
b. 1890 d. 1952

*Martha González
b. 1894 d. 1956

*Jerónimo Vásquez
b. 1903 d. 1990

*Guadalupe García
b. 1910 d. 1985

*Isaac Vásquez García
b. 1935

*María Gutiérrez
Montaño
b. 1937

*Estela Vásquez Gutiérrez
b. 1954

*Antonio Martínez
b. 1955

*Rosario Martínez Vásquez
b. 1975

*Antonio Martínez Vásquez
b. 1977

*Juan Ramón Martínez
Vásquez
b. 1979

*Guadalupe Vásquez
Gutiérrez
b. 1956

*Mario Martínez
b. 1958

*Maricela Martínez
Vásquez
b. 1984

*Alicia Vásquez Gutiérrez
b. 1958

*Jesús Hernández
b. 1958

*Ranferi Hernández
Vásquez
b. 1977

*Gladys Hernández
Vásquez
b. 1979

Malú Hernández Vásquez
b. 1981

Almanidia Hernández
Vásquez
b. 1982

Candy Hernández Vásquez
b. 1984

Yasmín Hernández
Vásquez
b. 1987

*Aida Vásquez Gutiérrez
b. 1960

*Manuel Alavéz
Lázaro
b. 1957

*Maribel Alavéz Vásquez
b. 1975

*Azucena Alavéz Vásquez
b. 1979

*Esmeralda Alavéz
Vásquez
b. 1983

*Gerónimo Vásquez
Gutiérrez
b. 1962

*Lila Luis Bautista
b. 1969

Wilmer Vásquez Luis
b. 1987

Liliana Vásquez Luis
b. 1992

*Ernesto Vásquez
Gutiérrez
b. 1964

*Margarita Alavéz
Gutiérrez
b. 1967

Mayra Vásquez Alavéz
b. 1990

Omar Vásquez Alavéz
b. 1992

*Ludivina Vásquez
Gutiérrez
b. 1973

*Faustino Ruíz
Lorenzo
b. 1968

Luis Ruíz Vásquez
b. 1991

Juan Isaac Ruíz Vásquez
b. 1993

Isaac Vásquez Gutiérrez
b. 1978

Gracieli Ruiz
b. 1975

Edwin Vásquez Ruiz
b. 1996

María Gloria Vásquez
García
b. 1936 d. 1964

Juan Vásquez García
b. 1938 d. 1946

174

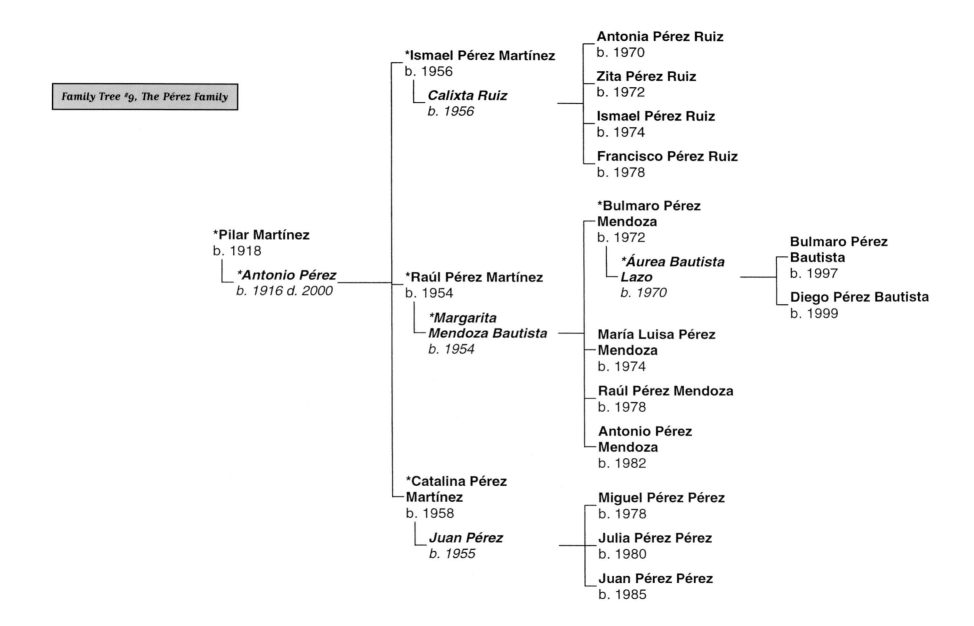

Family Tree #9, The Pérez Family

*Pilar Martínez
b. 1918
   *Antonio Pérez
   b. 1916 d. 2000

*Ismael Pérez Martínez
b. 1956
   Calixta Ruiz
   b. 1956

Antonia Pérez Ruiz
b. 1970

Zita Pérez Ruiz
b. 1972

Ismael Pérez Ruiz
b. 1974

Francisco Pérez Ruiz
b. 1978

*Raúl Pérez Martínez
b. 1954
   *Margarita Mendoza Bautista
   b. 1954

*Bulmaro Pérez Mendoza
b. 1972
   *Áurea Bautista Lazo
   b. 1970

Bulmaro Pérez Bautista
b. 1997

Diego Pérez Bautista
b. 1999

María Luisa Pérez Mendoza
b. 1974

Raúl Pérez Mendoza
b. 1978

Antonio Pérez Mendoza
b. 1982

*Catalina Pérez Martínez
b. 1958
   Juan Pérez
   b. 1955

Miguel Pérez Pérez
b. 1978

Julia Pérez Pérez
b. 1980

Juan Pérez Pérez
b. 1985

175

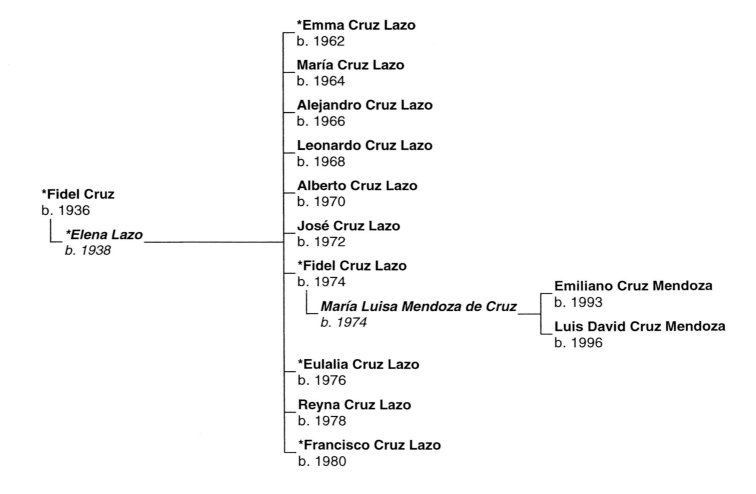

*Fidel Cruz
b. 1936

    *Elena Lazo
     b. 1938

*Emma Cruz Lazo
b. 1962

María Cruz Lazo
b. 1964

Alejandro Cruz Lazo
b. 1966

Leonardo Cruz Lazo
b. 1968

Alberto Cruz Lazo
b. 1970

José Cruz Lazo
b. 1972

*Fidel Cruz Lazo
b. 1974

    María Luisa Mendoza de Cruz
     b. 1974

Emiliano Cruz Mendoza
b. 1993

Luis David Cruz Mendoza
b. 1996

*Eulalia Cruz Lazo
b. 1976

Reyna Cruz Lazo
b. 1978

*Francisco Cruz Lazo
b. 1980

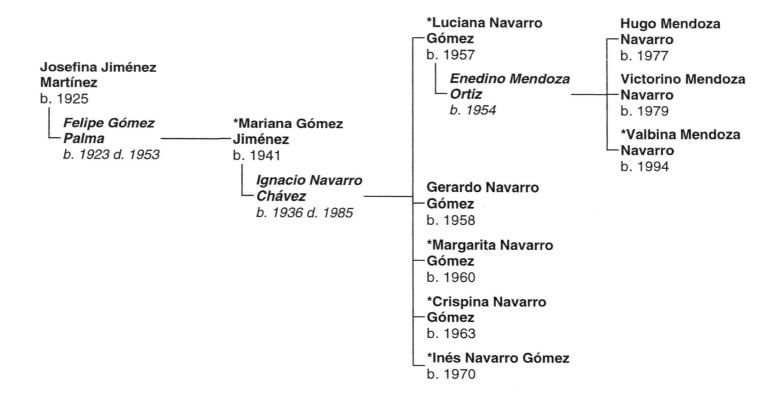

Josefina Jiménez
Martínez
b. 1925

*Felipe Gómez
Palma*
b. 1923 d. 1953

*Mariana Gómez
Jiménez
b. 1941

*Ignacio Navarro
Chávez*
b. 1936 d. 1985

*Luciana Navarro
Gómez
b. 1957

*Enedino Mendoza
Ortiz*
b. 1954

Gerardo Navarro
Gómez
b. 1958

*Margarita Navarro
Gómez
b. 1960

*Crispina Navarro
Gómez
b. 1963

*Inés Navarro Gómez
b. 1970

Hugo Mendoza
Navarro
b. 1977

Victorino Mendoza
Navarro
b. 1979

*Valbina Mendoza
Navarro
b. 1994

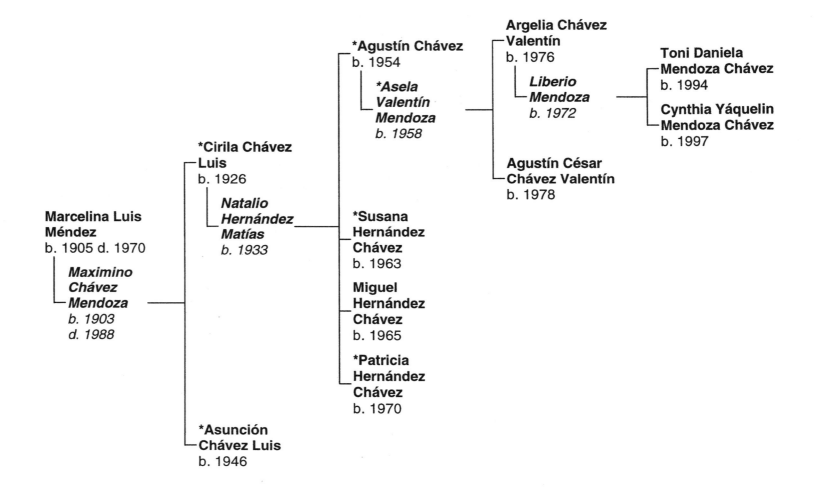

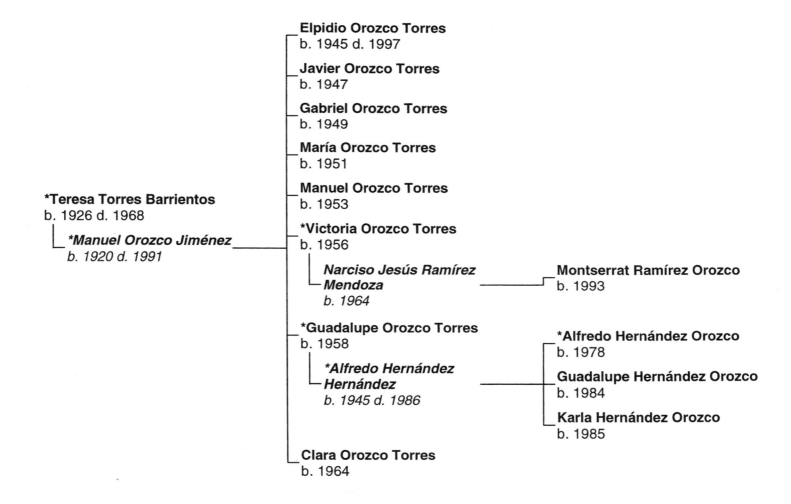

Elpidio Orozco Torres
b. 1945 d. 1997

Javier Orozco Torres
b. 1947

Gabriel Orozco Torres
b. 1949

María Orozco Torres
b. 1951

Manuel Orozco Torres
b. 1953

*Teresa Torres Barrientos
b. 1926 d. 1968

*Manuel Orozco Jiménez
b. 1920 d. 1991

*Victoria Orozco Torres
b. 1956

Narciso Jesús Ramírez
Mendoza
b. 1964

Montserrat Ramírez Orozco
b. 1993

*Guadalupe Orozco Torres
b. 1958

*Alfredo Hernández
Hernández
b. 1945 d. 1986

*Alfredo Hernández Orozco
b. 1978

Guadalupe Hernández Orozco
b. 1984

Karla Hernández Orozco
b. 1985

Clara Orozco Torres
b. 1964

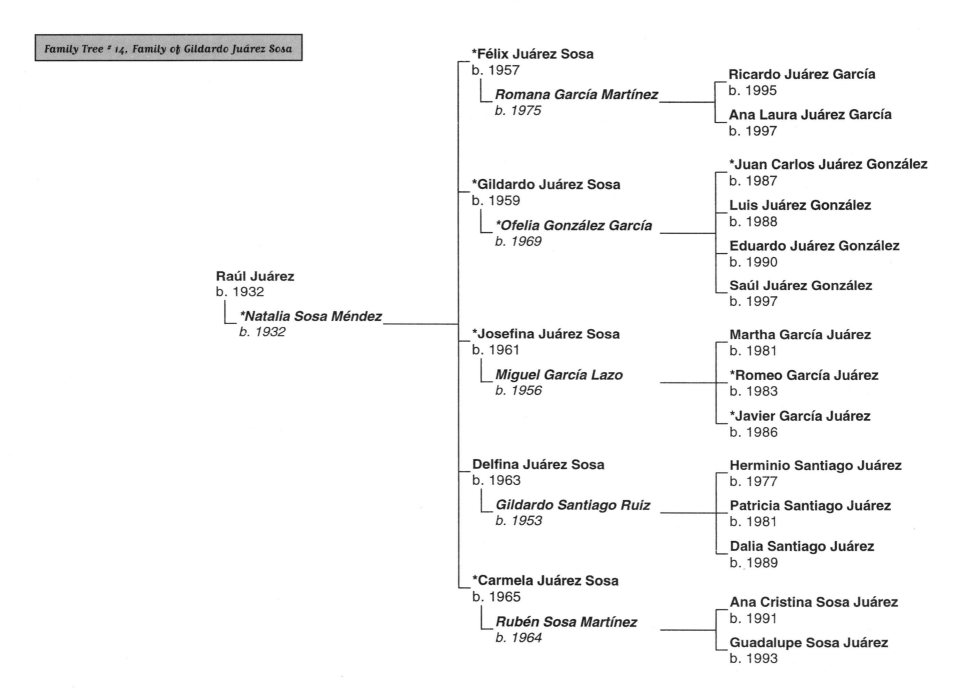

*Félix Juárez Sosa
b. 1957

Romana García Martínez
b. 1975

Ricardo Juárez García
b. 1995

Ana Laura Juárez García
b. 1997

*Gildardo Juárez Sosa
b. 1959

*Ofelia González García
b. 1969

*Juan Carlos Juárez González
b. 1987

Luis Juárez González
b. 1988

Eduardo Juárez González
b. 1990

Saúl Juárez González
b. 1997

Raúl Juárez
b. 1932

*Natalia Sosa Méndez
b. 1932

*Josefina Juárez Sosa
b. 1961

Miguel García Lazo
b. 1956

Martha García Juárez
b. 1981

*Romeo García Juárez
b. 1983

*Javier García Juárez
b. 1986

Delfina Juárez Sosa
b. 1963

Gildardo Santiago Ruiz
b. 1953

Herminio Santiago Juárez
b. 1977

Patricia Santiago Juárez
b. 1981

Dalia Santiago Juárez
b. 1989

*Carmela Juárez Sosa
b. 1965

Rubén Sosa Martínez
b. 1964

Ana Cristina Sosa Juárez
b. 1991

Guadalupe Sosa Juárez
b. 1993

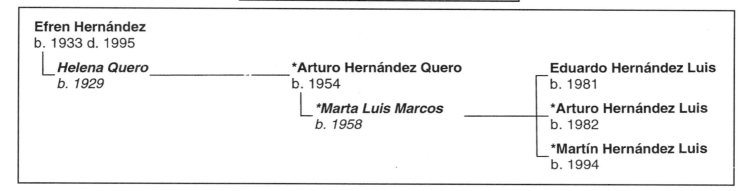

Family Tree #15, Family of Arturo Hernández Quero

Efren Hernández
b. 1933 d. 1995

Helena Quero
b. 1929

*Arturo Hernández Quero**
b. 1954

Marta Luis Marcos
b. 1958

Eduardo Hernández Luis
b. 1981

*Arturo Hernández Luis**
b. 1982

*Martín Hernández Luis**
b. 1994

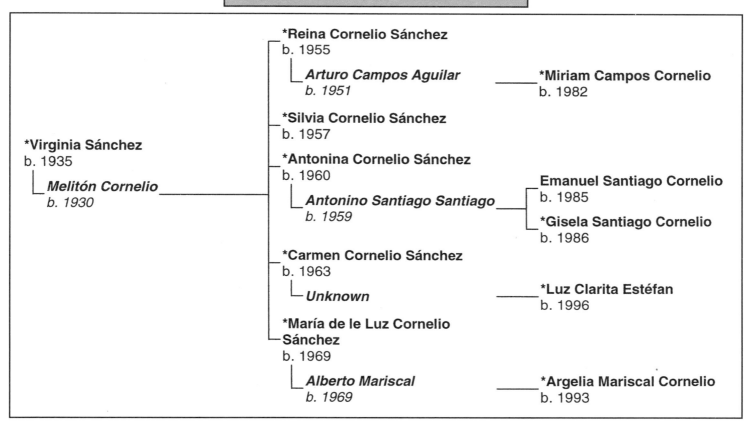

Family Tree #16, Family of Virginia Sánchez de Cornelio

*Virginia Sánchez**
b. 1935

Melitón Cornelio
b. 1930

*Reina Cornelio Sánchez**
b. 1955

Arturo Campos Aguilar
b. 1951

*Miriam Campos Cornelio**
b. 1982

*Silvia Cornelio Sánchez**
b. 1957

*Antonina Cornelio Sánchez**
b. 1960

Antonino Santiago Santiago
b. 1959

Emanuel Santiago Cornelio
b. 1985

*Gisela Santiago Cornelio**
b. 1986

*Carmen Cornelio Sánchez**
b. 1963

Unknown

*Luz Clarita Estéfan**
b. 1996

*María de le Luz Cornelio Sánchez**
b. 1969

Alberto Mariscal
b. 1969

*Argelia Mariscal Cornelio**
b. 1993

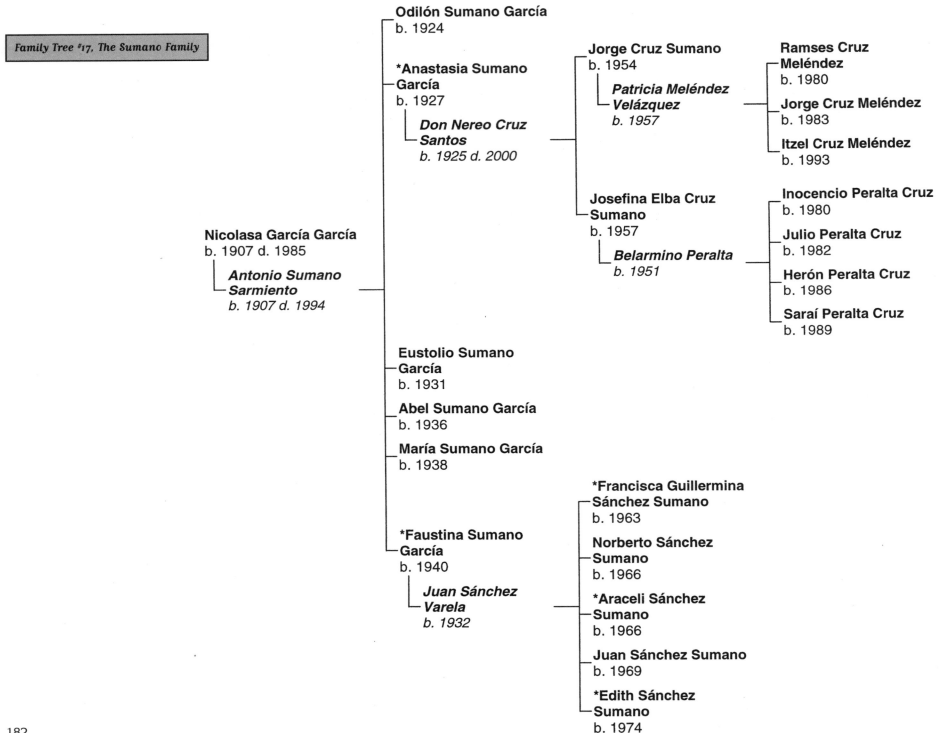

Family Tree #17, The Sumano Family

Nicolasa García García
b. 1907 d. 1985

Antonio Sumano Sarmiento
b. 1907 d. 1994

Odilón Sumano García
b. 1924

*Anastasia Sumano García
b. 1927

Don Nereo Cruz Santos
b. 1925 d. 2000

Jorge Cruz Sumano
b. 1954

Patricia Meléndez Velázquez
b. 1957

Ramses Cruz Meléndez
b. 1980

Jorge Cruz Meléndez
b. 1983

Itzel Cruz Meléndez
b. 1993

Josefina Elba Cruz Sumano
b. 1957

Belarmino Peralta
b. 1951

Inocencio Peralta Cruz
b. 1980

Julio Peralta Cruz
b. 1982

Herón Peralta Cruz
b. 1986

Saraí Peralta Cruz
b. 1989

Eustolio Sumano García
b. 1931

Abel Sumano García
b. 1936

María Sumano García
b. 1938

*Faustina Sumano García
b. 1940

Juan Sánchez Varela
b. 1932

*Francisca Guillermina Sánchez Sumano
b. 1963

Norberto Sánchez Sumano
b. 1966

*Araceli Sánchez Sumano
b. 1966

Juan Sánchez Sumano
b. 1969

*Edith Sánchez Sumano
b. 1974

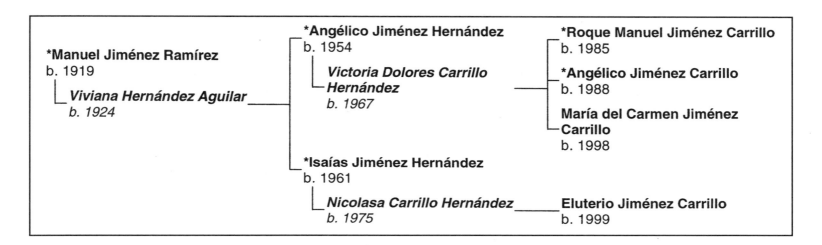

Family Tree #18, Family of Manuel Jiménez Ramírez

*Manuel Jiménez Ramírez
b. 1919

    Viviana Hernández Aguilar
    b. 1924

*Angélico Jiménez Hernández
b. 1954

    Victoria Dolores Carrillo Hernández
    b. 1967

*Isaías Jiménez Hernández
b. 1961

    Nicolasa Carrillo Hernández
    b. 1975

*Roque Manuel Jiménez Carrillo
b. 1985

*Angélico Jiménez Carrillo
b. 1988

María del Carmen Jiménez Carrillo
b. 1998

Eluterio Jiménez Carrillo
b. 1999

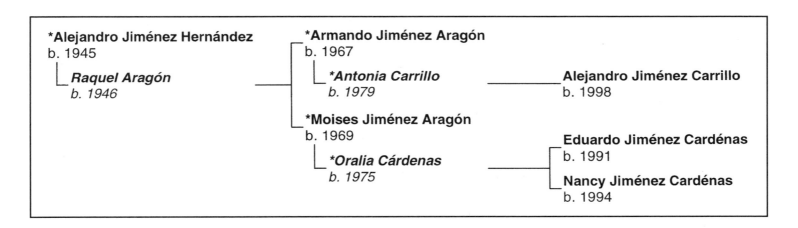

Family Tree #19, Family, of Armando and Moises Jiménez Aragón

*Alejandro Jiménez Hernández
b. 1945

    Raquel Aragón
    b. 1946

*Armando Jiménez Aragón
b. 1967

    *Antonia Carrillo
    b. 1979

*Moises Jiménez Aragón
b. 1969

    *Oralia Cárdenas
    b. 1975

Alejandro Jiménez Carrillo
b. 1998

Eduardo Jiménez Cardénas
b. 1991

Nancy Jiménez Cardénas
b. 1994

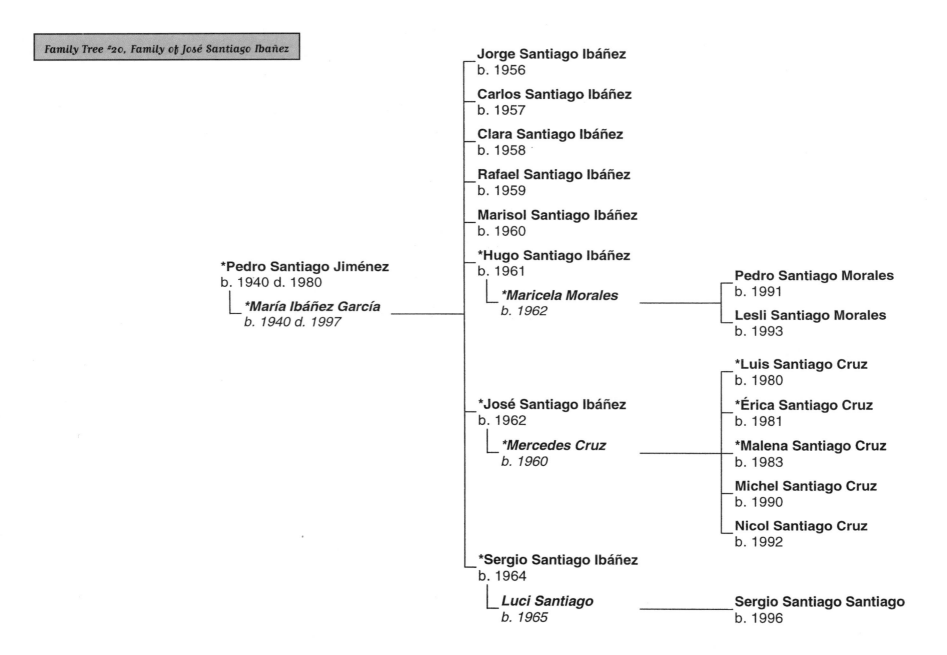

Jorge Santiago Ibáñez
b. 1956

Carlos Santiago Ibáñez
b. 1957

Clara Santiago Ibáñez
b. 1958

Rafael Santiago Ibáñez
b. 1959

Marisol Santiago Ibáñez
b. 1960

*Hugo Santiago Ibáñez
b. 1961

*Maricela Morales
b. 1962

Pedro Santiago Morales
b. 1991

Lesli Santiago Morales
b. 1993

*Pedro Santiago Jiménez
b. 1940 d. 1980

*María Ibáñez García
b. 1940 d. 1997

*José Santiago Ibáñez
b. 1962

*Mercedes Cruz
b. 1960

*Luis Santiago Cruz
b. 1980

*Érica Santiago Cruz
b. 1981

*Malena Santiago Cruz
b. 1983

Michel Santiago Cruz
b. 1990

Nicol Santiago Cruz
b. 1992

*Sergio Santiago Ibáñez
b. 1964

Luci Santiago
b. 1965

Sergio Santiago Santiago
b. 1996

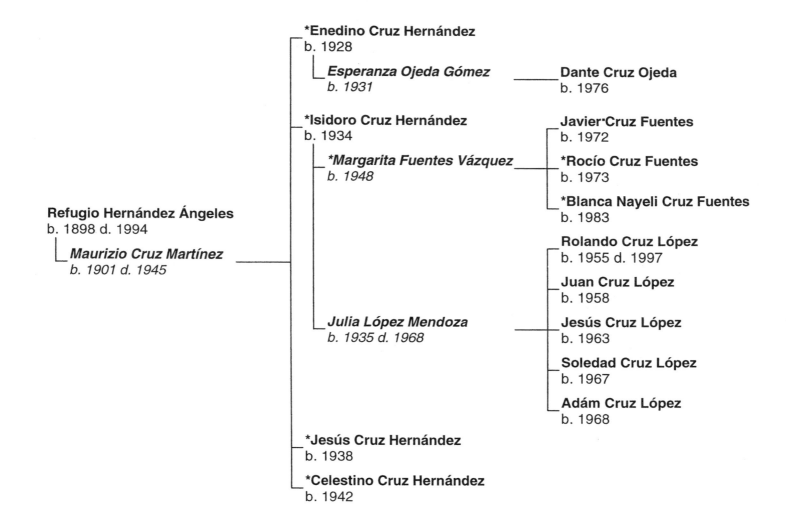

*Enedino Cruz Hernández
b. 1928

> **_*Esperanza Ojeda Gómez***   **Dante Cruz Ojeda**
> *b. 1931*   b. 1976

*Isidoro Cruz Hernández   **Javier·Cruz Fuentes**
b. 1934   b. 1972

> **_*Margarita Fuentes Vázquez***   ***Rocío Cruz Fuentes**
> *b. 1948*   b. 1973

*Blanca Nayeli Cruz Fuentes
b. 1983

Rolando Cruz López
b. 1955 d. 1997

Refugio Hernández Ángeles
b. 1898 d. 1994

> **_*Maurizio Cruz Martínez***
> *b. 1901 d. 1945*

Juan Cruz López
b. 1958

Jesús Cruz López
b. 1963

> **_*Julia López Mendoza***
> *b. 1935 d. 1968*

Soledad Cruz López
b. 1967

Adám Cruz López
b. 1968

*Jesús Cruz Hernández
b. 1938

*Celestino Cruz Hernández
b. 1942

185

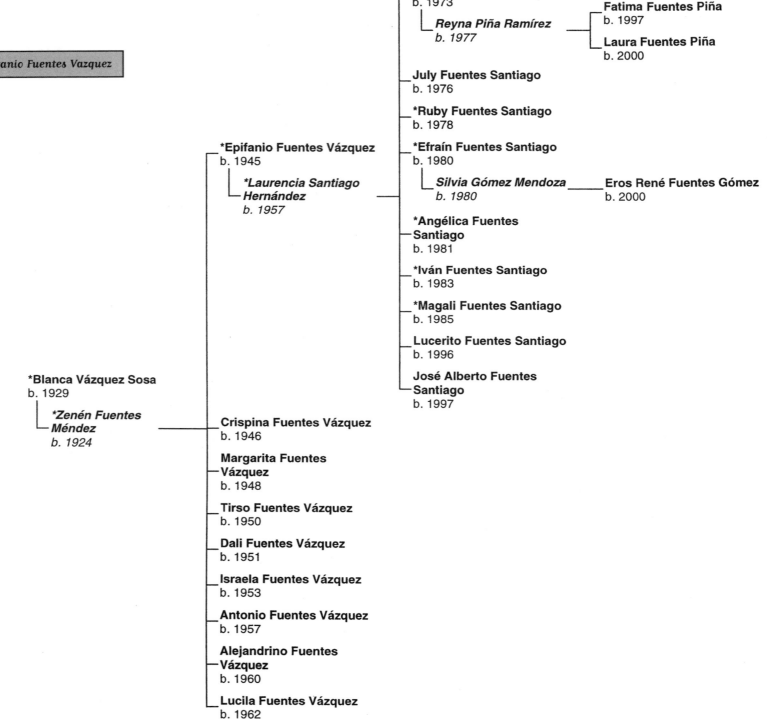

Family Tree #22, Family of Epifanio Fuentes Vazquez

*Zeni Fuentes Santiago
b. 1973

Reyna Piña Ramírez
b. 1977

Fatima Fuentes Piña
b. 1997

Laura Fuentes Piña
b. 2000

July Fuentes Santiago
b. 1976

*Ruby Fuentes Santiago
b. 1978

*Efraín Fuentes Santiago
b. 1980

Silvia Gómez Mendoza
b. 1980

Eros René Fuentes Gómez
b. 2000

*Angélica Fuentes Santiago
b. 1981

*Iván Fuentes Santiago
b. 1983

*Magali Fuentes Santiago
b. 1985

Lucerito Fuentes Santiago
b. 1996

José Alberto Fuentes Santiago
b. 1997

*Epifanio Fuentes Vázquez
b. 1945

*Laurencia Santiago Hernández
b. 1957

*Blanca Vázquez Sosa
b. 1929

*Zenén Fuentes Méndez
b. 1924

Crispina Fuentes Vázquez
b. 1946

Margarita Fuentes Vázquez
b. 1948

Tirso Fuentes Vázquez
b. 1950

Dali Fuentes Vázquez
b. 1951

Israela Fuentes Vázquez
b. 1953

Antonio Fuentes Vázquez
b. 1957

Alejandrino Fuentes Vázquez
b. 1960

Lucila Fuentes Vázquez
b. 1962

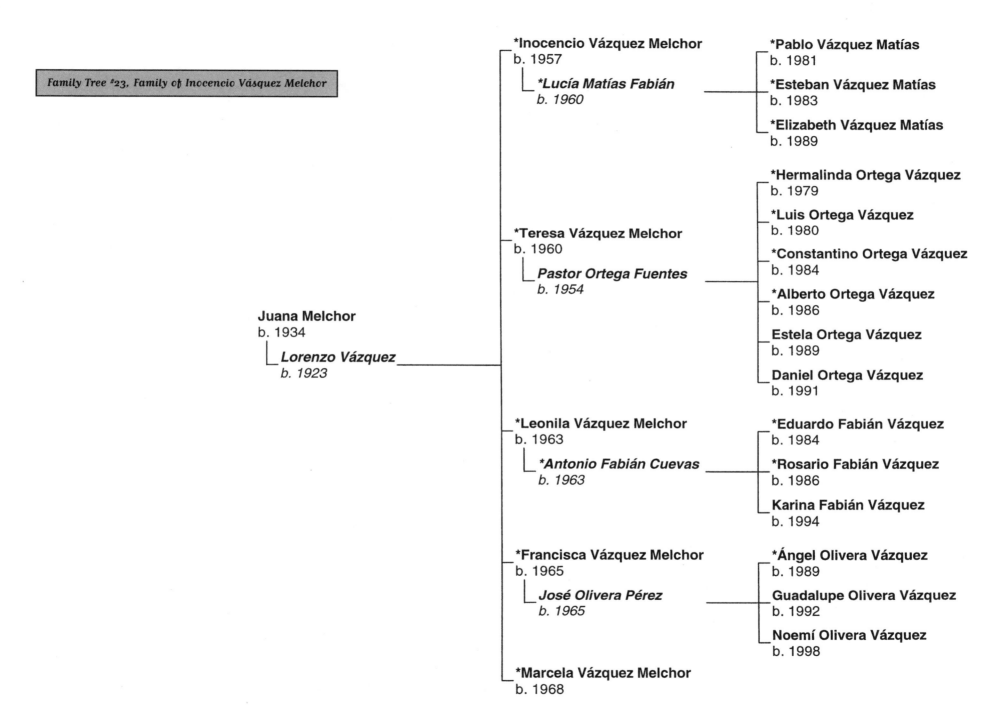

Family Tree #23, Family of Inocencio Vásquez Melchor

Juana Melchor
b. 1934
└ *Lorenzo Vázquez*
   b. 1923

*Inocencio Vázquez Melchor
b. 1957
└ **Lucía Matías Fabián*
   b. 1960

*Pablo Vázquez Matías
b. 1981

*Esteban Vázquez Matías
b. 1983

*Elizabeth Vázquez Matías
b. 1989

*Teresa Vázquez Melchor
b. 1960
└ *Pastor Ortega Fuentes*
   b. 1954

*Hermalinda Ortega Vázquez
b. 1979

*Luis Ortega Vázquez
b. 1980

*Constantino Ortega Vázquez
b. 1984

*Alberto Ortega Vázquez
b. 1986

Estela Ortega Vázquez
b. 1989

Daniel Ortega Vázquez
b. 1991

*Leonila Vázquez Melchor
b. 1963
└ **Antonio Fabián Cuevas*
   b. 1963

*Eduardo Fabián Vázquez
b. 1984

*Rosario Fabián Vázquez
b. 1986

Karina Fabián Vázquez
b. 1994

*Francisca Vázquez Melchor
b. 1965
└ *José Olivera Pérez*
   b. 1965

*Ángel Olivera Vázquez
b. 1989

Guadalupe Olivera Vázquez
b. 1992

Noemí Olivera Vázquez
b. 1998

*Marcela Vázquez Melchor
b. 1968

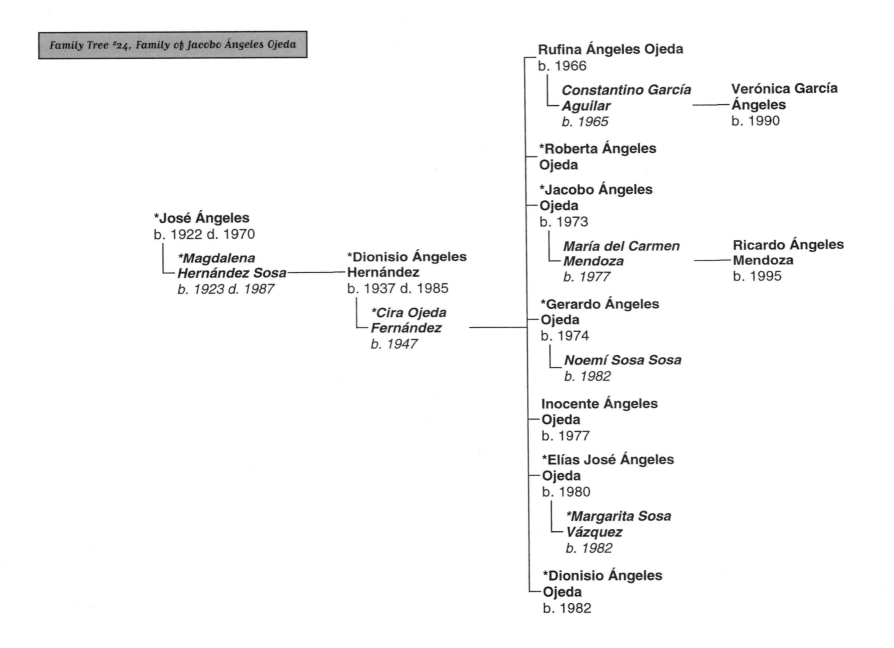

Rufina Ángeles Ojeda
b. 1966

    Constantino García Aguilar
    b. 1965

Verónica García Ángeles
b. 1990

*Roberta Ángeles Ojeda

*Jacobo Ángeles Ojeda
b. 1973

    María del Carmen Mendoza
    b. 1977

Ricardo Ángeles Mendoza
b. 1995

*José Ángeles
b. 1922 d. 1970

    *Magdalena Hernández Sosa
    b. 1923 d. 1987

*Dionisio Ángeles Hernández
b. 1937 d. 1985

    *Cira Ojeda Fernández
    b. 1947

*Gerardo Ángeles Ojeda
b. 1974

    Noemí Sosa Sosa
    b. 1982

Inocente Ángeles Ojeda
b. 1977

*Elías José Ángeles Ojeda
b. 1980

    *Margarita Sosa Vázquez
    b. 1982

*Dionisio Ángeles Ojeda
b. 1982

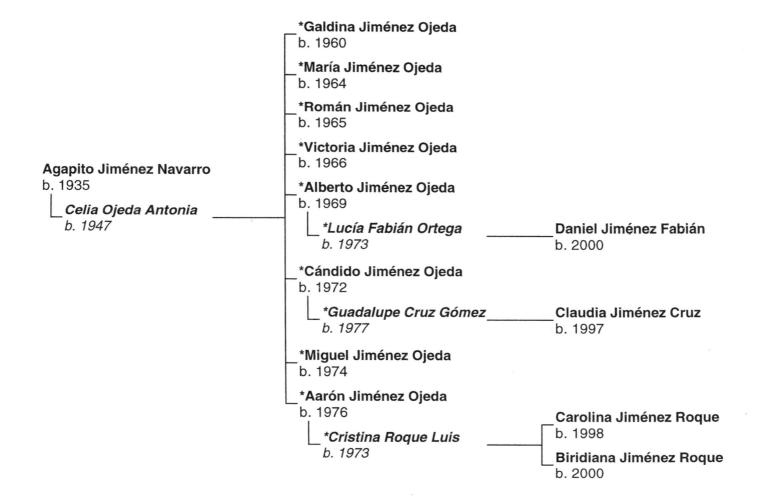

Agapito Jiménez Navarro
b. 1935

Celia Ojeda Antonia
b. 1947

*Galdina Jiménez Ojeda
b. 1960

*María Jiménez Ojeda
b. 1964

*Román Jiménez Ojeda
b. 1965

*Victoria Jiménez Ojeda
b. 1966

*Alberto Jiménez Ojeda
b. 1969

*Lucía Fabián Ortega
b. 1973

Daniel Jiménez Fabián
b. 2000

*Cándido Jiménez Ojeda
b. 1972

*Guadalupe Cruz Gómez
b. 1977

Claudia Jiménez Cruz
b. 1997

*Miguel Jiménez Ojeda
b. 1974

*Aarón Jiménez Ojeda
b. 1976

*Cristina Roque Luis
b. 1973

Carolina Jiménez Roque
b. 1998

Biridiana Jiménez Roque
b. 2000

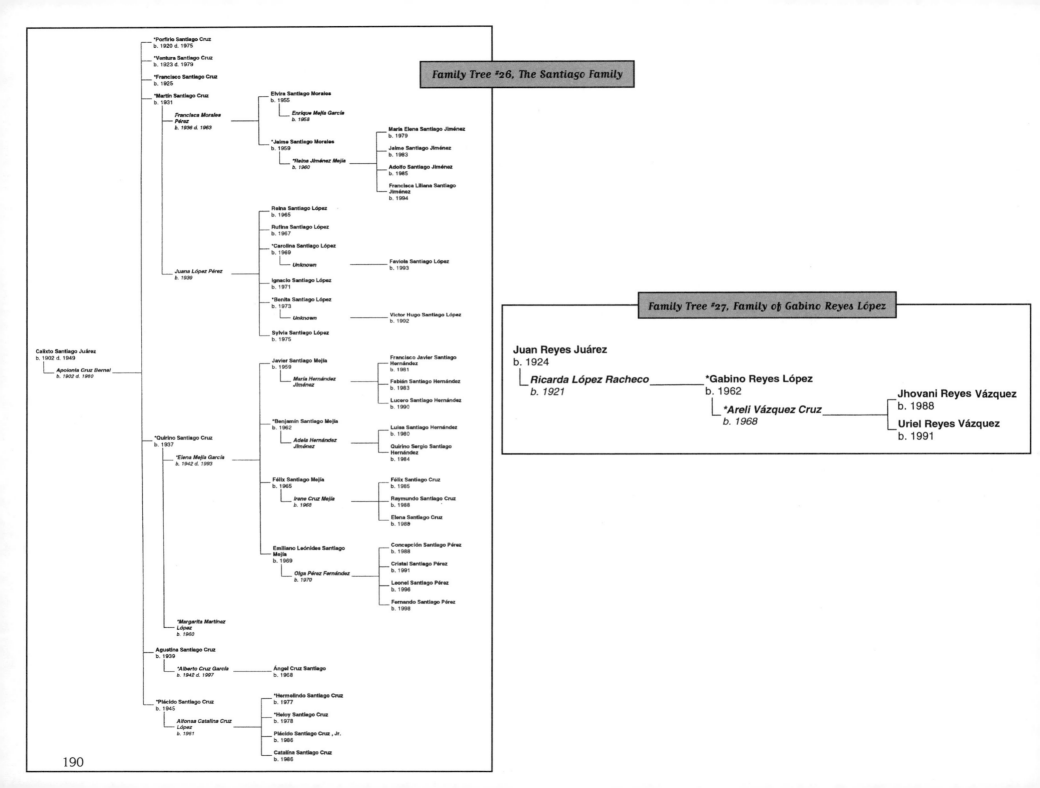

Family Tree #26, The Santiago Family

*Porfirio Santiago Cruz
b. 1920 d. 1975

*Ventura Santiago Cruz
b. 1923 d. 1979

*Francisco Santiago Cruz
b. 1925

*Martín Santiago Cruz
b. 1931

Francisca Morales Pérez
b. 1936 d. 1963

Elvira Santiago Morales
b. 1955

Enrique Mejía García
b. 1958

*Jaime Santiago Morales
b. 1959

Reina Jiménez Mejía
b. 1960

María Elena Santiago Jiménez
b. 1979

Jaime Santiago Jiménez
b. 1983

Adolfo Santiago Jiménez
b. 1985

Francisca Liliana Santiago Jiménez
b. 1994

Juana López Pérez
b. 1939

Reina Santiago López
b. 1965

Rufina Santiago López
b. 1967

*Carolina Santiago López
b. 1969

Unknown

Faviola Santiago López
b. 1993

Ignacio Santiago López
b. 1971

*Benita Santiago López
b. 1973

Unknown

Víctor Hugo Santiago López
b. 1992

Sylvia Santiago López
b. 1975

Calixto Santiago Juárez
b. 1902 d. 1949

Apolonia Cruz Bernal
b. 1902 d. 1980

*Quirino Santiago Cruz
b. 1937

Elena Mejía García
b. 1942 d. 1993

Javier Santiago Mejía
b. 1959

María Hernández Jiménez

Francisco Javier Santiago Hernández
b. 1981

Fabián Santiago Hernández
b. 1983

Lucero Santiago Hernández
b. 1990

*Benjamín Santiago Mejía
b. 1962

Adela Hernández Jiménez

Luisa Santiago Hernández
b. 1980

Quirino Sergio Santiago Hernández
b. 1984

Félix Santiago Mejía
b. 1965

Irene Cruz Mejía
b. 1968

Félix Santiago Cruz
b. 1985

Raymundo Santiago Cruz
b. 1988

Elena Santiago Cruz
b. 1988

Emiliano Leónides Santiago Mejía
b. 1969

Olga Pérez Fernández
b. 1970

Concepción Santiago Pérez
b. 1988

Cristal Santiago Pérez
b. 1991

Leonel Santiago Pérez
b. 1996

Fernando Santiago Pérez
b. 1998

Margarita Martínez López
b. 1960

Agustina Santiago Cruz
b. 1939

Alberto Cruz García
b. 1942 d. 1997

Ángel Cruz Santiago
b. 1968

*Plácido Santiago Cruz
b. 1945

Alfonsa Catalina Cruz López
b. 1961

*Hermelindo Santiago Cruz
b. 1977

*Heloy Santiago Cruz
b. 1978

Plácido Santiago Cruz , Jr.
b. 1986

Catalina Santiago Cruz
b. 1986

Family Tree #27, Family of Gabino Reyes López

Juan Reyes Juárez
b. 1924

Ricarda López Racheco
b. 1921

*Gabino Reyes López
b. 1962

Areli Vázquez Cruz
b. 1968

Jhovani Reyes Vázquez
b. 1988

Uriel Reyes Vázquez
b. 1991

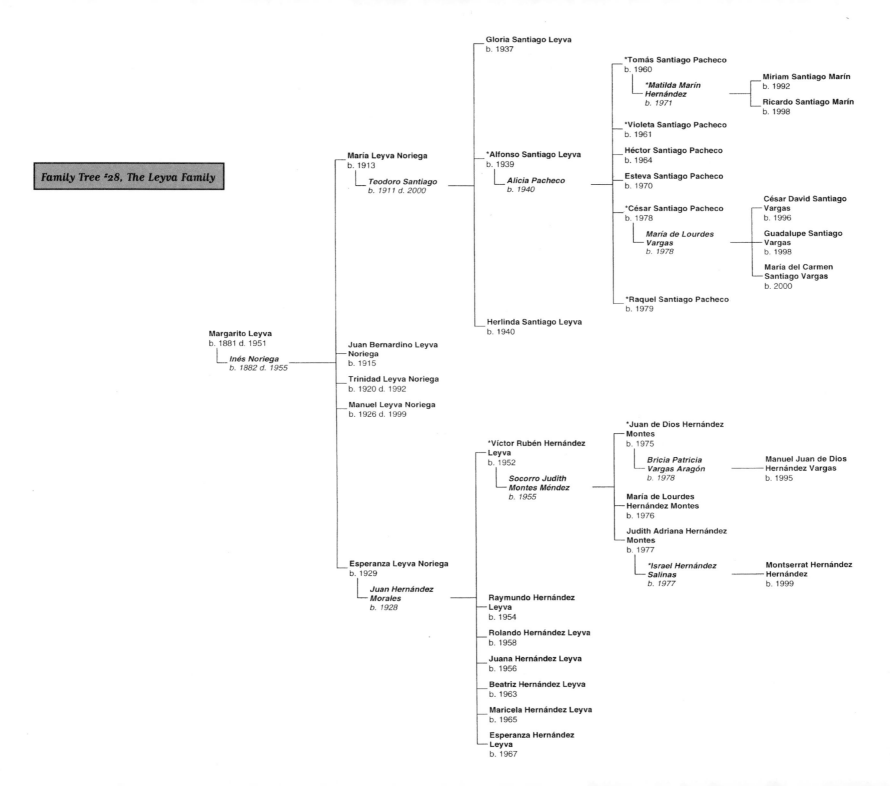

Family Tree #28, The Leyva Family

Margarito Leyva
b. 1881 d. 1951

Inés Noriega
b. 1882 d. 1955

María Leyva Noriega
b. 1913

Teodoro Santiago
b. 1911 d. 2000

Gloria Santiago Leyva
b. 1937

*Alfonso Santiago Leyva
b. 1939

Alicia Pacheco
b. 1940

*Tomás Santiago Pacheco
b. 1960

*Matilda Marín Hernández
b. 1971

Miriam Santiago Marín
b. 1992

Ricardo Santiago Marín
b. 1998

*Violeta Santiago Pacheco
b. 1961

Héctor Santiago Pacheco
b. 1964

Esteva Santiago Pacheco
b. 1970

*César Santiago Pacheco
b. 1978

María de Lourdes Vargas
b. 1978

César David Santiago Vargas
b. 1996

Guadalupe Santiago Vargas
b. 1998

María del Carmen Santiago Vargas
b. 2000

*Raquel Santiago Pacheco
b. 1979

Herlinda Santiago Leyva
b. 1940

Juan Bernardino Leyva Noriega
b. 1915

Trinidad Leyva Noriega
b. 1920 d. 1992

Manuel Leyva Noriega
b. 1926 d. 1999

Esperanza Leyva Noriega
b. 1929

Juan Hernández Morales
b. 1928

*Víctor Rubén Hernández Leyva
b. 1952

Socorro Judith Montes Méndez
b. 1955

*Juan de Dios Hernández Montes
b. 1975

Bricia Patricia Vargas Aragón
b. 1978

Manuel Juan de Dios Hernández Vargas
b. 1995

María de Lourdes Hernández Montes
b. 1976

Judith Adriana Hernández Montes
b. 1977

*Israel Hernández Salinas
b. 1977

Montserrat Hernández Hernández
b. 1999

Raymundo Hernández Leyva
b. 1954

Rolando Hernández Leyva
b. 1958

Juana Hernández Leyva
b. 1956

Beatriz Hernández Leyva
b. 1963

Maricela Hernández Leyva
b. 1965

Esperanza Hernández Leyva
b. 1967

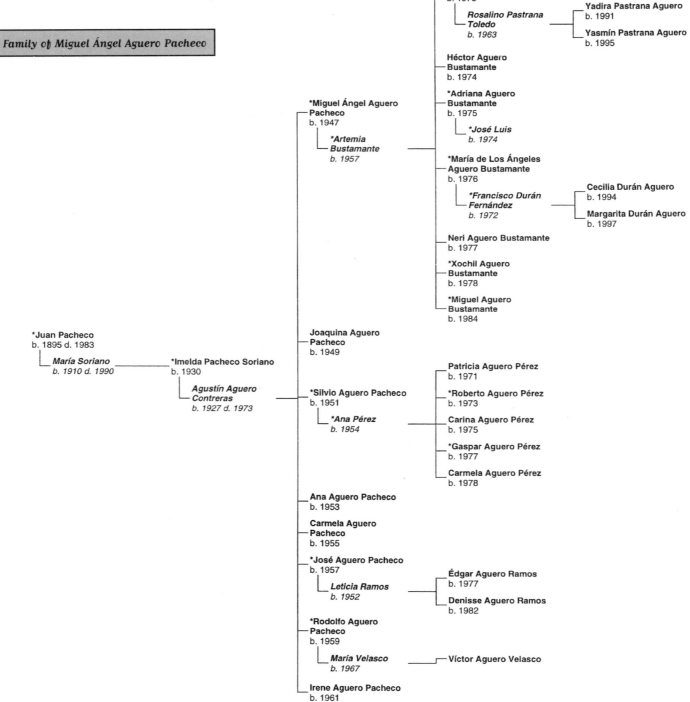

Family Tree #29, Family of Miguel Ángel Aguero Pacheco

*Andrea Aguero
Bustamante
b. 1973

  *Rosalino Pastrana
  Toledo
  b. 1963

Yadira Pastrana Aguero
b. 1991

Yasmín Pastrana Aguero
b. 1995

Héctor Aguero
Bustamante
b. 1974

*Adriana Aguero
Bustamante
b. 1975

  *José Luis
  b. 1974

*Miguel Ángel Aguero
Pacheco
b. 1947

  *Artemia
  Bustamante
  b. 1957

*María de Los Ángeles
Aguero Bustamante
b. 1976

  *Francisco Durán
  Fernández
  b. 1972

Cecilia Durán Aguero
b. 1994

Margarita Durán Aguero
b. 1997

Neri Aguero Bustamante
b. 1977

*Xochil Aguero
Bustamante
b. 1978

*Miguel Aguero
Bustamante
b. 1984

Joaquina Aguero
Pacheco
b. 1949

*Juan Pacheco
b. 1895 d. 1983

  María Soriano
  b. 1910 d. 1990

*Imelda Pacheco Soriano
b. 1930

  Agustín Aguero
  Contreras
  b. 1927 d. 1973

*Silvio Aguero Pacheco
b. 1951

  *Ana Pérez
  b. 1954

Patricia Aguero Pérez
b. 1971

*Roberto Aguero Pérez
b. 1973

Carina Aguero Pérez
b. 1975

*Gaspar Aguero Pérez
b. 1977

Carmela Aguero Pérez
b. 1978

Ana Aguero Pacheco
b. 1953

Carmela Aguero
Pacheco
b. 1955

*José Aguero Pacheco
b. 1957

  Leticia Ramos
  b. 1952

Édgar Aguero Ramos
b. 1977

Denisse Aguero Ramos
b. 1982

*Rodolfo Aguero
Pacheco
b. 1959

  María Velasco
  b. 1967

Víctor Aguero Velasco

Irene Aguero Pacheco
b. 1961

Maurilio Aguilar Pacheco
b. 1908

    Acacia Velasco Juárez
     b. 1917

Juan Aguilar Velasco
b. 1935

Georgina Aguilar Velasco
b. 1936

Salomón Aguilar Velasco
b. 1938

Amado Aguilar Velasco
b. 1939

Herlinda Aguilar Velasco
b. 1941

María Luisa Aguilar Velasco
b. 1943

Víctor Aguilar Velasco
b. 1944

Salvador Aguilar Velasco
b. 1945

Aurelio Aguilar Velasco
b. 1947

Soledad Aguilar Velasco
b. 1949

*Jesús Aguilar Velasco
b. 1950

*Ángel Aguilar Velasco
b. 1952 d. 1997

Manuela Aguilar Velasco
b. 1953

*Apolinar Aguilar Velasco
b. 1959

Family Tree # 31, Family of Justo Xuana Luis

*Severiano Xuana Hernández
b. 1914 d. 1979

Luz Luis Hernández
b. 1924 d. 1988

*Abad Xuana Luis
b. 1940

Catalina Gómez Mendoza ——— ***Antonio Xuana Gómez**
b. 1965

Inés Velasco Salmerón
b. 1950

*Floriberta Xuana Velasco
b. 1975

*Ana Xuana Velasco
b. 1976

*Víctor Xuana Velasco
b. 1977

*René Xuana Velasco
b. 1978

Rufino Xuana Luis
b. 1957 d. 1974

Viviana Xuana Luis
b. 1959

*Ventura Fabián Martínez
b. 1944

*Martín Fabián Xuana
b. 1978

*Norberto Fabián Xuana
b. 1979

María Eugenia Fabián Xuana
b. 1980

Juana Fabián Xuana
b. 1982

Teresa Fabián Xuana
b. 1985

Francisca Fabián Xuana
b. 1988

*Adrián Xuana Luis
b. 1959

*Justo Xuana Luis
b. 1964

Feliza Fabián Mendoza
b. 1960

*Silvia Xuana Fabián
b. 1979

*Edilberto Xuana Fabián
b. 1981

Justo Xuana Fabián
b. 1983 d. 1984

*Martín Xuana Fabián
b. 1985

*Justina Xuana Fabián
b. 1988

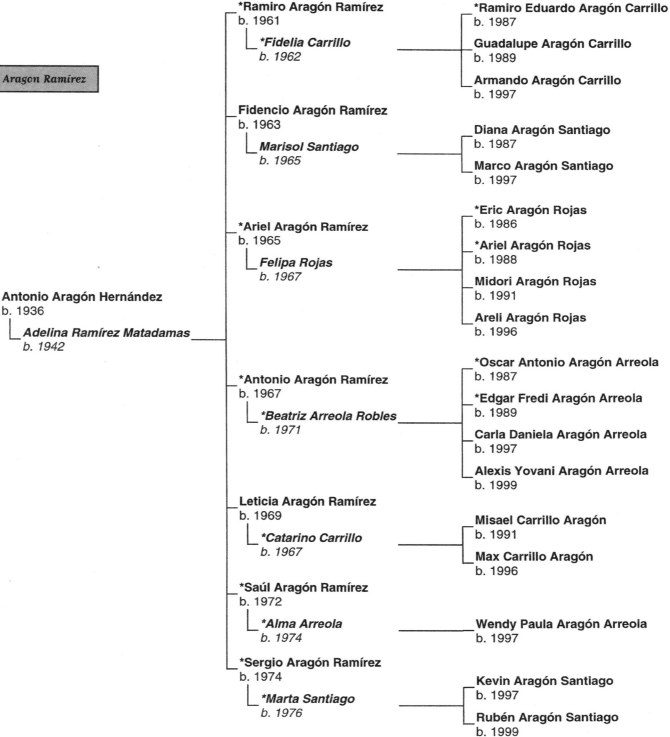

Family Tree # 32, Family of Antonio Aragon Ramírez

Antonio Aragón Hernández
b. 1936

Adelina Ramírez Matadamas
b. 1942

*Ramiro Aragón Ramírez
b. 1961

*Fidelia Carrillo
b. 1962

*Ramiro Eduardo Aragón Carrillo
b. 1987

Guadalupe Aragón Carrillo
b. 1989

Armando Aragón Carrillo
b. 1997

Fidencio Aragón Ramírez
b. 1963

Marisol Santiago
b. 1965

Diana Aragón Santiago
b. 1987

Marco Aragón Santiago
b. 1997

*Ariel Aragón Ramírez
b. 1965

Felipa Rojas
b. 1967

*Eric Aragón Rojas
b. 1986

*Ariel Aragón Rojas
b. 1988

Midori Aragón Rojas
b. 1991

Areli Aragón Rojas
b. 1996

*Antonio Aragón Ramírez
b. 1967

*Beatriz Arreola Robles
b. 1971

*Oscar Antonio Aragón Arreola
b. 1987

*Edgar Fredi Aragón Arreola
b. 1989

Carla Daniela Aragón Arreola
b. 1997

Alexis Yovani Aragón Arreola
b. 1999

Leticia Aragón Ramírez
b. 1969

*Catarino Carrillo
b. 1967

Misael Carrillo Aragón
b. 1991

Max Carrillo Aragón
b. 1996

*Saúl Aragón Ramírez
b. 1972

*Alma Arreola
b. 1974

Wendy Paula Aragón Arreola
b. 1997

*Sergio Aragón Ramírez
b. 1974

*Marta Santiago
b. 1976

Kevin Aragón Santiago
b. 1997

Rubén Aragón Santiago
b. 1999

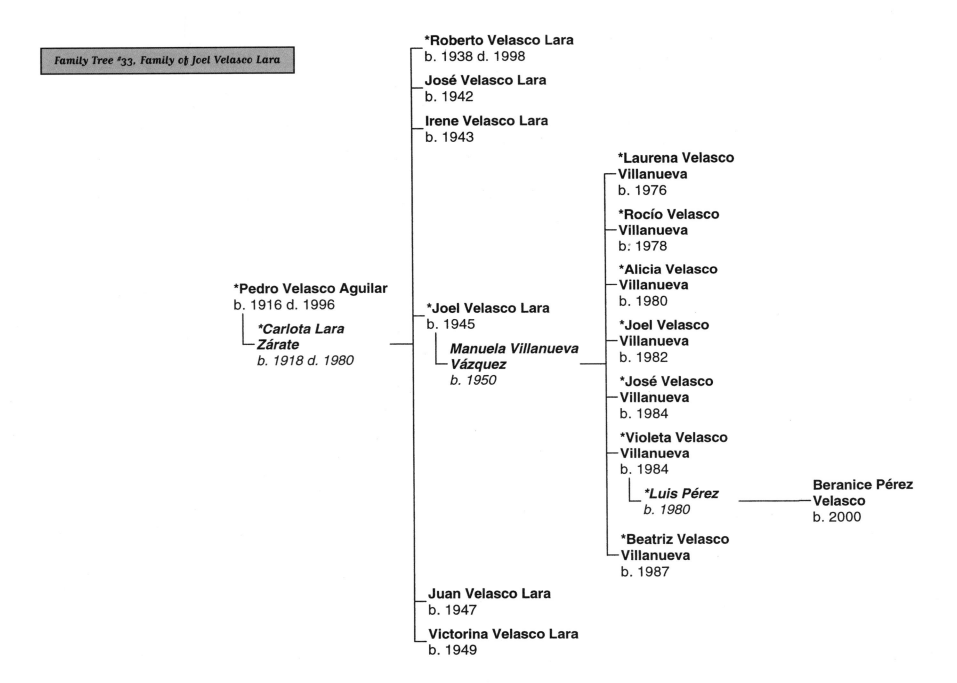

Family Tree #33. Family of Joel Velasco Lara

*Roberto Velasco Lara
b. 1938 d. 1998

José Velasco Lara
b. 1942

Irene Velasco Lara
b. 1943

*Pedro Velasco Aguilar
b. 1916 d. 1996

*Carlota Lara Zárate
b. 1918 d. 1980

*Joel Velasco Lara
b. 1945

Manuela Villanueva Vázquez
b. 1950

*Laurena Velasco Villanueva
b. 1976

*Rocío Velasco Villanueva
b: 1978

*Alicia Velasco Villanueva
b. 1980

*Joel Velasco Villanueva
b. 1982

*José Velasco Villanueva
b. 1984

*Violeta Velasco Villanueva
b. 1984

*Luis Pérez
b. 1980

Beranice Pérez Velasco
b. 2000

*Beatriz Velasco Villanueva
b. 1987

Juan Velasco Lara
b. 1947

Victorina Velasco Lara
b. 1949

196

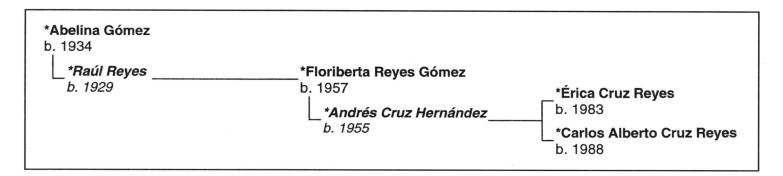

Family Tree #34, Family of Floriberta Reyes Gómez

*Abelina Gómez
b. 1934

└ ***Raúl Reyes** _____ ***Floriberta Reyes Gómez**
    b. 1929   b. 1957

                                 └ ***Andrés Cruz Hernández** _____ ***Érica Cruz Reyes**
                                     b. 1955   b. 1983
                                                                       └ ***Carlos Alberto Cruz Reyes**
                                                                         b. 1988

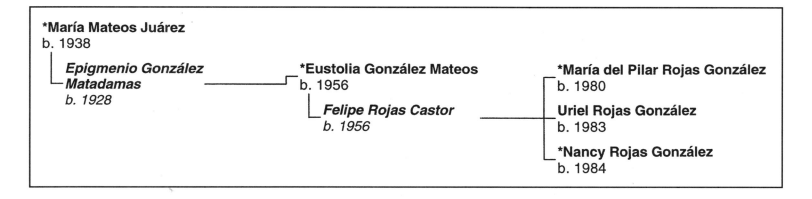

Family Tree # 35, Family of Eustolia González Mateos

*María Mateos Juárez
b. 1938

└ **Epigmenio González Matadamas** _____ ***Eustolia González Mateos** _____ ***María del Pilar Rojas González**
    b. 1928   b. 1956   b. 1980

                                     └ **Felipe Rojas Castor** _____ **Uriel Rojas González**
                                       b. 1956   b. 1983

                                                                     └ ***Nancy Rojas González**
                                                                     b. 1984

*David Villafañe
b. 1928 d. 1970

└ ***Felicitas Acevedo Clemente**
b. 1933

*Antonio Villafañe Acevedo
b. 1947

└ ***Enriqueta López Oliver**
b. 1952

*Guadalupe Villafañe López
b. 1969

└ **Federico Gabriel López**
b. 1969 d. 1998

*Anahí Villafañe López
b. 1986

*Alejandra Gabriel Villafañe
b. 1990

*Gisela Gabriel Villafañe
b. 1991

*Montserrat Gabriel Villafañe
b. 1992

*Manuel Villafañe López
b. 1973

*Marco Antonio Villafañe López
b. 1977

*Verónica Villafañe López
b. 1978

└ **Juan Raúl Santiago**
b. 1978

*Nancy Lizbeth Santiago Villafañe
b. 1994

*Érica Janet Santiago Villafañe
b. 1996

*Daniel Alejandra Villafañe López
b. 1985

Alicia Villafañe Acevedo
b. 1954

*David Villafañe Acevedo
b. 1961

María Villafañe Acevedo
b. 1963

Juan Villafañe Acevedo
b. 1965

*Octaviano Villafañe Acevedo
b. 1966

Angelina Villafañe Acevedo
b. 1969

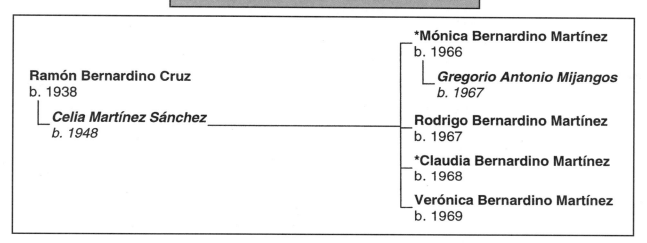

Family Tree #37, Family of Mónica Bernardino Martínez

Ramón Bernardino Cruz
b. 1938

    Celia Martínez Sánchez
    b. 1948

*Mónica Bernardino Martínez
b. 1966

    Gregorio Antonio Mijangos
    b. 1967

Rodrigo Bernardino Martínez
b. 1967

*Claudia Bernardino Martínez
b. 1968

Verónica Bernardino Martínez
b. 1969

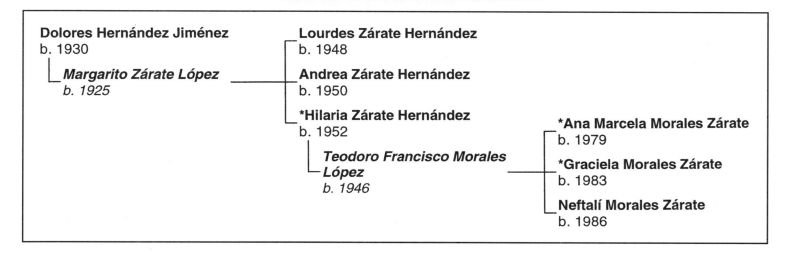

Family Tree #38, Family of Hilaria Zárate Hernández

Dolores Hernández Jiménez
b. 1930

    Margarito Zárate López
    b. 1925

Lourdes Zárate Hernández
b. 1948

Andrea Zárate Hernández
b. 1950

*Hilaria Zárate Hernández
b. 1952

    Teodoro Francisco Morales López
    b. 1946

*Ana Marcela Morales Zárate
b. 1979

*Graciela Morales Zárate
b. 1983

Neftalí Morales Zárate
b. 1986

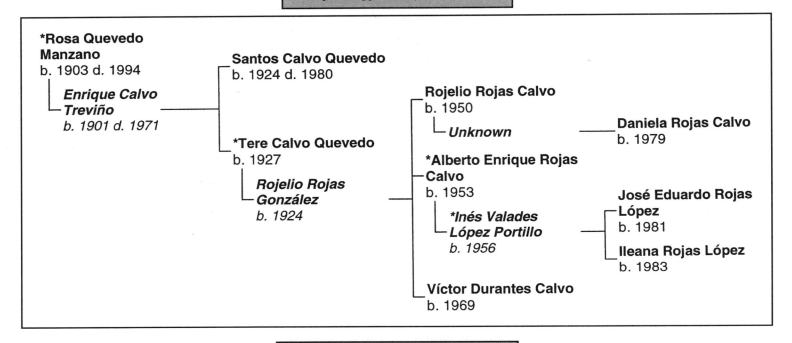

*Rosa Quevedo Manzano
b. 1903 d. 1994

   Enrique Calvo Treviño
   b. 1901 d. 1971

Santos Calvo Quevedo
b. 1924 d. 1980

*Tere Calvo Quevedo
b. 1927

   Rojelio Rojas González
   b. 1924

Rojelio Rojas Calvo
b. 1950

   Unknown

Daniela Rojas Calvo
b. 1979

*Alberto Enrique Rojas Calvo
b. 1953

   *Inés Valades López Portillo
   b. 1956

José Eduardo Rojas López
b. 1981

Ileana Rojas López
b. 1983

Víctor Durantes Calvo
b. 1969

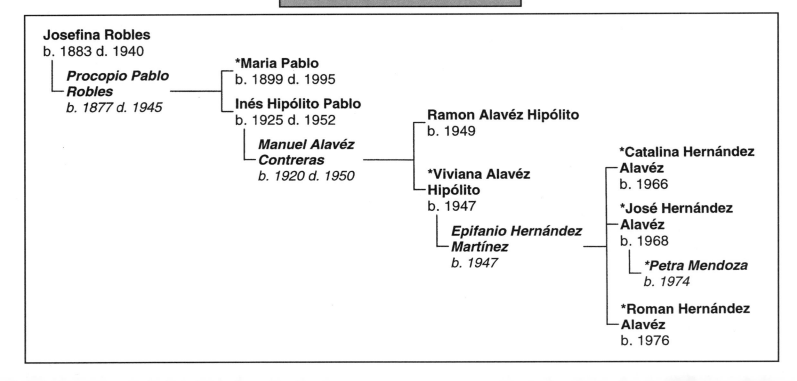

Josefina Robles
b. 1883 d. 1940

   Procopio Pablo Robles
   b. 1877 d. 1945

*Maria Pablo
b. 1899 d. 1995

Inés Hipólito Pablo
b. 1925 d. 1952

   Manuel Alavéz Contreras
   b. 1920 d. 1950

Ramon Alavéz Hipólito
b. 1949

*Viviana Alavéz Hipólito
b. 1947

   Epifanio Hernández Martínez
   b. 1947

*Catalina Hernández Alavéz
b. 1966

*José Hernández Alavéz
b. 1968

   *Petra Mendoza
   b. 1974

*Roman Hernández Alavéz
b. 1976

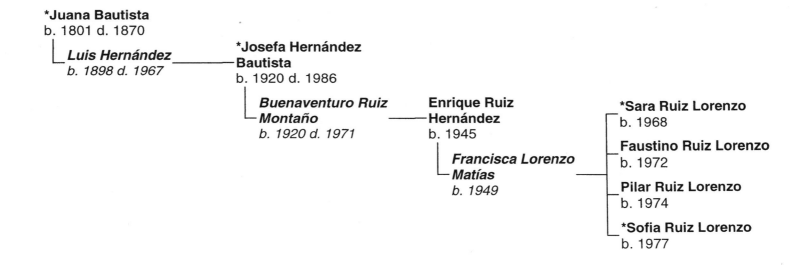

Family Tree #41, Family of Sofía Ruíz Lorenzo

*Juana Bautista
b. 1801 d. 1870

Luis Hernández
b. 1898 d. 1967

***Josefa Hernández
Bautista**
b. 1920 d. 1986

*Buenaventuro Ruiz
Montaño*
b. 1920 d. 1971

**Enrique Ruiz
Hernández**
b. 1945

*Francisca Lorenzo
Matías*
b. 1949

*Sara Ruiz Lorenzo
b. 1968

Faustino Ruiz Lorenzo
b. 1972

Pilar Ruiz Lorenzo
b. 1974

*Sofia Ruiz Lorenzo
b. 1977

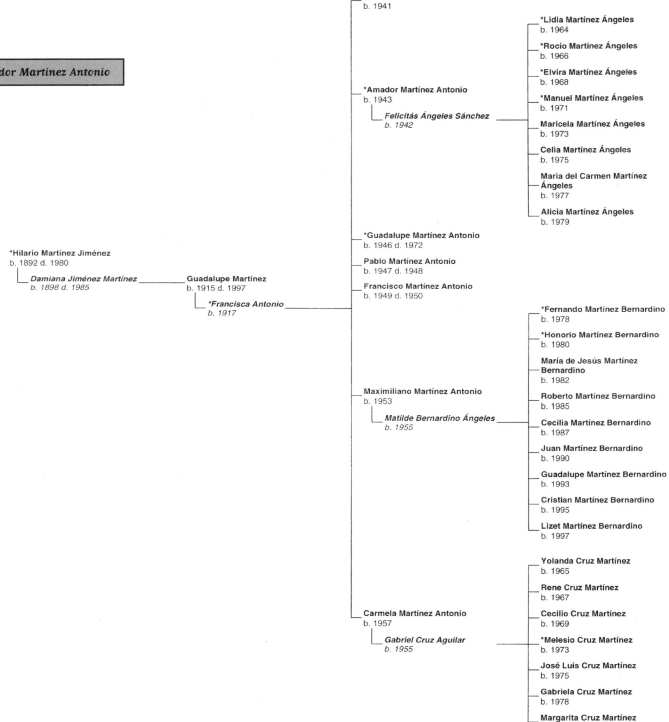

Family Tree #42, Family of Amador Martinez Antonio

*Rufina Martínez Antonio
b. 1941

*Amador Martínez Antonio
b. 1943
    Felicitás Ángeles Sánchez
    b. 1942

*Lidia Martínez Ángeles
b. 1964

*Rocio Martínez Ángeles
b. 1966

*Elvira Martínez Ángeles
b. 1968

*Manuel Martínez Ángeles
b. 1971

Maricela Martínez Ángeles
b. 1973

Celia Martínez Ángeles
b. 1975

Maria del Carmen Martínez Ángeles
b. 1977

Alicia Martínez Ángeles
b. 1979

*Guadalupe Martínez Antonio
b. 1946 d. 1972

Pablo Martínez Antonio
b. 1947 d. 1948

Francisco Martínez Antonio
b. 1949 d. 1950

*Hilario Martínez Jiménez
b. 1892 d. 1980
    Damiana Jiménez Martínez
    b. 1898 d. 1985

Guadalupe Martínez
b. 1915 d. 1997
    *Francisca Antonio
    b. 1917

Maximiliano Martínez Antonio
b. 1953
    Matilde Bernardino Ángeles
    b. 1955

*Fernando Martínez Bernardino
b. 1978

*Honorio Martínez Bernardino
b. 1980

María de Jesús Martínez Bernardino
b. 1982

Roberto Martínez Bernardino
b. 1985

Cecilia Martínez Bernardino
b. 1987

Juan Martínez Bernardino
b. 1990

Guadalupe Martínez Bernardino
b. 1993

Cristian Martínez Bernardino
b. 1995

Lizet Martínez Bernardino
b. 1997

Carmela Martínez Antonio
b. 1957
    Gabriel Cruz Aguilar
    b. 1955

Yolanda Cruz Martínez
b. 1965

Rene Cruz Martínez
b. 1967

Cecilio Cruz Martínez
b. 1969

*Melesio Cruz Martínez
b. 1973

José Luis Cruz Martínez
b. 1975

Gabriela Cruz Martínez
b. 1978

Margarita Cruz Martínez
b. 1980

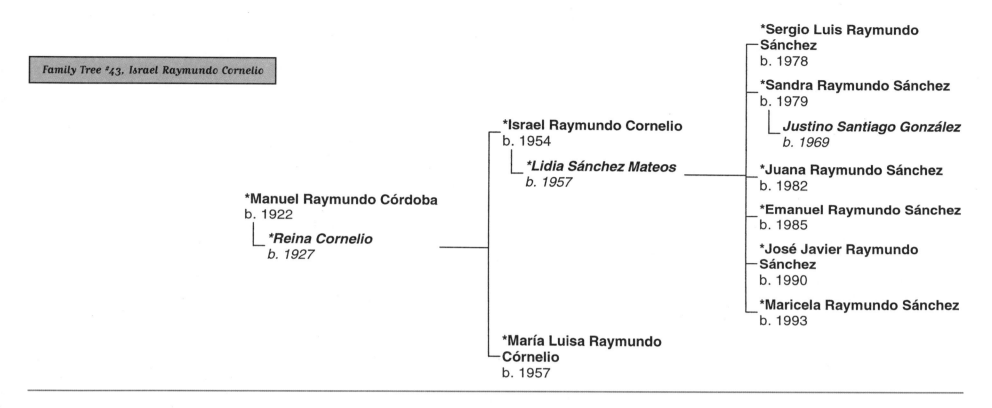

*Manuel Raymundo Córdoba
b. 1922

    *Reina Cornelio
    b. 1927

*Israel Raymundo Cornelio
b. 1954

    *Lidia Sánchez Mateos
    b. 1957

*Sergio Luis Raymundo Sánchez
b. 1978

*Sandra Raymundo Sánchez
b. 1979

    Justino Santiago González
    b. 1969

*Juana Raymundo Sánchez
b. 1982

*Emanuel Raymundo Sánchez
b. 1985

*José Javier Raymundo Sánchez
b. 1990

*Maricela Raymundo Sánchez
b. 1993

*María Luisa Raymundo Córnelio
b. 1957

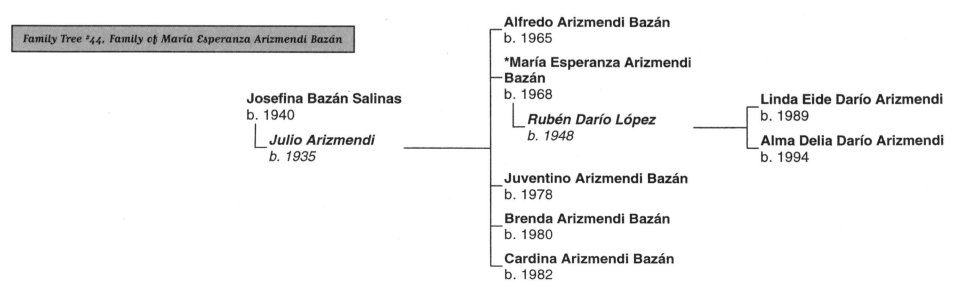

Josefina Bazán Salinas
b. 1940

    Julio Arizmendi
    b. 1935

Alfredo Arizmendi Bazán
b. 1965

*María Esperanza Arizmendi Bazán
b. 1968

    Rubén Darío López
    b. 1948

Linda Eide Darío Arizmendi
b. 1989

Alma Delia Darío Arizmendi
b. 1994

Juventino Arizmendi Bazán
b. 1978

Brenda Arizmendi Bazán
b. 1980

Cardina Arizmendi Bazán
b. 1982

Featured Artist Families and Types of Folk Art Arranged by Pueblo

Arrazola (more formally San Antonio Arrazola)
Woodcarving
Manuel Jiménez Ramírez and his sons, Isaías and Angélico
Armando and Moises Jiménez Aragón
José ("Pepe") Santiago Ibáñez

Miniatures (woodcarving)
Antonio Aragón Ramírez and his brothers Sergio and Saúl

Atzompa (more formally Santa María Atzompa)
Terra Cotta Ceramics
The Blanco Family
Luis García Blanco
Irma García Blanco
Alicia Leticia García Blanco
Bertha Blanco Nuñez
Avelino Blanco Nuñez

The Vásquez Cruz Family
Delfina Cruz Díaz and Ernesto Vásquez Reyes
Angélica Vásquez Cruz
Enedina Vásquez Cruz
Luis Vásquez Cruz

Green Glazed Ceramics
Guadalupe Aguilar Guerrero and her daughters Teresa and
Juana Lorenzo

Multi-Color Glazed Ceramics
The Regino Porras Family
Dolores Porras and Alfredo Regino Ramírez
Irma Regino Porras
Norberto Regino Porras and his wife Rosa Elena García López
Aurelia Regino Porras

Miniatures (Ceramics)
Joel Velasco Lara and his wife Manuela Villanueva Vázquez
Avelino Blanco Nuñez

Coyotepec (more formally known as San Bartolo Coyotepec)
Black Ceramics
The Pedro Martínez Family

Antonio Eleazar Pedro Carreño
Cecilia Martínez Barranco
Carlomagno Pedro Martínez
Adelina Pedro Martínez
Magdalena Pedro Martínez
Abel Pedro Martínez
Amando Pedro Martínez
Antonio Eurípides Pedro Cardozo

The De Nieto Castillo Family
Dona Rosa Real Nieto
Don Valente Nieto Real
Rafaela Castillo Cardozo
Erasmo Nieto Castillo and his wife, Rita Rosillo Andrés Calderón
Jorge Nieto Castillo and his wife, Alejandrina Galán Morga
Javier Nieto Castillo and his wife, María Moto
Fernando Nieto Castillo

Miniatures (Black Ceramics)
Floriberta Reyes Gómez and her husband, Andrés Cruz Hernández
Eustolia González Mateos

La Unión (more formally known as La Unión Tejalapam)
Woodcarving
The Santiago Family
Martín Santiago Cruz
Quirino Santiago Cruz
Plácido Santiago Cruz
Jaime Santiago Morales

Gabino Reyes López

Mitla
Woven Cotton Cloth
Gildardo Juárez Sosa
Arturo Hernández Quero

Oaxaca City and its immediate environs
Jewelry
The Calvo Rojas Family
Tere Calvo Quevedo
Alberto Calvo Rojas

Woven Cotton Cloth
    Guadalupe Orozco Torres
Tin Work ("Hojalata")
    The Leyva Family
    Alfonso Santiago Leyva
    Víctor Ruben Leyva

    Miguel Ángel Aguero Pacheco

Carousels and Ferris Wheels
    Antonio Villafañe Acevedo

Corn Husk Figures ("Totomoxtle")
    Mónica Bernardino Martínez
    Hilaria Zárate Hernández

Day of the Dead
    María Esperanza Arizmendi Bazán

Ocotlán (more formally known as Ocotlán de Morelos)
Red Painted Ceramics
    The Aguilar Alcántara Family
    Isaura Alcántara Díaz
    Guillermina Aguilar Alcántara
    Josefina Aguilar Alcántara
    Irene Aguilar Alcántara
    Concepción Aguilar Alcántara
    Jesús Aguilar Alcántara
    Demetrio García Aguilar

Cutlery and Swords
    Apolinar Aguilar Velasco

San Antonino (more formally known as San Antonino Castillo Velasco)
Embroidery
    Virginia Sánchez and her daughters, Reina, Silvia, Antonina, Carmen and María de la Luz

Dried Flowers
    Israel Raymundo Cornelio and his wife Liliana Sánchez Mateos

San Juan Chilateca
Embroiderery
    The Sumano Family
    Anastasia Sumano García
    Faustina Sumano García

San Martín (more formally known as San Martín Tilcajete)
Woodcarving
    Isidoro Cruz Hernández

    The Fuentes Family
    Epifanio Fuentes Vázquez
    Zeni Fuentes Santiago
    Efraín Fuentes Santiago
    Iván Fuentes Santiago
    Zenén Fuentes Méndez

    Jacobo Ángeles Ojeda

    María Jiménez Ojeda

    Inocencio Vázquez Melchor

Miniatures (Woodcarving)
    Justo Xuana Luis
    Marcela Vázquez Melchor

Santa Cruz Papalutla
Basketry
    Amador Martínez Antonio

Santo Tomás (more formally known as Santo Tomás Jalieza)
Woven Cotton Belts, Handbags and Placemats
    The Navarro Gómez Family

    The Chávez Family
    Cirila Chávez Luis and Patricia Hernández Chávez
    Agustín Chávez and his wife Asela Valentín Mendoza

Teotitlán del Valle
Rugs and Wallhangings
    The Vásquez Family
    Isaac Vásquez García
    Ernesto Vásquez Gutiérrez
    Aida Vásquez Gutiérrez

    Bulmaro Pérez Mendoza

    Fidel Cruz Lazo and his wife María Luisa de Mendoza Ruiz
Candles
    Viviana Alavéz Hipólito
    Sofía Ruíz Lorenzo

Shops and Markets in Oaxaca City and Its Pueblos

Oaxaca City

Markets
all are open daily, but the Mercado de Abastos is especially active on Saturdays
Mercado de Artesanías (juncture of Zaragoza and J.P. Garcia)
Mercado de Abastos (juncture of Periférico and Avenida Central)
Mercado de Benito Juárez (juncture of Las Casas and 20 de Noviembre)
Mercado de 20 de Noviembre (juncture of 20 de Noviembre and Mina)

Streets to Roam
Macedonio Alcalá
García Vigil
5 de Mayo
Gurrión

Shops
hours are generally 9:00 a.m. – 2:00 p.m. and 4:00 - 7:30 p.m.

Spectrum of Folk Art and Handicrafts
ARIPO (García Vigil #809)
El Arte Oaxaqueño (Mina #317, corner of Mina and J.P. García)
Artesanía Cocijo (Leona Vicario #117)
Artesanías de Oaxaca (Plazuela A. Gurrion "D," near corner of Macedonio Alcalá)
Chimalli (García Vigil #513A)
Corazon del Pueblo (Macedonio Alcalá #307, second level)
Fonart (Crespo #114)
La Mano Mágica (Macedonio Alcalá #203)
Mujeres Artesanas de las Regiones de Oaxaca A.C., (or MARO) (5 de Mayo #204)

Complexes of shops
Arte y Tradición (García Vigil #406)
Plaza Santo Domingo (Macedonio Alcalá #407)

Jewelry
Antiguedades (Abasolo #107)
La Bodega del Fraile (Macedonio Alcalá #501)
El Diamante (García Vigil #104)
Joyeria Luzma (Macedonio Alcalá #102-1)
Kanda (Calle 5 de Mayo #209)
Oro de Monte Alban (Macedonio Alcalá #403 and 503 and Calle C Gurrión S/N)
Taller del Orfebre (Macedonio Alcalá #205 and 206D)
Tere (Avenida Hidalgo #600W)
Xipe (5 de Mayo #315)

Rugs and Wallhangings
El Cactus Co. (Macedonio Alcalá #401)
Sarapes Arte y Tradición (García Vigil #406)

Woodcarving
Artesanías Teresita (Macedonio Alcalá # 401A)
Hecmafer Bazar Artesanal (5 de Mayo #301)

Books
Amate Books (Macedonio Alcalá #307)
Codice (Trujano #508)
Libreria Granen Porrua (Macedonio Alcalá #104)
Proveedor Escolar (Independencia #1001)

Pueblos

Markets
Etla: Wednesday
Zaachila: Thursday
Ocotlán: Friday
Tlacolula: Sunday

Pueblo Maps
with Locations of Featured Artists
(in alphabetical order)

Map A: Arrazola (San Antonio Arrazola)
Map B: Atzompa (Santa María Atzompa)
Map C: Coyotepec (San Bartolo Coyotepec)
Map D: La Unión (La Unión Tejalapam)
Map E: Mitla
Map F: Ocotlán (Ocotlán de Morelos)

Map G: San Antonino (San Antonino Castillo Velasco)
Map H: San Juan Chilateca
Map I: San Martín (San Martín Tilcajete)
Map J: Santa Cruz Papalutla
Map K: Santo Tomás (Santo Tomás Jalieza)
Map L: Teotitlán (Teotitlán del Valle)

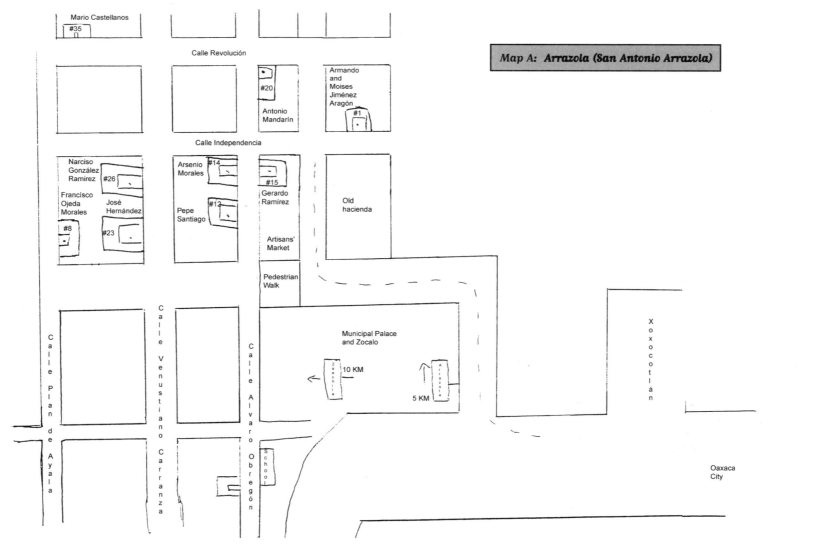

Map A: Arrazola (San Antonio Arrazola)

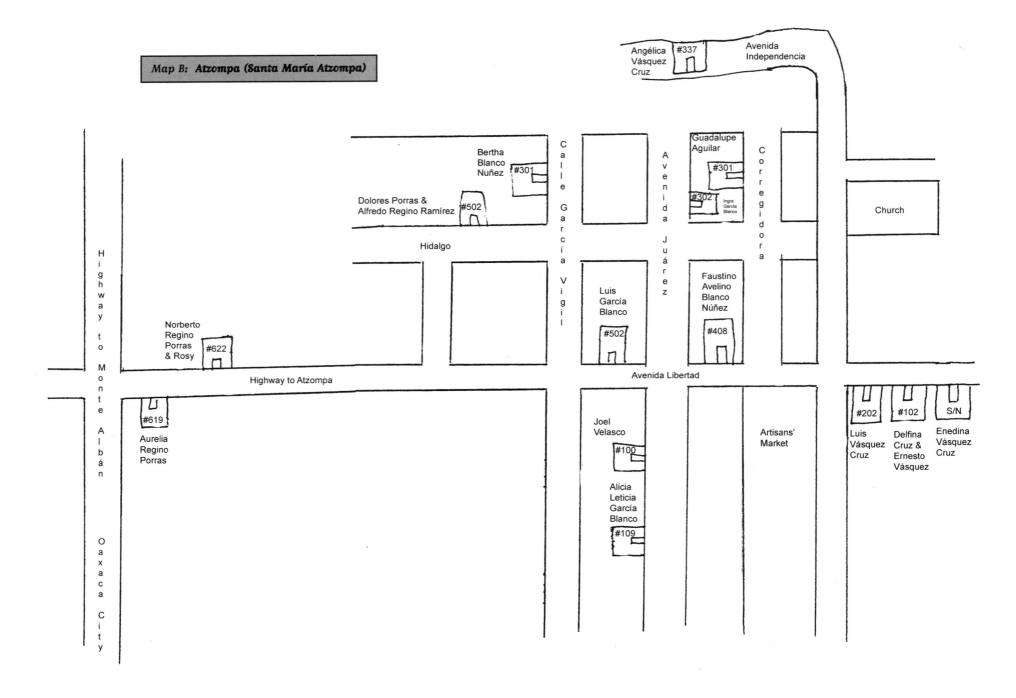

Map B: **Atzompa (Santa María Atzompa)**

Angélica Vásquez Cruz #337

Avenida Independencia

Bertha Blanco Nuñez #301

Dolores Porras & Alfredo Regino Ramírez #502

Calle García Vigil

Hidalgo

Avenida Juárez

Guadalupe Aguilar #301

#302 Ingra García Blanco

Corregidora

Church

Norberto Regino Porras & Rosy #622

Luis García Blanco #502

Faustino Avelino Blanco Núñez #408

Highway to Atzompa

Avenida Libertad

Highway to Monte Albán Oaxaca City

#619

Aurelia Regino Porras

Joel Velasco #100

Alicia Leticia García Blanco #109

Artisans' Market

#202

Luis Vásquez Cruz

#102

Delfina Cruz & Ernesto Vásquez

S/N

Enedina Vásquez Cruz

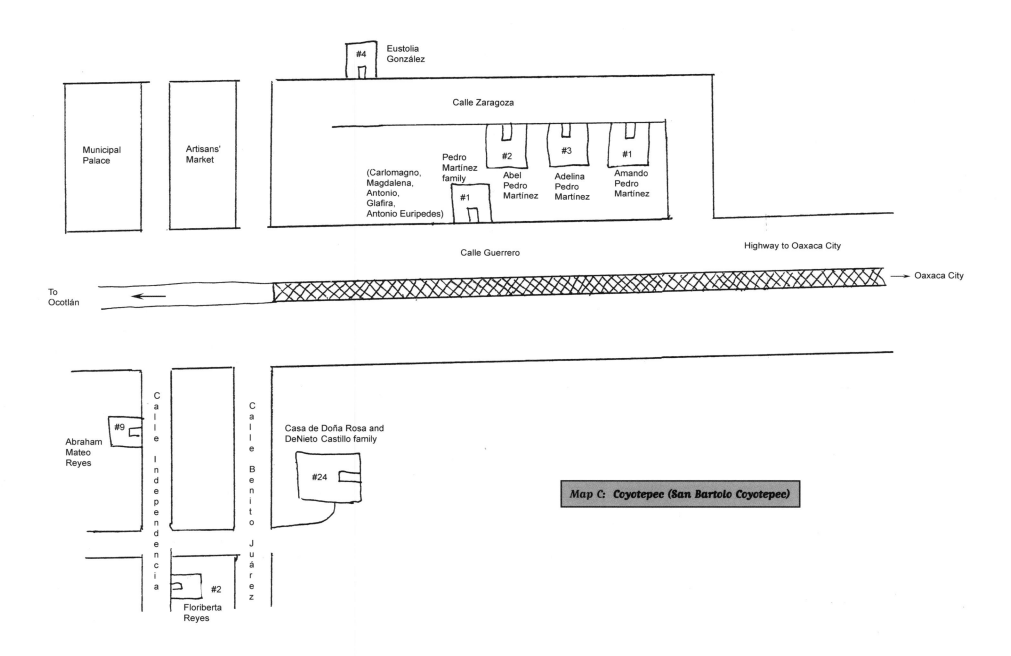

Eustolia
González

#4

Calle Zaragoza

Municipal
Palace

Artisans'
Market

Pedro
Martínez
family

#2

#3

#1

(Carlomagno,
Magdalena,
Antonio,
Glafira,
Antonio Euripedes)

Abel
Pedro
Martínez

Adelina
Pedro
Martínez

Amando
Pedro
Martínez

#1

Calle Guerrero

Highway to Oaxaca City

To
Ocotlán

Oaxaca City

Calle Independencia

Calle Benito Juárez

#9

Abraham
Mateo
Reyes

Casa de Doña Rosa and
DeNieto Castillo family

#24

Map C: Coyotepec (San Bartolo Coyotepec)

#2

Floriberta
Reyes

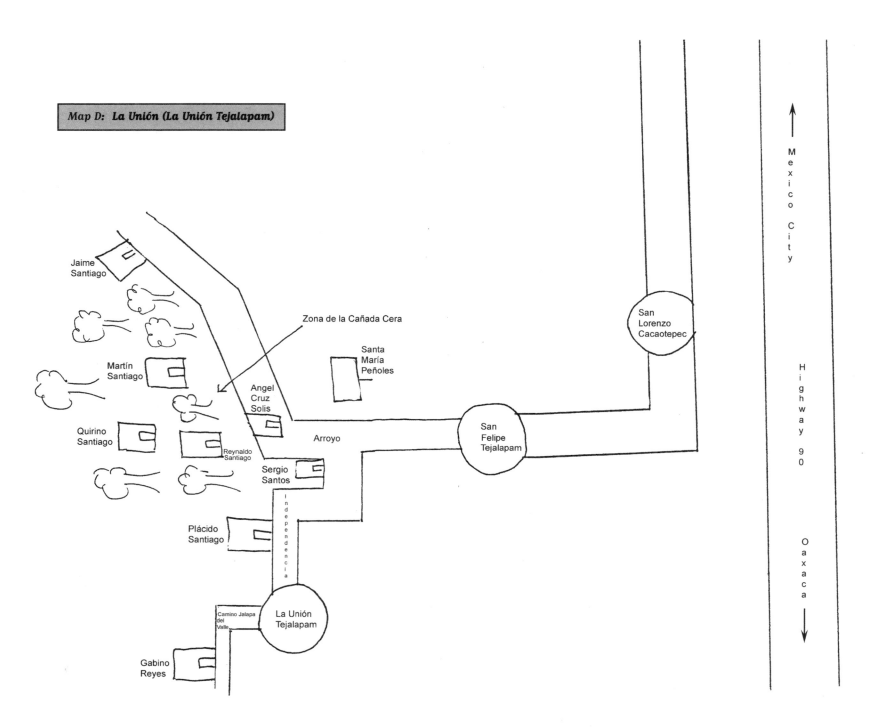

Map D: *La Unión (La Unión Tejalapam)*

Jaime Santiago

Zona de la Cañada Cera

Santa María Peñoles

San Lorenzo Cacaotepec

Martín Santiago

Angel Cruz Solis

Quirino Santiago

Reynaldo Santiago

Arroyo

San Felipe Tejalapam

Sergio Santos

Independencia

Plácido Santiago

La Unión Tejalapam

Camino Jalapa del Valle

Gabino Reyes

Mexico City

Highway 90

Oaxaca

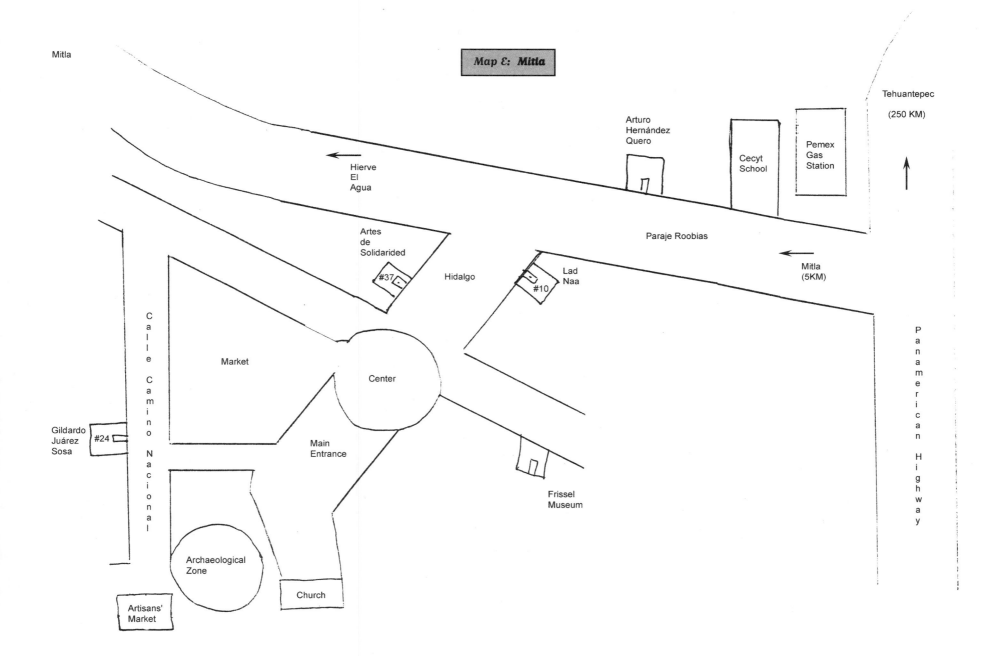

Mitla

Map Ɛ: Mitla

Tehuantepec
(250 KM)

Arturo
Hernández
Quero

Cecyt
School

Pemex
Gas
Station

Hierve
El
Agua

Paraje Roobias

Artes
de
Solidarided

#37

Hidalgo

#10

Lad
Naa

Mitla
(5KM)

Calle Camino Nacional

Market

Center

Gildardo
Juárez
Sosa

#24

Main
Entrance

Frissel
Museum

Panamerican Highway

Archaeological
Zone

Church

Artisans'
Market

211

Map F: Ocotlán (Ocotlán de Morelos)

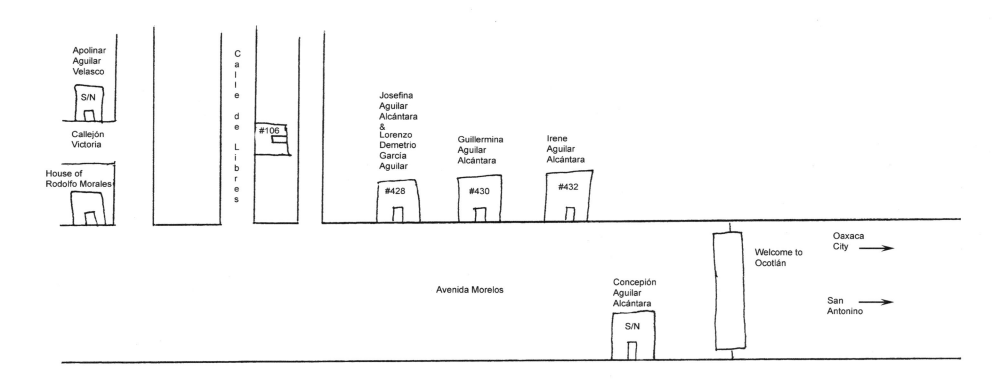

Apolinar
Aguilar
Velasco

S/N

Callejón
Victoria

House of
Rodolfo Morales

Calle de Libres

#106

Josefina
Aguilar
Alcántara
&
Lorenzo
Demetrio
García
Aguilar

#428

Guillermina
Aguilar
Alcántara

#430

Irene
Aguilar
Alcántara

#432

Welcome to
Ocotlán

Oaxaca
City ⟶

San
Antonino ⟶

Avenida Morelos

Concepión
Aguilar
Alcántara

S/N

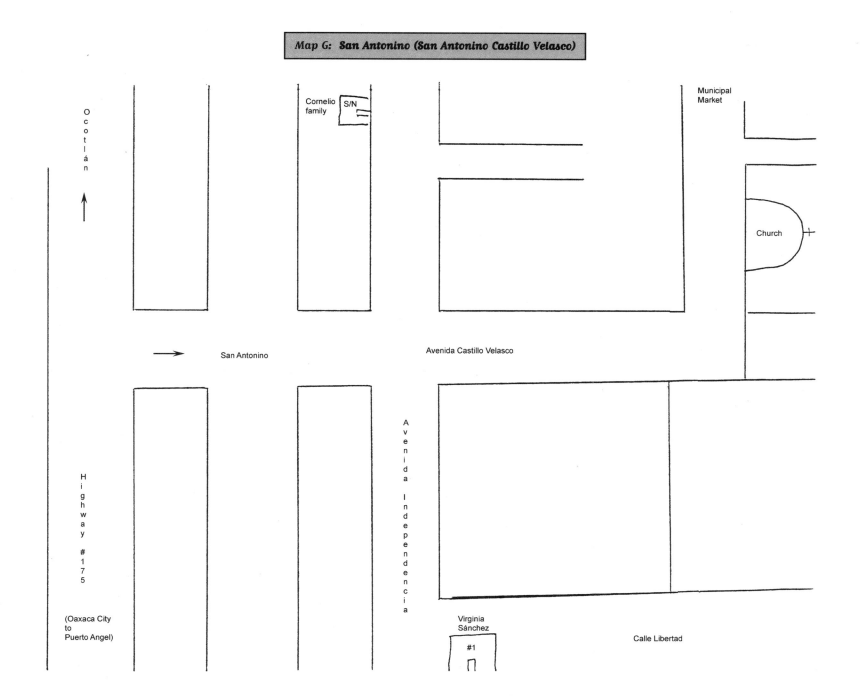

Map G: **San Antonino (San Antonino Castillo Velasco)**

Ocotlán

Municipal Market

Cornelio family

S/N

Church

San Antonino

Avenida Castillo Velasco

Highway #175

Avenida Independencia

(Oaxaca City to Puerto Angel)

Virginia Sánchez

#1

Calle Libertad

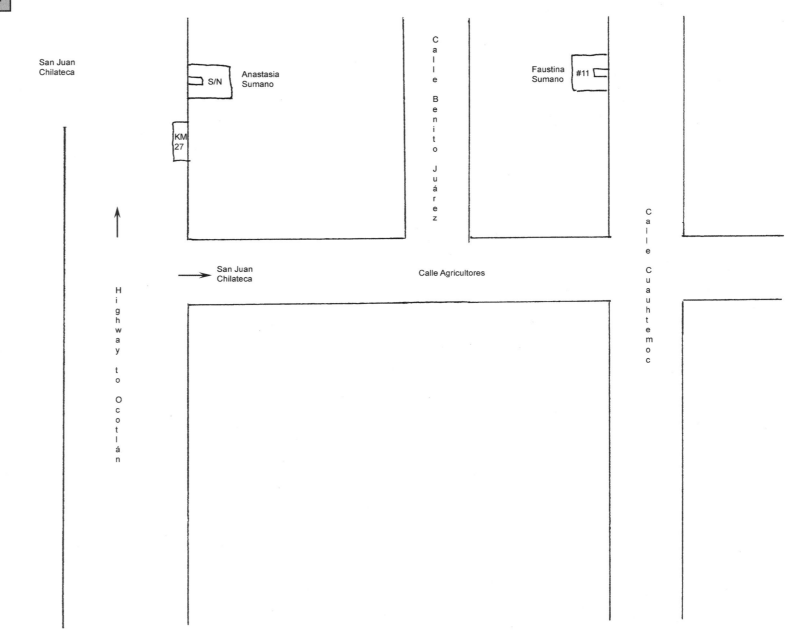

San Juan
Chilateca

S/N

Anastasia
Sumano

KM
27

C a l l e   B e n i t o   J u á r e z

Faustina
Sumano

#11

↑

H i g h w a y   t o   O c o t l á n

→ San Juan
Chilateca

Calle Agricultores

C a l l e   C u a u h t e m o c

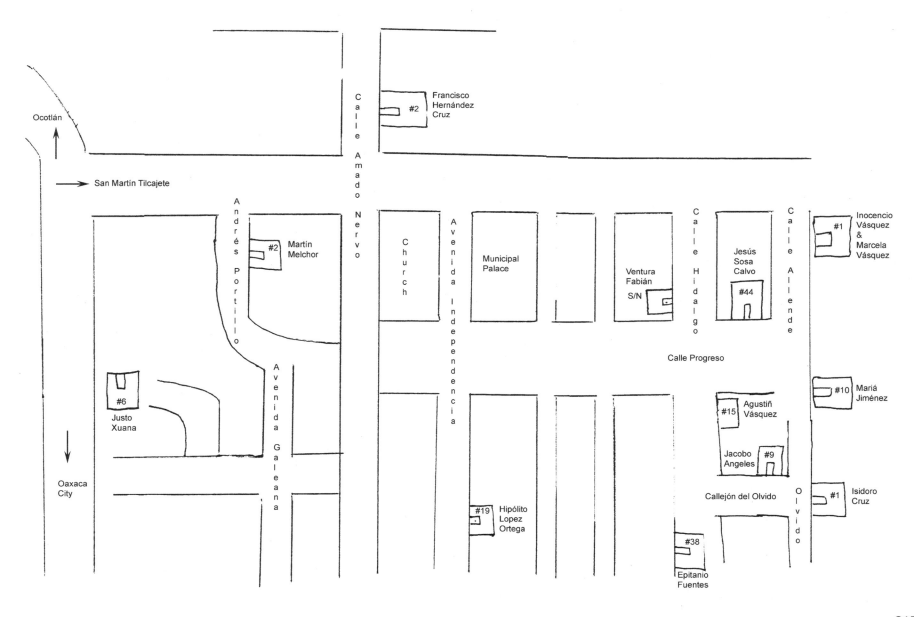

Map I: **San Martín (San Martín Tilcajete)**

215

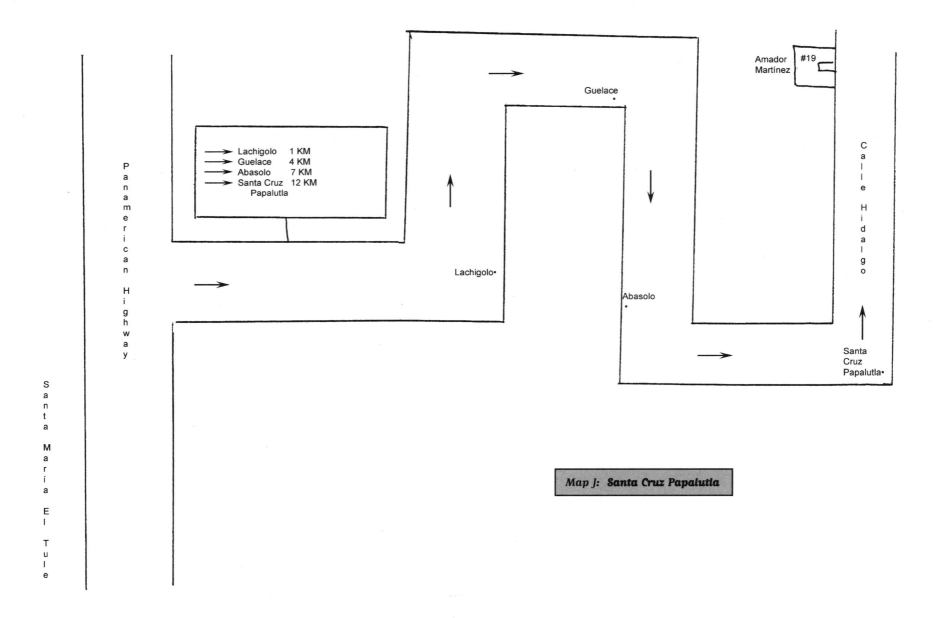

Panamerican Highway

Santa María El Tule

Lachigolo 1 KM
Guelace 4 KM
Abasolo 7 KM
Santa Cruz 12 KM
Papalutla

Guelace

Amador Martínez #19

Calle Hidalgo

Lachigolo•

Abasolo•

Santa Cruz Papalutla•

Map J: *Santa Cruz Papalutla*

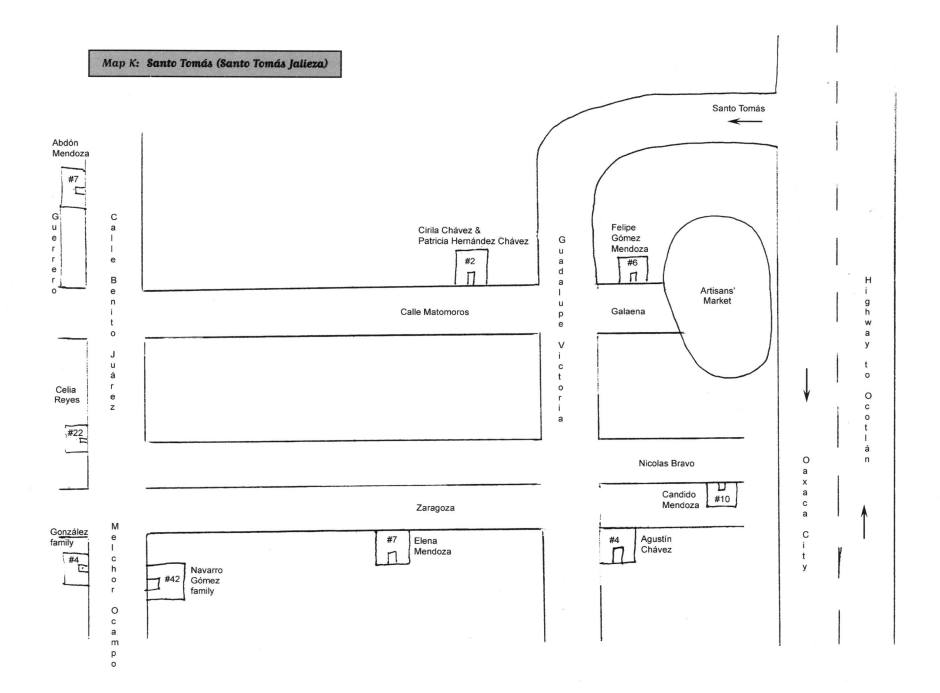

Map K: Santo Tomás (Santo Tomás Jalieza)

Abdón Mendoza

#7

Guerrero

Calle Benito Juárez

Celia Reyes

#22

González family

#4

Melchor Ocampo

Cirila Chávez & Patricia Hernández Chávez

#2

Calle Matomoros

Zaragoza

Navarro Gómez family

#42

#7 Elena Mendoza

Guadalupe Victoria

Santo Tomás

Felipe Gómez Mendoza

#6

Artisans' Market

Galaena

Nicolas Bravo

Candido Mendoza

#10

#4 Agustín Chávez

Highway to Ocotlán

Oaxaca City

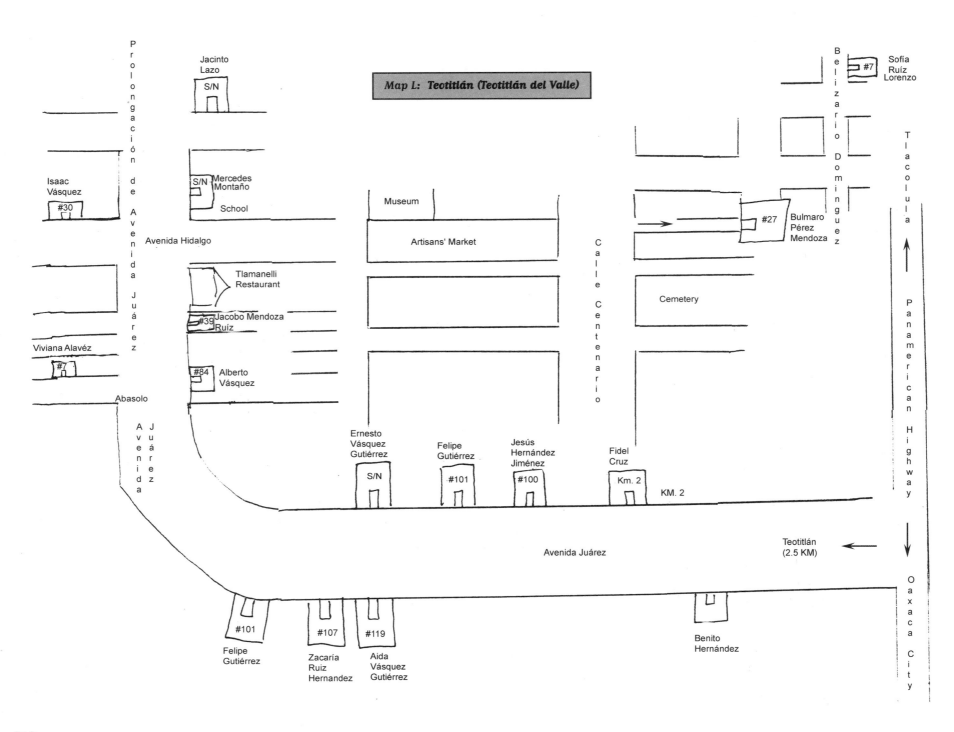

Map L: *Teotitlán (Teotitlán del Valle)*

Notes

Introduction

[1]Some pueblos encompass more than one type of folk art ,and some types of folk art are created in more than one pueblo. See the map of pueblos surrounding Oaxaca City that follows the Introduction.

[2]With rare exceptions (noted within the text), indigenous artists speak only Spanish. Negotiating purchases is possible with a combination of writing numbers and pointing. However, if you do not have a modest command of Spanish, a translator greatly enriches what you can learn about the artist's work and family life. Drivers such as our assistant, Constantino (Tino) Jiménez López, who know the pueblos intimately and have relationships with specific artists greatly enhance the experience. Most are quite inexpensive and well worth the hiring. They can also help arrange secure packing of treasured purchases for airplane transport or ground shipment.

[3]There are many fine artists to whom we have not had the good fortune to find our way, or who we did not include because of serendipitous events or the constraints of travel time or limited spece. The reader may supplement our selections by consulting our lists of additional fine artists in some classes of folk art and handicrafts. These follow the artists we feature. Other sources of information are collections of the many excellent folk art shops in the city of Oaxaca and more specialized books we have referenced on particular classes of folk art. Meandering into homes we do not mention and asking for suggestions will also yield pleasant surprises. Finally, visits to the major indigenous markets of Oaxaca allow further immersion in its folk arts.

[4]We typically present members of a family from eldest to youngest, except where several live in the same household. In this case they are organized on the basis of geographical proximity.

[5]Information about sightseeing, accommodations, dining, transportation, and the like is beyond the scope of our book. However, we have compiled a list of excellent books on these subjects that appears in the Bibliography on page 222.

[6]There is some overlap among these classes. For example, there are miniatures in ceramics, woodcarving, baskets, and decorative tin. Artists whom we feature specifically because of their reputation for producing miniatures are included in the section on miniatures. In addition, many classes of folk art and handicrafts are produced for or inspired by the Day of the Dead year round, including ceramics, tin work, and woodcarving. There are also several types of work that are created expressly for this purpose by artisans who specialize in their production. Because of the profound significance of this holiday, and the manner in which it permeates Oaxacan culture, we present a photographic collage of examples of the folk art and handicrafts it inspires, some by outstanding artists featured in other chapters.

[7]In Mexico of recent generations, each person has two surnames. The first is his father's initial surname. A woman does not take her husband's surname upon marriage. In everyday use it is common to refer to an individual by his initial surname alone. When a mother is an especially renowned artist, an individual may use her first surname to call attention to this lineage.

Glossary

agobe: mixture of clay and other natural substances (such as volcanic ash and ground stone) based in clay that are sometimes used to add color to ceramic pieces

alcatraz: callas lily, a type of flower that has a long white tube-like blossom (10 centimeters) and a long green stem (approximately 1 1/2 feet). Several of Diego Rivera's best-known paintings feature figures holding these flowers

alebrije: a word improperly used to refer to all painted woodcarved pieces; it is more accurately applied to pieces that are fantasy figures, such as two-headed serpents and winged horses, sometimes with a threatening tone)

alfarería: workshop

artesanías: handicrafts

atole: corn-based drink

azucena: daisy

borracho: drunkard

borrego: lamb

calenda: celebratory procession

carizo: a reed similar to bamboo used for basketry

catrinas: female figures with skeleton faces, often elegantly dressed, created for the Day of the Dead

cempasuchil: a flower that is a relative of the marigold, used especially during the Day of the Dead

centavo: cent, equivalent to one hundredth of a peso (there are approximately nine pesos to a dollar)

cochineal: tiny mites from the nopal cactus that are dried and ground to create dyes ranging from rose to deep purple, most often used for woven rugs and wallhangings

comal: flat ceramic plate used for making tortillas

cooperativa: cooperative

copal: the type of wood used most often for carving

cresta de gallo (also called **borla**): cockscomb, a brilliant red flower used especially during the Day of the Dead

desilado: the open crocheted portion of embroidered wedding dresses, usually at the juncture of the yolk and sleeve but sometimes on the trunk portion as well

enamorados: romantic loved ones, sometimes featured in ceramics

esmalte: a gold colored substance that provides a dramatic contrast in painted decoration of woodcarving

esmeril: emery, used for polishing knives and swords

flores inmortales: dried flowers (literally immortal flowers)

Fridas: ceramic female figures inspired by Frida Kahlo

frijoles: beans

frutero: ceramic fruit bowl

grecas: stepped fret geometric patterns derived from ancient ruins, especially those of Mitla, that are used in many types of folk art such as weaving, ceramics, and jewelry

greta: glaze that appears yellow prior to firing but creates the rich green tone of green-glazed pottery of Santa Maria Atzompa

Guelaguetza: an extraordinary celebration of traditional regional dances performed in memorable costumes; it takes place in Oaxaca City on the two Mondays immediately following July 18th, the birthday of Benito Juárez

hazme si puedes: literally, make me if you can, but here referring to the band of small human figures stitched across the bottom of the yolk portion of wedding dresses

hojalata: tin work

hojalatero: tin maker

huipil: traditional sleeveless blouse consisting of a loose, squared shape with openings for the head and arms

jacaranda: a popular tree in Mexico with purple flowers and very large seeds

jara: jug

loza verde: green glazed ceramics typically produced in Santa María Atzompa

mariachi: a musician in a strolling band, usually consisting of brass and string instruments, who generally wears lively garments

marimba: an elongated percussion instrument similar to a xylophone

mescal: an alcoholic drink made from the maguey plant

metate: a free-standing stone platform with legs on which a long round stone (similar to a rolling pin) is repeatedly rolled to grind spices and other natural materials for cooking and preparation of dyes

mil rayas: literally, a thousand stripes, but here referring to a multi-striped pattern

mole: sauce for chicken and meat, made of ingredients such as chocolate, chili, peanuts, sesame seeds, and innumerable other spices

montañitas: literally, little mountains, but here referring to a pattern

mucho cariño: with a lot of love

muertos: skeletons in human activity, in honor of the Day of the Dead

muñeca: literally doll, but more broadly the term for human figures in many types of folk art

musgo de roca: a type of lichen found on rocks near Teotitlan, used for dying wool a range of colors, from salmon to beige

nahual: an indigenous belief (with variations by pueblo) about the integral relationship between humans and animals, for example, that an animal spirit serves as an individual's protector from birth or that humans transform into animal spirits at night

negro brillante: shiny black surface in black ceramics of San Bartolo Coyotepec

novias: sweethearts

ocote: a soft wood used for carving, as well as for kindling to start fires

pastillaje: a type of ceramic decoration created by adding clay to the surface of the piece

petate: a woven straw mat

pueblo: village

quinceaños: the special celebration that takes place at the 15th birthday, comparable to a Sweet Sixteen

rebozo: woven shawl, in cotton or wool

renacimiento: rebirth

retablo: three-dimensional altar-like scenes, religious and otherwise, within boxes that are mounted behind doors, resembling a cabinet configuration

sabino: a type of tree

sierra: mountain ranges

sueño: dream

símbolo de la lluvia: literally, symbol of rain, but here referring to a particular ancient symbol incorporated in weavings

tapetes: patterned pieces of woolen weaving, used for rugs or wallhangings

tepeizcuintle: literally mountain dog, a type of design appearing in some work of the pre-Hispanic era and in current folk art based on designs of this period

Terrenos de Atzompa: fields in the pueblo of Santa María Atzompa

tortilla: a pancake-like food, made primarily from ground corn, used for many types of dishes, such as tacos, enchiladas, quesadillas

traje: regional costume

zompantle: a type of wood used for carving, especially for masks because it is very soft

zocalo: town square

Bibliography

Folk Art

Artes de México, 35. *Textiles de Oaxaca*. 1996.

Artes de México, 44, *Ojalata*. 1999.

Barbash, Shepard. *Oaxacan Woodcarving: The Magic in the Trees*. San Francisco: Chronicle Books, 1993.

Barbash, Shephard. These magicians carve dreams with their machetes. *Smithsonian Magazine*, May, 1991, pp. 118-129.

Fernández, Cándida de Calderón. *Great Masters of Mexican Folk Art*. New York: Harry N. Abrams, Inc., 2001.

Fomento Cultural Banamex, A. C. *Great Masters of Mexican Folk Art*. New York: Harry N. Abrams, Inc., 2001.

Forcey, John M. *The Colors of Casa Cruz: An Intimate Look at the Art and Skill of Fidel Cruz Award Winning Textile Weaver*. Oaxaca: Impresos Árbol de Vida, 1999.

Klein, Kathryn (Ed.). *The Unbroken Thread: Conserving the Textile Tradition of Oaxaca*. Getty Conservation Institute, 1998.

Mulryan, Lenore H. *Mexican Figural Ceramists*. Monograph #16, Museum of Cultural History, UCLA, 1982. (especially the sections on Teodora Blanco and Josefina Aguilar)

Oettinger, Marion. *Folk Treasures of Mexico*. New York: Harry N. Abrams, Inc., 1990.

Peden, Margaret S. *Out of the Volcano*. Washington and London: Smithsonian Institution Press, 1991.

Rojas, Bernardo V. *Artesanías Artísticas de Oaxaca, Mexico*. Facultad de Filosofía y Educación, Universidad de Chile, 1964.

Sandoval, Judith. *Shopping in Oaxaca*. Oaxaca: Sedetur, Gobierno del Estado de Oaxaca, 1998.

Sayer, Chloe. *Arts and Crafts of Mexico*. San Francisco: Chronicle Books, 1990.

Stanton, Andra F. *Zapotec Weavers of Teotitlán*. Santa Fe: Museum of New Mexico Press, 1999.

Toneyama, Kojin. *The Popular Arts of Mexico*. New York and Tokyo: Weatherhill/Heibonsha. (foreword and notes by Carlos Espejel, Director, Museo Nacional de Artes e Industrias Populares, Mexico City, 197).

Ward, William E. & Ward, Evelyn S., *Folk Art of Oaxaca: The Ward Collection*. Cleveland Institute of Art, 1987.

Wasserspring, Lois. *Oaxacan Ceramics: Traditional Folk Art by Oaxacan Women*. San Francisco: Chronicle Books, 2000.

Travel and Contemporary Culture

Andrade, Mary J. *Through the Eyes of the Soul: Day of the Dead in Mexico*. San Jose, CA: La Oferta Review Newspaper, Inc., 1996.

Hopkins, Barbara. *Oaxaca Crafts and Sightseeing*. Mexico, D. F. Minutiae Mexicana, S.A. de C. V., 1999.

Mallan, C. & Mallan, O. *Colonial Mexico*. Chico, California: Moon Press, 1998.

Martínez, Zarela. *The Food and Life of Oaxaca: Traditional Recipes from Mexico's Heart*. New York: Macmillan Publishing, 1997.

Sayer, Chloe. *The Mexican Day of the Dead*. Boston and London: Shambhala Redstone Editions, 1994.

Trilling, Susana. *Seasons of My Heart: A Culinary Journey through Oaxaca, Mexico*. Ballantine Publishing Group, 1999.

Whipperman, Bruce. *Oaxaca Handbook*. Emeryville, CA: Avalon Travel Publishing, 2000.

History, Archaeology and Sociology

Blanton, Richard E.; Feinman, Gary M; Kowalewski, Stephen A.; Nicholas, M. *Ancient Oaxaca: The Monte Alban State*. Cambridge University Press, 1999.

Campbell, Howard; Binford, Leigh (Editor); Bartolome, Miguel (Editor); Barabas, Alicia (Editor). *Zapotec Struggles: Histories, Politics, and Representations from Juchitan, Oaxaca*. Smithsonian Institution Press, 1994.

Cohen, Jeffrey H. *Cooperation and Community: Economy and Society in Oaxaca*. Austin: University of Texas Press, 1999.

Dennis, Philip. *Intervillage Conflict in Oaxaca*. New Brunswick and London: Rutgers University Press, 1987.

Giordano, Carlos. R. *Oaxaca: Archaeology, Colonial Art, Traditions*. Florence: Casa Editrice Bonechi, 1999.

Higgins, Michael James James & Coen, Tanya L. *Streets, Bedrooms, and Patios: The Ordinariness of Diversity in Urban Oaxaca*. Austin: University of Texas Press, 2000.

Holmes, William H. *Archaeological Studies Among the Ancient Cities of Mexico: Monuments of Chiapas, Oaxaca and the Valley of Mexico*. Books on Demand, 1997.

Marcus, Joyce & Flannery, Kent V. *Zapotec Civilization: How Urban Society Evolved in Mexico's Oaxaca Valley, 1996*.

Mullen, Robert J. *The Architecture and Sculpture of Oaxaca. 1530s-1980s*. Arizona State University, Center for Latin American Studies, 1997.

Paddock, J. *Ancient Oaxaca: Discoveries in Mexican Archeology and History*. Stanford University Press, 1966.

Stephen, Lynn. *Zapotec Women*. Austin: University of Texas Press, 1991.

Index